Lean On Me

Lean On Me

The Power of
Positive Dependency
in Intimate Relationships

DR. MARION SOLOMON

Kensington Books

KENSINGTON BOOKS are published by

Kensington Publishing Corp.
850 Third Avenue
New York, NY 10022

First Kensington Trade Paperback Printing: March, 1996
ISBN 1-57566-019-9

Printed in the United States of America

To Matthew, with love and appreciation

Contents

Acknowledgments

This book is an outgrowth of many years of thinking, dialoguing, and writing about relationships of all kinds. It was built upon the wisdom of many people. My name is on the cover because I took the time to write down ideas that have been generating much discussion in the mental health community.

I am indebted foremost to my mentors and teachers from whom I learned about the importance of the early interactions between babies and parents in organizing the ways that we relate throughout life—Heinz Kohut, Otto Kernberg, Daniel Stern, and the many other speakers at our UCLA Mental Health Training series. I am indebted also to James Grotstein and Joan Lang, my coeditors of *The Borderline Patient: Emerging Concepts in Diagnosis, Etiology, Psychodynamics, and Treatment,* for their help in synthesizing many diverse ideas about mental health and personality disturbances.

Jean Baker-Miller and her colleagues from the Stone Center at Wellesley College helped to clarify issues of women's growth in connection. Janet Surrey and Stephen Bergman added to my thinking about how men and women use connections to meet important dependency needs.

Margaret Ryan contributed substantially to the organization of the book. I am grateful for the gift of her company and her superb skills. From the beginning she has been instrumental in helping me think through the many alternative paths to understanding the process that intimate relationships go through. She is a most perceptive guide and enjoys playing with complex ideas. Without her input, this would be a different book, twice as long and half as clear.

I am particularly grateful to friends who were involved with me from the beginning of this project: Rita Lynn, who brought concepts from the Institute of Group and Family Analysis in London, for always being available to explore issues and offer encouragement; Robert Rodman, for the concept of mature dependency and dialogues on what is curative. I appreciate the friends who have read different versions of the manuscript along the way—Madeline Taylor, Barbara Zax, Lee Hausner, Caron Broidy, Nancy Addison, Ivan Gabor, Carol Francis, James Gottfurcht, Deborah Berger-Reiss, and Anthony Gerard—and the input from colleagues in the Tuesday Breakfast Group who meet monthly to discuss couples therapy, Robert and Celia Anderson, Ronald Alexander, Walter Brackelmanns, Pearl Brown, Saul Brown, Helen Reid Brown, and Ronald Levine.

I thank Sheila Cluff for providing such a perfect environment for writing, exercise, and dialogue at the Oaks at Ojai.

A special thanks to Susan Barrows-Munro at W. W. Norton for her help and support of my previous book, *Narcissism and Intimacy: Love and Marriage in an Age of Confusion,* and for giving me two great gifts when she introduced me to Margaret Ryan and Linda Chester.

My agent, Linda Chester, has been tremendously supportive, constantly encouraging me, and was instrumental in moving me from writing for mental health professionals to translating ideas in ways that are clear and understandable to a larger audience. I owe a great deal to Linda and her assistant, Lori Fox, for all their effort on behalf of this book.

I am grateful to Sandy Gelles-Cole, the editor who took this manuscript under her wing and in one month's time did a fantastic editing job, reassuring me repeatedly that it would be completed on schedule—and it was. I give her credit for turning this into a book that does not require training as a psychologist to comprehend and use.

I thank Judith Regan, my editor at Simon and Schuster, for her interest and involvement in this project and for being available when I call—despite her incredibly busy schedule.

I thank the special people who have long been part of my personal support system: Steve Levine, computer consultant extraordinaire, who often dropped what he was doing evenings and weekends to find and retrieve sections lost in the deep recesses of the computer; and Mary Raffety, who typed dozens of revisions as the ideas in the book changed and took form, and who worked overtime many Sundays to get the manuscript finished on time.

Most significantly, I am grateful for the help and encouragement of my family. My husband, Matthew, the love of my life, I thank for his constant support, and for listening to my ideas as they took form. Even more I am indebted to him for being the person whose solid presence I can lean on. His loving support in good times and times of trial goes beyond words of appreciation.

I thank my two wonderful children, Bonnie and Glenn, who so willingly shared their insights with me and who gave me the perspective of the younger generation.

Introduction

A friend just left. It is very late at night and I've been ready for sleep for an hour. But she is my friend and I listen as she cries about the end of her affair, and what she feels is the end of love for the rest of her life.

Nancy had been going with Jeff since he separated from his wife a year ago. But Jeff had not fully let go of his marriage, even though he promised marriage to Nancy. Now, a year later, there were no signs of divorce proceedings. Nancy kept telling him her feelings, expecting him to understand and respond to her needs. Finally, she realized that Jeff was still in love with his wife, and so they had parted, and Nancy is bereft. "Why do I *need* him so much? Why do I do this to myself? What's wrong with me? Why can't I be content by myself?" she asks me tearfully.

As Nancy goes on berating herself for the pain she feels over losing love, I can hear her underlying belief that her dependence on this relationship means that she is childish and needy. She thinks that she should be able to fill her needs by herself.

Nancy, like many people today, is trying hard to be independent, to not need others, to love herself more completely. "When I can love myself, I will be ready for a real relationship," Nancy says, as though reciting something she has learned. "Why did I fall into this *same* trap again, depending on a man to make me feel good?" And so Nancy beats herself up further, adding self-doubt and self-dislike to the pain of losing the man she loves. Believing as she does that being independent and capable of standing alone is a prerequisite to mature adulthood, Nancy sees her dependence on others for love and fulfillment as a sign of weakness. Loving too much is the problem, she asserts through her sniffles. She has to learn to take care of herself *first*.

I disagree. Loving too much is not Nancy's problem, nor is it depending on others. In fact, both of these can be cures for our "me"-centered, independence-driven, narcissistically focused society. It is time to consider a new path to love, and one that works—not a solitary path of independence, not a pathological path of codependence, but a mutually beneficial collaboration between partners that I call *positive dependence.*

Positive dependence is not simply a matter of taking care of one another, although that sometimes happens. Dependence even in childhood is much more than caretaking. We depend upon others to provide a reflection of ourselves, to help us define who we are, to recognize our worthiness. We need others who can attune themselves to our feelings and understand and accept us as we are, not as what we ought to be for them. When we have positive dependence in relationships, we can trust that we are known, understood, loved, and accepted.

During the course of more than thirty years as a therapist, I have developed a growing conviction that therapists are on the wrong track when we teach people that in order to achieve mental health we must become independent, autonomous, self-sufficient, and self-actualized. Letting others become dependent on us is typically viewed as negative, unless, of course, they are children.

Because we equate dependence with the need of a child for a parent, it is easy to see why we think growing up means being independent. But in fact, no one is independent of the need for others. Self-sufficiency to the exclusion of loving and needing another is no more possible than a life lived independently of oxygen or water (psychoanalyst Heinz Kohut suggested this more than twenty years ago in a presentation at UCLA entitled "Narcissism: The Psychology of the Self." We are a species dependent on others to survive, to thrive, and to grow to our full potential.

The men and women who come to me for couples therapy are often frustrated in their attempts to develop and maintain intimate relationships. Attempting to understand why so many were disappointed in their search for love, I looked to relationships that I knew were working. I spent a number of years assessing couples who described themselves as satisfied in their relationships and with their help examined what made their relationships work. Invariably, partners in these working relationships felt they were with someone they could depend upon, someone who could be trusted not to hurt or shame them by pointing out all their vulnerable points. They felt appreciated for their positive attributes and accepted even with their weaknesses. They knew they were loved, not as perfect, healthy human beings but as perfectly human and vulnerable individuals. Rather than trust only my vague assessment, I questioned them on their family histories, the background of their relationships, and the day-to-day "operations" of their lives together. Some of the responses I received said it all:

"He was the first *mother* I ever had," said a dynamic, successful woman about her husband of twenty-eight years. Another man who said that his marriage was the first good relationship he had ever had in his life told me, "She knew I was eighteen years older and had four kids with a lot of baggage, but she loved me without conditions."

Some aspects of working relationships included feeling affirmed, understood, accepted (warts and all), respected, trusted, emotionally connected, and open to each other's needs. If these partners did not always get what they wanted, they were able to negotiate differences. They accepted that some differences would always exist and that there will be times of stress. They knew they were not alone, that their partners were there to share the joys of success and the burden of troubles that every relationship must go through. This nurturing and trust that each felt from the other, I concluded, are the basic aspects of positive dependency.

More astonishing to me was the realization that many of these couples had individual histories that were no more nor less damaged than patients I was seeing in therapy. I did not know why their early traumas had not interfered with their partnerships. I have learned that, for many people, their intimate relationship is itself the therapeutic agent, a source of healing and personal growth.

What I learned from assessing these successful working partnerships, I took back to the couples I saw in therapy. Through our therapeutic journey together, we began to reexamine the needs of each partner and their expectations of the relationship. When we looked for ways to provide for a mutually healthy dependency, we found that not only did their relationship improve, but so did each individual's self-esteem, sense of accomplishment, and feelings of well-being.

What I present in this book is the result of a journey that many brave couples took with me into the depths of their hearts and minds. What they discovered and shared with me and with each other broke through lifelong failures of trust and lack of empowerment that had made their relationships precarious, unsatisfying, and at times quite destructive. This was a sometimes exciting, sometimes painful exploration that we embarked on together. We examined periods of childhood development most concerned with the development of loving relationships. We used the exercises in the last chapter of this book to uncover and understand more about the personal imprints of each partner.

There are periods when the imprints for relationships become established and become our models for relating. These imprints are personal patterns of relating that we develop early in life through our connections with important others. For reasons that I will discuss in this book, these primary imprints for human connection remain with us as we become involved in each new relationship throughout life.

We are imprinted during the course of the primary interactions in our lives, the first relationships with parents and other early caretakers. What we learn as babies about trust, security, love, or their opposites are imprinted from these days and carried forever in our bodies and minds. Painful interactions leave an internal residue of pain. Caring, attuned responsiveness leaves an internal experience of trust in relationships. What we learned to expect and how we learned to respond become our personal generalized patterns of relating in loving or non-loving ways. Once our way of relating is imprinted, unless something new changes our expectations, our love relationships in times of stress become hardened. The inherent value of positive dependency is that through a relationship it is possible to modify these imprinted patterns of interacting, and to heal old wounds.

There are ways to promote changes in our models for intimacy. If we know what we need, acknowledge that we depend on important others to respond caringly to these needs, and are willing to do the same for a partner, significant changes can occur. These are the messages that I learned from successful couples and with my patients in therapy. The longer I work with this focus on intimate relationships as part of a therapeutic partnership, the more convinced I become that *a healing relationship can be any relationship in which people have a commit-*

ment to work together and a basic caring and respect for one another. If these necessary conditions exist, problems of the relationship such as money, work, sex, children, in-laws, can be resolved. More astounding, early psychological damage that occurred to the individuals and that may have been brought into the current partnership can often be resolved.

My practice revolves around the treatment of relational problems. I work primarily with couples who come in together, with individuals who want to find new ways to be in relationships, and through group therapy in which the focus is on exploring the ways that people interact, learn to depend on one another, or avoid being close and interdependent. I work with marital partners and with unmarried couples grappling with problems of intimacy. But healing relationships can be any loving bonded connection between two or more people who are important to each other. The issues are the same for gay and lesbian partners who are trying to understand and deepen their relationships.

The case histories in this book are drawn from my records of the past twenty-five years of working with couples. I write about my work in order to maintain a sense of clarity about what is happening in the treatment, where we have been and where we are going. I often invite my patients to read about themselves, to point out information that I have missed, to challenge me where I have misunderstood them. My patients are my collaborators in this book. The names have been changed and details of their lives have been altered or modified to protect their identities. But the important details of journeys to their past are presented. I thank each of these couples for all that they have given me, both at the time when we worked together and now as I share what I have found.

Part 1 Everyone Needs Someone

1 The Myth of Self-Sufficiency

For one human being to love another: that is perhaps the most difficult of all our tasks, the ultimate, the last test and proof, the work for which all other work is but preparation. For this reason young people, who are beginners in everything, cannot yet know love: they have to learn it. With their whole being, with all their forces, gathered close about their lonely, timid, upward-beating heart, they must learn to love.

—Rainer Maria Rilke, *Letters to a Young Poet*

Rule #1 for Positive Dependency:
Remember that your partner needs love as much as you do. Give signs of love generously with your praise, compliments, hugs, gifts, passion, prayer.

"We are born alone and we die alone," concluded Carl, a patient in group therapy, after he described how his third wife had served him with divorce papers. Demonstrating little emotion, Carl asserted his ability to manage "quite well" without having to depend on anyone. But Carl was not managing well at all. In a misguided attempt to protect himself against being hurt once again, he was not allowing himself to feel his rejection and loneliness. Instead, he was working sixty hours a week and had developed an ulcer. He did not understand that a healthy relationship requires both partners to *depend* on one another. In fact, he was so terrified of feeling dependent, he had short-circuited every intimate relationship he had attempted in the last thirty years. I have seen this pattern in the series of relationships he has had on and off over the three years that I've been counseling him.

Because he was financially successful, whenever a woman expressed interest in him, he assumed she was after his money. Ironically, when he met Lois, a woman who clearly had no interest in his money because of her own financial situation, he said she would probably leave him and then proceeded to behave in ways to test her "staying power." He was demanding, was critical of her friends and of people she admired, didn't show up one night for a date. "I'm very busy; she should understand," he said. When she didn't and refused to see him again, it confirmed his stance that it is a mistake to depend on anyone.

In most of his relationships, he is in control. People he employs do his bidding or he gets rid of them. Once again Carl was doing what he always did with the women he considered good enough for him: he tested and found her flawed. Like many people, Carl fears closeness and dependency and has learned ways to ward off the danger of allowing his basic needs to surface. In this way, he has managed to re-create and reenact his childhood experience with cold, unresponsive grandparents who raised him after his parents had died in a plane crash.

For Carl, and for many like him, life has become a frustrating search for ways to fill what is missing or to hide from a deep, intense need for love. The erroneous idea that we are all born alone and should be able to function alone in order to be "self-sufficient" is one of the myths that permeates our self-oriented society.

Numerous pop-psychology books tell us that separation, self-sufficiency, and independence are the hallmarks of maturity and the prerequisites to true intimacy. Many of us have already taken the road that beckons toward independence, but found instead that it can lead to isolation. When this happens, we assume that *we* are at fault—that we have not learned how to be fully independent.

As increasing numbers of lonely people look to therapy for solutions to their unhappiness, self-sufficiency at all levels of functioning continues to be presented as the epitome of psychological health and the answer to many relationship problems. The solution many psychology books and psychotherapists offer to combat loneliness and isolation is to be strong enough to stand alone. In essence, we are exhorted: "Don't depend on others to love and affirm you. Know what *you* want. Find it within yourself. Be your own best friend. Heal yourself. Only then will you be mature and ready for love."

Ironically, promoting this unbalanced view of life has encouraged a descent into traps of *dis*connection and *dis*contentment. The irony is that *feeling secure in oneself* is built upon a solid network of interdependent *relationships*. The human personality becomes mature through these relationships, *not* solely through the experience of autonomy and independence. There is a basic human need for positive, dependent connection, not only early in life, but throughout adulthood. Autonomy, self-worth, self-actualization, and self-esteem are all developed within the context of interpersonal connections. Psychology helps through a therapeutic relationship. The self is defined through its interactions with others. Unfortunately, ignoring this reality has led to the hermetic, self-absorbed orientation of our society and to the disturbing feelings of isolation experienced by so many. The myth is that we can "love ourselves to health and happiness," but instead we are "loving" ourselves to loneliness and isolation. That is why I open this chapter with my first of ten rules for healthy interdependence.

#1: Remember that your partner needs love as much as you do. Give signs of love generously with your praise, compliments, hugs, gifts, passion, prayer. When the truth includes words of love, speak freely. Feel free to address your partner with a special name and talk often about why you feel such deep love. Note things that are simple and often forgotten that will enhance the ego of the one you love.

Not only do we depend on others for such validation and not only is it healthy to be able to lean on someone, but it is a fair assumption that our partner also needs love and many manifestations of love.

The common wisdom of our culture suggests that we are supposed to love ourselves despite what others may think of us. The problem with this belief is that it excludes a fundamental human truth: the feeling of being worthwhile begins through relation with others; through the adoring gaze of a new mother's eye in our earliest years; in school, through the approval of teachers and the comradeship of our peers; and later, from the feeling that one is loved by another person or is a valued member of a community. *Healthy dependency begins with the awareness that we need to be connected to another person who values us.* We all depend on such connections in order to feel good and to be healthy. When these connections are insufficiently fulfilled, we become "needy" at best, physically and emotionally disturbed at worst.

Unfortunately, we have learned to equate dependency with "neediness." But neediness occurs only *after denial* of our normal human need to depend on one another. The more this need is ignored or disallowed, the needier—and more demanding—we become. In fact, the reason that so many people veer off into what is often labeled as "sick" patterns of codependent relating is precisely because normal human dependency needs—which are inborn and lifelong—have been denied a healthy outlet or insufficiently fulfilled.

No Man or Woman Is an Island

How did our natural human need for dependency become so distorted? For an answer, we have to go back several decades.

The social revolution of the sixties was triggered, in part, by the confusion of traditional values that peaked in the 1950s. I know about those values because I lived them.

Many women who were married in the 1950s thought of marriage as our life's goal. We believed the myth that we could depend on "our man," and on our society's structures, for our future, for emotional and financial security. We wanted a family as on *Ozzie & Harriet* or the husband we had seen on *Father Knows Best*.

When I married in 1956, Betty Friedan had not yet written *The Feimine Mystique*, nor had Gloria Steinem decided to give feminism a voice of its own through *Ms.* magazine. The sexual revolution was still awaiting the pill to free women from the threat of unwanted pregnancy. Helen Gurley Brown, the publisher of *Cosmo*, was still Helen Gurley, writing *Sex and the Single Girl*, and I was a married woman studying psychology.

When I entered the field of mental health in the sixties, I found myself in the midst of a revolution. Manners, values, and sexual morality seemed in constant flux. I watched friends and colleagues throw themselves into each new idea, therapy, and freedom; usually they emerged confused, disappointed, and lonely.

"Stop complaining about your husband," Fritz Perls scolded one member of an Esalen workshop I attended. "Shit or get off the pot. . . . If you're not happy, leave him." And she did.

The qualities that enabled a person to be independent appeared to conflict with those that enabled a person to connect intimately. It was Perls who gave us the motto of the sixties:

> *I do my thing and you do your thing.*
> *I am not in this world to live up to your expectations,*
> *And you are not in this world to live up to mine.*
> *You are you and I am I;*
> *If by chance we find each other, it's beautiful.*
> *If not, it can't be helped.*

According to Perls (and others), my responsibility to my parents or spouse should not interfere with doing what is right for *my* personal growth. "Do your own thing" was the first commandment of the "me" generation. Young men and women flocked to encounter groups with the goal of finding their "true selves." We spent a lot of time looking for these true selves, reading books, seeing therapists, learning to state our needs clearly. Only by tenaciously pursuing our own interests, proclaimed the popular wisdom of the day, could we have healthy relationships with others. But—*surprise*—relationships began to flicker into oblivion as adults marched off to do their own thing and find their "inner selves."

The message of Fritz Perls and other gurus of the sixties is part of the ground upon which our modern psychological culture is built. The encounter-group movement declined, but a version of the encounter-group philosophy survived to become part of the mainstream. In the subsequent years, the mass culture promoted the underlying message that any desire for intimate, dependent relationships demonstrated a *lack* of self-development rather than a normal and healthy human need.

Healthy development, we have been told, mandates that we disentangle ourselves from all the ties that bind—those with mothers, fathers, siblings, spouses, children, grandparents. Harboring too great a need for others has been identified as a destructive, lingering feeling from childhood, to be overcome through self-discovery and self-love.

As less-stringent divorce laws made it easier to terminate unsatisfying relationships and plunge into self-oriented pursuits, a common question arose, one that was rarely asked a generation earlier: "Am I better off without this relationship? Am I better off *alone?*" The answer, increasingly, was yes. And why shouldn't it have been so? Each time a relationship hits a snag, it hurts. There's all that pain and work involved in getting a partnership to its next positive plateau. When one is trained to tune only into one's own growth and needs, it is much easier to go it alone and lean on oneself rather than to help the relationship grow. The expansion of no-fault divorce foreshadowed the widespread use of "irreconcilable differences" to unilaterally justify declarations of independence that, in essence, terminated relationships. It no longer seemed to matter that one mate's declaration of independence could be disaster for the other mate or for the children.

Today, being parents together is no longer a good enough reason to remain in an unhappy relationship. "Your mom and I are getting a divorce," Fred told his children as he packed a suitcase and prepared to leave their home. "We don't love each other anymore, but I will always love you." Twenty years later his daughter still breaks into tears each time she talks about how her father became increasingly distant and seemed to have divorced her as well. "If he loved me, he would not have left. . . . I must have done something wrong," she says as she tries to overcome the loss and the grief that has never left her since her parents' "most-civilized divorce."

The "Me Generation" handled the problem of widespread divorce by contending that children are somehow better off with divorced parents than with unhappy parents. True for some, perhaps, but seriously untrue for many others. Judith Wallerstein's book *Second Chances* offers us quite a different picture, presenting evidence to support the contention that divorce is by no means "no-fault" and, in fact, can

inflict lifelong damage upon many children and adults. Clearly, we
have preferred to hear about independence and not *inter*dependence.
Like Bruce, who is described below, we have wanted to believe that
we could "do our own thing" and that nobody would be hurt.

Hungry for Love

Bruce was a thirty-four-year-old patient when I first saw him. We
worked together for two years and I heard from him occasionally when
he referred a friend or relative to me. He had a brief marriage and quick
divorce while in medical school, and his second marriage seemed
shaky at the time I met him. When he came into therapy, he had been
married eight years to his second wife and was also having an ongoing,
serious affair. He came to therapy because of his pattern of restlessness
in intimate relationships. Bruce made it clear from the beginning that
he was adept at "doing his own thing," but he thought he might need
a "little tune-up" or a "sounding board" so he could figure out this
"little problem" that was bothering him. But when he started to talk, he
quickly went to the despair he was feeling about his life. "I'm looking
for something, but I don't know what. I feel as if I have this huge cavity
inside that needs filling. For a while, a new relationship fills me up—
but it never lasts."

Now, in his reentry in therapy, Bruce described himself as "hungry
for love." Occasionally, the hungry place was filled, but mostly he felt
empty inside. He was bored with his marriage and with his life. Although he loved his girlfriend, Amy, and did not want to lose her, he
also felt an "internal pressure" to remain in his marriage. Bruce described a deep fear of being alone, but explained his indecision about
his future relationships in more concrete terms: "If I divorce my wife,
Mary, to begin a third marriage, I would have to give up my home, my
children, and my standard of living."

Bruce had already gone through the same scenario eight years before when, at the age of twenty-six and after three years of marriage, he
had fallen in love with Mary, who became his second wife. He had
wasted no time; they had married the weekend after he divorced his
first wife.

"How do I know," Bruce wondered, "that I won't find myself in the same position a few years from now?" It was a good question. He rightly feared that he would experience the same emptiness and lack of vitality with Amy that prevailed in his current relationship with Mary. His deep depression in part reflected his insight that he was caught in a vicious cycle.

Bruce felt a pressing need to relate at a deep level; he felt that he needed an intimate relationship, but lacked the ability to sustain the connection over time. Bruce was caught in an old pattern, learned early in his life and endlessly replayed. He managed to avoid facing his dependency needs by maintaining a pseudo-independence. From this stemmed his false sense of self-sufficiency. "I'm an independent person," he reminded me often, counting off the accomplishments and awards he had achieved during his career in his particular medical specialty. On his card his M.D. was followed by a string of letters attesting to his four subspecialties. Of course, his love hunger was neither easily certified nor easily satisfied.

Despite his success and high-functioning facade, Bruce could not deny the string of relationship failures both outside and within his marriages. Nor could he deny that his failure to connect intimately had serious ramifications for his family. His pose of self-sufficiency was being emulated by his teenage son, who used the popular slogan "I've got to do my own thing" to disconnect from his parents, from school, and from any semblance of responsibility to others.

Is This Virtual Reality?

At the time that I first met Bruce, the message of self-sufficiency permeated the field of psychology and society in general. But it made me suspicious. It seemed the more we professed our autonomy and independence, the less content we seemed to be. Society's ills made this apparent. Drug use was rampant, the divorce rate was rising, men and women seemed more at odds than ever before. Clearly, some important values were missing in the messages being communicated by the new psychologies.

Soon after completing my training as a mental-health professional, I began to question the "truths" or premises on which the field was being directed. When I solicited viewpoints from teachers, Gestalt therapists, transactional analysts, self-actualization advocates, Rogerians, and other "humanistic" psychologists, they all agreed that the ideals of mental health are *personal growth* and *overcoming the traumas of childhood.* No one spoke about adult relationships as being central to one's self-development. Rather, we were taught that the self is strengthened not in relation to intimate partnerships, families, and communities, but through increased independence. The goal of therapy is not to help us connect to others, but to become singularly self-sufficient, self-contained—and, as it turns out, isolated.

I watched as my colleagues' intimate relationships ruptured and terminated. I looked at my own relationship with my husband and decided to ask some different questions. Instead of asking, "How do I become a totally fulfilled, *self-sufficient,* happy individual?" I asked questions from a more interpersonal perspective:

- Do I have to love myself first in order to love another? Or do I have to feel loved by someone else in order to love myself?
- Is being dependent on another person really negative? Is it childish? Does it impede personal growth?
- How do we create fulfilling relationships in which we respond to *one another's* needs?
- If our dependency needs were not met in childhood, does that mean we will necessarily have unhappy adult relationships?
- How many people do I know who recall a happy childhood?
- Is there a future for love?

Listening and Responding Creatively to Dependency Needs

When I married Matt, neither of us would have been considered paragons of mental health. I was anxious and insecure about my intellectual abilities. When I got up to talk in class, my voice came out as a whisper. My future father-in-law said I was "meek as a lamb." For a time, I wondered why this wonderful man, Matthew, had chosen me, and I wondered when he would realize his mistake. I did not think much about *his* history, his need for security and loyalty in a relationship, his dependency needs. I only knew how safe I felt when he protected me against his father's criticism. I knew when he made it clear that I was number one in his life that I could relax and let him see who I was below the surface, and I was gratified when he, in turn, shared with me a few things that were part of his private world. I did not know then that much of his private world would remain private. At the time I only knew that I was in love. Only after I began to examine relationships for my professional growth did I come to understand how and why we had found each other, responded to each other, and fallen in love with each other. Looking back after thirty-eight years of marriage and thirty years of therapeutic experience, I recognize the factors that worked for us. Without recognizing it, we were responding to each other's core needs and feelings, powerful ones that emanated from early childhood and resurfaced in intimate bonds of adulthood. We were attending to each other's dependency needs without shame or blame.

Matt and I both came from unhappy families, and the way in which we fit together as adults would not pass the me generation's test of self-actualized behavior. But the fact is that the relationship continues to thrive after thirty-eight years. And it has been well tested: we have survived crises produced by changing social mores as well as the daily challenges of balancing two careers against the demands of child rearing. My experience as half of this couple is what caused me to rethink principles I had been taught to take for granted.

After the first rush of sharing our private thoughts we rarely discussed our relationship. Matt did not talk much about his feelings and I soon learned that pressuring him to do so would not improve our relationship. So I watched and listened. Gradually I learned. I knew that his mother had died when he was three. Although his father had a series of girlfriends after his wife's early death, he had been deeply affected by the loss of his young wife and reacted by never allowing himself to need another person. Matt's father was a salesman who conveniently spent much of his time traveling throughout the country while Matt and his sister went to live with various relatives for three to six months at a time. As a child, Matt was described as being "deep in his thoughts," introspective, independent, unemotional, and a hard worker.

Matt has shared only a few memories of his childhood with me: believing as a small child that his mother was watching him from heaven; living in eight different places in the years after his mother died; never knowing when the next move would take place; never being able to feel attached to a friend or a teacher. From the scant amount he was able to recall, I knew that the instability and impermanence that characterized his upbringing had been painful enough to defy memory.

Looking back at my early years, I was a child of what is considered a united home. I recall growing up in an emotionally distant but physically together family. My parents were determined to improve their financial situation, although it meant working long hours in a growing family business. Their goals were to become successful, educate the children, make their son a doctor, and marry their daughter to a doctor. The oldest son, as in many families, was my parents' pride and joy. He received most of our family's emotional energy. Throughout my growing-up years, I felt isolated, unloved, and unlovable. One scene I recall from my childhood was when I was three or four years old. I was watching my father and brother working together, building a sailboat. Feeling left out, I said simply, "Daddy, talk to me." He answered, "When you're as old as David, I'll talk to you." I thought that I would never be as old as David, and at that point I decided that I would never be smart enough for my father to talk to me. In school I struggled to overcome my feeling that I couldn't learn as well as other people. I felt dumb. I read few books as a child, a few fairy tales, and lots of comics.

As long as I told myself that my brother was loved because he was the smart one, my self-image could not change. The people I depended upon did not love me, I thought. My solution was, *Don't depend on others*. I had learned not to expect much from people and they responded as I expected. I was quiet, shy, and afraid that people would think of me as inadequate.

My parents did not want me to go to college, even though I fought hard to go. Years later, my father told me that he was trying to save me from the "heartbreak of failure." Once in college, I was not a superior student by any means. Actually, I used few of my inner resources and talents until I met Matt.

Matt was the first person I trusted with the "hidden" me. Probably I first trusted him because when I shared my ideas about politics, history, philosophy—the musings of a twenty-year-old—he did not correct me. I wanted to open up further. Whereas my father would have said, "You will understand when you grow up," Matt assumed I *was* grown-up. He liked my ideas. It was certainly a new experience. When Matt started to talk to me and *listen* to me, I was able to blossom. He treated me as though I had something to contribute. I saw in Matt an idealized father, who reassured me that I was smart and competent. In return, I gave Matt safe, reliable, loving nurturing; because I felt I could depend on him, I could also be loyal to him, assuring him of the permanence of our relationship.

Many professionals in the mental-health field might contend that my husband and I had an unhealthy relationship—after all, you're not supposed to mother your husband and father your wife. But we did not provide only those qualities for each other; we also have been and continue to be lovers, friends, and parents. My point is that, throughout the years, we expected to share insecurities as well as successes and to meet one another's dependency needs in positive, mutually fulfilling ways.

In fact it is through my own relationship's ups and downs that I developed my Rule #1. By showering Matt with the manifestations of love, I got back the love I wanted. In effect, we together learned *how* to love each other.

Healthy dependency for adults requires that both partners be aware and protective of one another's vulnerable areas. One tactic I have intuitively recognized that I must never employ—even if we are fighting—is to talk about leaving or to threaten to leave. I know that, because of Matt's early losses, even a hint of impermanence would severely undermine the trust we have built. Matt, for his part, knows my most vulnerable area—a fear of lack of competence. Despite plenty of opportunities, he has never said, "That's a stupid idea." We nurture each other. I depend on Matt's willingness and ability to attune to my needs, and he depends on my *reciprocal sensitivity*. This doesn't mean that I necessarily fulfill each and every one of his needs that surfaces, nor that he fills all of mine. It means that, over time, we have learned which needs are negotiable or flexible and which are not.

Matt and I have very different needs at the end of the day. He likes to stay home and read or watch the *MacNeil/Lehrer Newshour* or *60 Minutes*—or just quietly read a book. I, on the other hand, after sitting in my office all day listening and trying to understand what I am hearing, need to end my day going out to dinner and talking. I like to talk. I am in a talking profession. But mostly when I work, I actively listen. So Matt and I have different styles—his is quiet contemplation, and mine is ongoing stimulation. As we come together at the end of the day, we check with each to see how we are feeling. We have learned to assess whose needs are greater at the moment. Whose needs get priority tonight, got priority last night, last week? We try to maintain a pretty even balance. I know that he wishes to please me, and I recognized long ago that I would have to reciprocate if I wanted him to continue. I looked for what I could give this very self-contained man who didn't easily display needs.

I realized early in our marriage that Matt needed messages that our relationship would be secure, that he would be affirmed and cared for, that I would not leave, as his mother had done by dying, or as his father had done by traveling to earn a living during the Depression. In his own way—and he certainly never verbalized it—Matt recognized that I needed positive messages about my abilities. Even though we each had wounds from our early lives, we also had the willingness to give emotional sustenance to each other. In a process that continues to this day, our mutual giving has helped to heal our old wounds.

Sometimes I watch Matt listening to me with his eyes clouded over. I could complain that he is tuning me out, or I can acknowledge that I am talking too much and boring him. One day when I was in the midst of explaining my theory of how men and women handle dependency needs differently, Matt said, "I'm pretty sick of hearing about men and women and relationships." That's my life's work, I thought, and he's bored with it. But rather than feeling angry, I looked at it from his perspective. It was time to stop talking on and on about my ideas and get on to a more active stage of working with them.

I also realized that it is important to have other outlets for thinking about this subject; so I organized some discussion groups with friends who are interested in the subject of relationships. I had gone as far as I could in my internal dialogue and needed others to help validate my ideas. At the same time, I got the message that it was time to tune into his needs and interests—charities, education, resolving the problems of the inner cities, finding ways to provide life-span learning to healthy senior citizens. And in the process, I have learned to give him plenty of quiet contemplative times without complaining that he is not available. In this exchange between us is revealed the dynamics of forming positive, healing partnerships. Later in the book we will examine other aspects of development that can be bolstered in ways like this.

Taking the Pathology Out of Relationships

It is not difficult to recognize each other's vulnerabilities. When I work with couples in therapy, it often becomes evident that partners know each other as well as or sometimes better than each knows him or herself. In the play *Who's Afraid of Virginia Woolf?* Martha and George are extremely attuned to each other, but they choose to use their knowledge to hurt and punish. Each continues to injure the other rather than risk losing in their ongoing battle. But it is not lack of sensitivity to each other's needs and vulnerabilities that has caused their perpetual wars.

In this drama we see how a couple's understanding of each other's needs can escalate into poisoned words culminating in what truly is a toxic relationship. The partners in Albee's play hurt each other by pushing sensitive buttons—and they can hurt each other precisely because they know each other's vulnerabilities so well and choose to jab at these wounds. Imagine what this relationship would be like if George and Martha chose instead to soothe each other's wounds—to heal. Perhaps it wouldn't be great drama, but the couple would be healthier and the individuals within it more whole.

If we judge our partners to be withholding, sick, needy, or demanding, then we will react accordingly. If we attribute to our partners a normal need to be nurtured, understood, and accepted, then we will interpret the messages we receive in an entirely different light, and we can give and receive love. The very same behavior can be labeled in either positive or negative terms, and that choice of labels or viewpoints then greatly influences the outcome of the interaction.

With a divorce rate over 50 percent and with men and women complaining equally that they cannot seem to find a mate who will meet their needs, it is time to rethink what we expect of relationships. It is not that relationships fail because men have "commitment phobias" or women have "Cinderella complexes." Relationships fail because the current rules of our society force a choice between being strong, independent, and having self-esteem versus being emotionally nurtured in a dependent relationship. These days, if you choose to take care of your partner's deep needs, you may be labeled codependent and encouraged to join a support group to cure you of unhealthy caretaking tendencies!

I believe that our blanket denial of normal dependency needs has created an impossible polarity that leaves us either "self-sufficient" or codependent. We value and accept only half of ourselves—the half that is competent and independent. The other half is labeled undesirable or even sick. This forced choice between supposedly competing and contradictory needs causes symptoms to emerge that often reveal our hidden emotional modus operandi.

Randi: Who Will Be There for Me?

Randi, recently divorced and with joint custody of a two-year-old child, came into therapy with symptoms of depression. She is a successful businesswoman who started sewing and designing as a teenager and by the age of twenty-five worked her way up to owning a national business focused on clothes for young adults. Married for three years to a musician who spent weeks at a time on the road, Randi decided she wanted a divorce. "He isn't there for me, so I may as well take care of myself," she said. And she was able to do it. Financially independent, she appears to be strong, competent, and perfectly capable of handling her life. There was no shortage of men for this tall, blond, very seductive twenty-six-year-old dynamo.

What the world didn't see were the increasing bouts of depression.

As we explored what went wrong in her marriage, she told me about her current boyfriend, a record producer. "Finally I found someone who seemed strong, but soon he wanted to put his head in my lap and tell me about his ex-wife and his troubles with his kids. Every time I get to know a man well, he starts telling me his troubles and worries. *Then* he wants to make love! I am so angry at men. They just want sex and mothering. What about what I need? Who will be there for me? I know that I am strong. But sometimes I just want to relax and know I am safe with somebody, and it never happens." Thus, she revealed the source of her depression.

Randi told me that all of her relationships with men were in one way or another similar. "It was like that with my husband," she said. "At first he seemed powerful and successful. I thought that I would finally have someone I could count on. I am good at giving, but I need someone strong. It turned out he was weak. When I let him know what a disappointment he was, that all he wanted was to be babied, he got angry and abusive. He relapsed into his coke habit. Finally, I just got so bored, I couldn't stand it. I knew it was time to get out. I didn't want to be codependent. I know too many women who put up with that. I don't need a relationship with any man if it's going to be like that."

Meanwhile, she keeps dating and looking, not realizing the extent to which she has become part of the problem. Randi focused her complaints on her partner's dependency needs while denying her own. "Why can't you be there for me?" is her silent question, described only in terms of anger and depression. Perhaps her husband was weak, perhaps her boyfriend was troubled, but by focusing on these aspects of their characters she locked each relationship into a losing battle with each partner struggling to have needs met. When these needs aren't met, there may be physical or psychological repercussions, sometimes even substance abuse as with her current boyfriend, or depression.

Randi's relationship problems are not simply an outgrowth of an unhappy childhood or of a codependent relationship. Her battle between independence and dependence is an inner struggle in which unmet dependency needs leave her feeling a deep angst, sadness, hurt, emptiness, and despair that she can't assuage because she doesn't think that she or the men in her life should have these needs (i.e., for nurturing, soothing) or have to depend on each other to meet such needs. In short, Randi is denying herself the benefits that can emanate from a healthy expression of Rule #1. If she unbegrudgingly gave in to her partner's need for love and tenderness, she would be able to get her needs met. A partner who feels loved is more loving.

Loosening the Chains of the Past

Freudian theory dictates that our past determines our present. We have also been told that, to heal the wounds of the past, we have to go back to those old traumas, remember them or even relive them, to understand how our adult behavior has been caused by them. Unfortunately, in gaining this tremendous insight into our past, there is a tendency to assign blame: "My mother was overprotective and clingy and therefore I am a dependent, needy adult. . . . My father was never there for me and therefore I can't trust men now."

Supposedly, the tracing of our wounded history will free us to become independent, self-actualized people—able to exist happily, completely on our own, loving ourselves and healing our "inner child." Having once achieved this, we find that love follows naturally, or so the story goes.

Many who follow these precepts wonder why the process does not lead to happy relationships. My experience as a therapist (and my experience in dealing with my childhood wounds) has taught me that neither achieving insight nor assigning blame brings healing. Insight brings intellectual comprehension of how the pieces in the puzzle fit together, and blame creates glue that keeps the pieces stuck together in their old pattern. The thing that leads to healing is *loving, interdependent connections with others in the present.*

In an interview with Bill Moyers, Sam Keen, best-selling author of *Fire in the Belly: On Being a Man*, talked about reaching a point in his marriage when he realized, with tremendous frustration, that he would never be able to change his wife. Certain characteristics that annoyed him or enraged him or even hurt him would not yield to his manipulations. His illusions lost, he asked himself, "Can I still love this person *with* these 'flaws'? Once you cross that dividing line between fantasy [I can change this person] and reality [I can't change this person]," Keen declared with vigor, "that's when things get interesting. That's when things finally get real and you start to learn what it really means to love."

Men and women have traveled different paths toward adulthood, but both sexes have ended up feeling wounded, cheated, and increasingly isolated from one another. We cannot rewrite our developmental history by merely loving *ourselves* to health. Healing is not something we do alone. Emotional wounds develop in relationships, and the healing of those wounds also requires relationships. These can be heterosexual, homosexual, or nonsexual, loving relationships with friends, mentors, teachers, therapists, religious leaders, and a host of others in close personal bonds. Loving adults can touch the core needs of one another and heal the inner wounds of childhood. Alone, I cannot make myself healthy. Alone, I cannot love myself enough.

Much of the family-therapy field focuses on the childhood roots of marital problems. When a marriage is in trouble, we typically try to help the partners become more independent and mature so that their individual childhood wounds will not interfere with their current relationship. But lack of independence and the contamination of childhood wounds do not necessarily ensure failure in relationships. More often than not, it is the denial of our need to depend on our partners, and the resulting inability to share in healing one another's wounds, that become the seeds of later failures. *Dependence on others for nurturance, acceptance, and affirmation is not a pathological symptom.* Because we have come to believe that it is "sick" to have needs, dependent behavior that is quite normal is perceived as a disability. It is imperative that we learn how to distinguish between positive dependency and dependent behavior that is unhealthy or destructive.

Relationship Busting in the Age of Codependence

The belief that dependence upon intimate connections with others is a sign of weakness is the foundation for a widespread movement christened codependence in which people became dependent on a relationship that is dysfunctional. Recovery from codependency requires a willingness to disengage from unhealthy patterns.

What I call *relationship busting* has become part of the fallout of this worthwhile movement, which had the original purpose of exposing abuse and raising society's awareness that many people are caught in relationships that are physically and emotionally damaging. Unfortunately, an important aspect of human nature has been endangered along the way: our primary, unchanging need for healthy dependency and for enduring, committed involvement.

Profile of Codependence

The profile of the codependent person comprises a dizzying number of characteristics. Among other things, those who are identified as codependent may:

- overextend themselves by feeling responsible for too many things
- feel harried and pressured
- find themselves doing things they don't really want to do
- not know what they want or need
- feel bored, empty, and worthless unless there is a problem to solve or someone to help
- feel safest when giving
- anticipate other people's needs
- feel anxiety, pity, and guilt when other people have a problem
- feel compelled to help another person solve a problem
- feel responsible for other people
- feel sad because they spend their whole lives giving to other people
- resent others' lack of reciprocity
- become confused when their "help" isn't effective or appreciated
- believe they are somehow responsible for how another person feels

- find that other people become impatient or angry with them for the way they feel
- abandon their routine to respond to or do something for somebody else
- feel angry, victimized, unappreciated, and used

These are characteristics of codependence that I found in books by Anne Wilson Schaef; in *Co-Dependence: Misunderstood—Mistreated,* and Melody Beattie in *Co-Dependent No More.* Clearly, these characteristics fit many people. In fact, many of them fit all of us. We need to ask, Why is it sick to anticipate others' needs? To feel anxiety or pity when we recognize the problems of another? To put another's needs before our own? Some of the traits on the list apply to people who might be content in their lives and satisfied in their relationships. Others are qualities that apply to people whose unhappy relationships have led to emotional problems. Simply making a list of character traits and then identifying them as indicators of "codependency" does not help much. But it does help convince us to be wary of the *need* to depend on another as part of giving and receiving love.

The codependency movement has rightly identified unhealthy relationships in which one partner is abusive and the battered partner struggles to please. To go from identifying truly abusive attitudes, however, to the assumption that caretaking itself is pathological requires a gigantic leap in logic. Each individual's wounds has an effect on the relationship. Sadly, instead of addressing these wounds, many of us have become wary of all caretaking needs and have started to disengage from genuine relationships, which by their nature imply a form of mutual dependence. In essence, the baby has been thrown out with the bathwater. Intimate relationships cannot exist in an atmosphere devoid of caretaking and dependency. We need to look at the positive aspects of the very same qualities that have been banned as codependent. Try thinking about yourself in terms of the following. Notice the feelings that surface while filling out the following inventory as compared to how you felt reading the earlier list of characteristics labeled "codependent."

Am I a Positive Dependent?

	Never	Sometimes	Often	Always
It is easy for me to sense what others are feeling and to respond.	___	___	___	___
I enjoy taking care of my mate because I like the appreciation I get in return.	___	___	___	___
I find it uncomfortable to not respond when I see someone I love in need.	___	___	___	___
I am good at solving problems and I enjoy trying to help my friends with their various situations.	___	___	___	___
I get a sense of exhilaration when I am able to respond in a caring way to others.	___	___	___	___
I know that I have an impact on those close to me, and I like being sensitive to that.	___	___	___	___
Helping others brings out the best in me.	___	___	___	___
I can depend on my partner to care about how I feel.	___	___	___	___
I like the feeling that we are a team.	___	___	___	___
If a friend asks me for help, it is easy for me to adjust my routine.	___	___	___	___
Giving help in some way, being there for someone else, gives me a nourishing spiritual feeling.	___	___	___	___

If you have answered "often" or "always" throughout this checklist, you are already experiencing the positive aspects of healthy dependency and caretaking. If not, you might be missing something worth reading more about.

The Survival of Love

Loving too much is not a disease. Providing support and nurturance is not unhealthy, nor is needing support and nurturance. They are among the most important components of intimate, caring relationships. The perception that normal caretaking is automatically unhealthy must be reversed in our modern culture if love is to survive.

When past needs and defenses against being needy result in conflict or confusion, it is *healthy* to work on these difficulties in a relationship that has the potential for love. To have a strong desire to express and to receive love is healthy, *not sick.* Ironically, the real danger occurs when women and men label themselves as "overly dependent" and try to cure themselves by *needing less.* Often, this translates into giving less but expecting more.

Alcoholics Anonymous identifies addiction as a disease that responds to the process of *recovery,* which is a battle that is waged over an illness that is never permanently overcome. Instead, the organization contends that it can only be dealt with one day at a time. Because recovery is an ongoing process, a *permanent* part of one's life, attendance at meetings and, of course, complete abstinence from the addictive substance are necessary for recovery.

But what abstinence is required of the "women who love too much"? What of women who have a strong need to be caretakers? Should they be "in recovery" from needing love? *Nobody can recover from needing love!*

In the idealized world of pop psychology, caretaking and nurturing are sometimes defined as diametrically opposed to autonomy and maturity. Indeed, the message of the codependence movement blends deceptively well with the traditional view of mature development as the ability to function independently, without the need of others. We are supposed to move from early childhood through increasing degrees of separation and individuation, striving to be able to stand alone, to be strong without needing support from others.[1] "Autonomous functioning" has been heralded by many as the ultimate goal of maturity. There is little room in these goals for normal adult feelings of dependency, for periods of healthy caretaking, for a balanced experience of separateness and relatedness.

How can such messages possibly prepare anyone for a loving relationship? If one actually achieved the goals of mental health and maturity, so defined, the resulting "cure" would, in fact, resemble what in my previous book *Narcissism and Intimacy*[2] is identified as a "narcissistic disorder"—which means that the afflicted person is not able to sustain intimate relationships!

Well-being and self-esteem do not develop as a result of being alone. Rather, the capacity to function alone is an outgrowth of feeling loved and nurtured in a bonded, secure relationship. We learn patterns of relating early in childhood and tend to re-create them repeatedly throughout our lives. Indeed, most partners choose each other with the unconscious hope of repeating what was good and repairing what was bad or lacking in their earliest relationships. Whatever was learned in our primary relationships about love, trust, and safety, that helps us to join in the world of others, becomes our model for relating. Just as blueprints are needed to lay the basic foundation of a building, the foundation of our intimate relationships are based on early instilled blueprints for love, our relational imprints.

Relationship patterns that are imprinted in the early years play a large part in our connections with important others. These primary imprints for love remain with us as we become involved in each new relationship throughout our lives.

In Part 2, you will learn more about the ways that we all develop imprints for love. In Part 3, you will find exercises that help you and your partner recognize your own unique imprints for relating.

In the next chapter, we will see how models for human connection develop during our earliest, most dependent years and influence us for the rest of our lives. We will also learn that early injury does not have to cause unhappy adult relationships. In fact, nurturing our intimate relationships in the present is the means by which emotional wounds from childhood can be healed.

2 Wounded Men, Wounded Women

Rule #2 for Positive Dependency:

There are many levels of "truth" from the surface message to the deepest core emotions. In every adult there is a wide range of dependency needs stemming from childhood. Listen for the imprinted messages of childhood to help you understand the true meaning of your partner's words.

D o these statements sound familiar?

"I would get married if only I could find a woman I could trust."

"What's the matter with men? They never want to be close."

"I've been let down so many times that I keep my guard up until I know I won't get hurt."

With so many people protecting themselves against being hurt by love, it is no wonder that so many of us feel alone—even when we are involved in a relationship. If we cannot depend on others *not* to hurt us, our only alternative is to wear a protective shell of emotional guardedness. But human beings are not meant to be alone. The whole of human evolution is bound up with society and with social relationships. We need people in our lives and we need to be able to *depend* on them. We develop the capacity for healthy aloneness only when we know we are loved and that someone is there for us. An innate need for relationships drives us from the time that we are born to the time that we die. When adults do not feel that they are accepted, valued, and affirmed by important others, they become frustrated and unhappy.

From the beginning of life, babies who do not feel secure in a safe, loving relationship can become emotionally disturbed and may spend a lifetime trying to repair the damage. As adults, *healthy human beings get their needs filled through mutual, healthy, dependent relationships.* Indeed, from infancy to adulthood, we never stand alone and we never really lose our need for others. In many cases, *denying* or *pathologizing* our basic needs creates the seemingly impenetrable barriers to intimacy and long-term stable relationships that plague us today.

Marriage, more than any other adult relationship, parallels both the successes and failures of our early experiences—experiences steeped in the dependency needs of the baby and the child. With fateful precision, adults re-create in their marriages the patterns of emotional dependency, positive and negative, that they developed in the homes of their parents. In every adult there is a wide range of dependency needs stemming from childhood. This leads to Rule #2 for positive dependency. Listen for the imprinted messages of childhood to help you understand the true meaning of your partner's words. You will discover that there are many levels of "truth" from the surface message to the deepest core emotions.

The relationship of husband and wife closely resembles, in many ways, the relationship of parent and child. In many aspects, marriage reproduces adult versions of the infant-mother bond. In order to be healthy, both relationships require a balance of close, dependent contact with a measure of separateness and independence. Because these two relationships—parent and child, husband and wife—are so central to the human experience, they provide arenas of interaction in which individuals can realize their best and their worst selves. You can see, as marriage mirrors childhood, the importance of understanding our partner's deepest truths and feelings. With understanding we don't stumble unknowingly into wounds that we didn't realize were there.

A Self of One's Own

The self-esteem that is so often considered a prerequisite to healthy relating is actually the *outgrowth* of a series of interdependent relationships that ideally begin at birth. A child gains a sense of self through interactions with his or her parents. These interactions are like a mirror in which the developing child perceives him- or herself. If the mirror (the parent's response) reflects a positive image, feelings of self-esteem develop. A baby who cannot depend on parental responses to be loving or caring will not grow up to have a solid sense of self.

Over the past three decades or so, an impressive body of infant research has demonstrated that, from the earliest moments of life, the experience of being able to depend on others is necessary for every baby's emotional as well as physical health. Even given adequate care of their physical needs, infants who do not receive ample, loving emotional contact and touching often fail to thrive, falling behind in all aspects of their development. Closeness between mother and baby is so crucial an experience for survival that British pediatrician and psychoanalyst Donald W. Winnicott once commented, "There is no such thing as an infant." Infants, he explained, exist only as a part of a mother-child pair. A human baby is so helpless that it cannot survive without a mother (or substitute caretaker) who responds positively to the baby's emotional and physical needs.[3]

The pervasive assumption, popular among mental health professionals and lay people alike, that the needs of early life somehow vanish as our capacity for mature behavior emerges is a fundamental error. I find it paradoxical that, although psychotherapists recognize the crucial equation between receiving loving care and the development of independence in infants and children, from adolescence onward we recognize and encourage only half of this equation— independent functioning.

Daniel Stern, a renowned pediatrician and infant researcher, is one of the experts who contends that the developmental phases of infancy and childhood are not stages that we pass through and outgrow; rather, *they continue to exist throughout life.*[4] I agree. More than that, I see the continuation of our earliest needs into adult life every day in my consulting room. The continuing existence of these early needs is not the problem. Our automatic disavowal of them, shame in feeling them, or disgust in seeing them in others is what creates problems.

The following diagram may help you to see where you fit in the spectrum of dependency needs and help you identify ways that you defend against being dependent. You may find that your current or past partners show signs of similar or complementary patterns, which shall be discussed in later chapters.

We each learn certain styles of relating. Your particular form becomes your basic imprint, and you are likely to return to it time and again. For example, do you feel ashamed to admit it when you are hurt by what someone says? Do you become anxious when you are the center of attention? Do people you care about complain that you keep yourself emotionally distant? Do you feel unsatisfied and always want more in your relationships? Do you want to hide at social events? These are your unique ways of feeling, ways that you have probably carried all your life. If you want to understand how they affect your ability to depend on others, look at the Spectrum of Dependency chart on page 50.

Dependency is not immaturity, an unhealthy regression, or a sign of pathology. Dependency exists along a spectrum from health to pathology. Positive dependency allows you to maintain close bonds, to feel open and connected without fear of being swallowed up, to share special experiences that enhance intimacy, to experience yourself as enhanced within the context of something larger, a relationship, a community, a family in which you take pride. Unhealthy dependency takes its form from the defenses used to avoid the danger of needing someone else. In its severe forms, it may be a narcissistic grandiosity or pseudo-independence: "I am the center, and you, whom I depend upon to fill my needs, are an object, a thing to be used by me as I wish. I cannot depend on a real person because you may then use me, demand from me, drain me. So when I feel dependent, you must cease to exist as a real, live other person in my life." This is narcissistic thinking.

Other forms of unhealthy dependency may occur when what I need from you is clear, but I fear that I cannot get it. You have the power to say no to me or to reject and shame me for allowing weakness and neediness to show, so I must get rid of those infantile parts and show only my strong, powerful parts. I will cross the barriers between us and give you all the bits of me that I hate. Then I can hate it in you. I do this

Spectrum Of Dependency

Signs of Defensive Dependency

(You have mastered ways of keeping others at a distance)

Signs of Positive Dependency

(You can maintain closeness and be vulnerable with others)

Signs of Defensive Dependency	Signs of Positive Dependency
An *"anxious attacher"* You often feel insecure and suffer from fear of abandonment in every relationship. You may have a general feeling of emptiness that helps you hide from an inner chaos.	A *"secure attacher"* You are connected to the people around you and feel fully "present" during experiences together.
A *"boundary buster"* You lack emotional boundaries between yourself and others. Sometimes you feel confused between what you are feeling and what others feel.	An *"empathic attuner"* Your boundaries are solid but not rigid, and, when you want, permeable. You can let in other people and other viewpoints. You have a sense of security, a cohesive set of values and beliefs; yet can take in new information.
A *"fragile connector"* You may, under stress, feel emotionally overloaded and be perceived as "prickly," difficult, or easily angered.	A *"caring connector"* You have positive interests that can be engaged when you are alone and also be shared with others.
A *"defensive distancer"* You may be a "loner" who isolates from others out of fear or oversensitivity to being hurt. It is a pseudo-independence that protects you from the danger of intimacy.	A *"healthy togetherness"* You feel both an I-ness and a we-ness, feeling whole and independent within the context of a relationship.

by maintaining control at all times. What I fear most is losing control and feeling needy, helpless, and impotent.

Another form of unhealthy dependency is to substitute the need for people with a need for things; drugs, sex, TV, computers, pornography, and a multitude of other objects provide comfort and security to make me feel more stimulated or more calm, or deadening me to the pain of not having needs met.

In a fourth damaging form of dependency, the neediness is strong and dependence is colored by intense anxiety, insecurity, and fears of abandonment. The person with an inability to form attachments or one who repeatedly forms "push-pull" attachments may have suffered from a failure of bonding early in life. There is never a comfortable fit in such a relationship. If I am too close I feel swallowed up or smothered. If I pull away to be safe, I soon feel totally isolated and urgently seek to reconnect. "I can't live with her, I can't live without her" is a common reaction in such a relationship. It sometimes seems that this is a common theme of human relationships.

The Evolution of Our Dependency Needs

Human beings evolved in groups. Our evolutionary history suggests that dependency on others is an inherent biological fact. Throughout time, neither individuals nor families have been completely self-sufficient. Until recent centuries, human beings lived in small groups whose members literally depended upon each other for survival. With few exceptions, people spent the entire span of their lives in close proximity to others in a band of closely related families. We come from a heritage in which individuals are part of a family, a tribe, or a village. Our ancestors worked and played together in small communities where privacy was minimal. Together they worshiped, participated in community social and religious events, and depended on one another for survival and sustenance. The community was the basic social structure. Being cast out of the band was the harshest of punishments because it condemned the individual to a solitary life and death. In most instances, those who lived to reproduce were those who avoided isolation and chose to stay close to others. They have passed on to us as their legacy, the tendency to seek social contact.

As we approach the turn of the century, American culture no longer requires such obvious communal interdependence for survival. We have far less need to live together in order to grow food, build shelters, and ward off death. As a consequence, we have come to the erroneous conclusion that we can live and survive alone. Indeed, we believe we *ought* to be able to do so. Privacy has become an important badge of modern Western societies. For most of human history, it was necessary to be together; in recent centuries, being separate has become a luxury that we have come to prize. This separateness, however, is largely an illusion. We delude ourselves into believing that, just because we no longer need others to hunt with us or defend our homes, we don't *need* each other. But the truth is, at every level of society and in every sector, we still need human connection: we still depend on each other. In fact, our need for each other is a direct link to our earliest days of infancy, when our existence depended on others. Perhaps as adults we feed and clothe ourselves, but other emotional and even biological drives dictate that our need to depend on others does not end just because we aren't infants anymore.

Understanding Your Imprints for Relating

During the first three years of life we learn particular patterns of behavior, primarily through interaction with important caretakers—usually our mothers and fathers. Once learned, these imprinted patterns shape the way we feel about ourselves as well as the way we relate to others; in turn, these imprints shape our dependency needs. That is why (as in Rule #2) it is so important to understand the imprints that underlie both your own and your mate's behavior.

Among our earliest imprints are the wordless records of our experiences in giving and receiving love, which serve as our personalized guidelines for relating. When early development is relatively supportive and "normal," our imprints record only the wounds that we are all subject to: the infant's discovery that he or she is not the center of the universe, the day-to-day discomfort of tolerating momentarily unfulfilled needs, and the insults of socialization (toilet training, restraining food-throwing behaviors, etc.). All of these uncomfortable restrictions are integrated into our relational imprints.

Some developmental experiences are not so easily handled: emotional unavailability of caretakers, neglect, abuse, chaos in the home that causes anxiety—these are all serious wounds that are also integrated into our imprints, together with the coping mechanisms each child uses as a means of protective defenses against the pain of the wounds. These defenses are organized within the developing relational imprints and become part of a repertoire for coping with stressful interactions over the course of life. In this way, our imprints map our relationships as well as our defenses against emotional pain. I have identified four imprints that organize key repetitive patterns of relating:

1. *The Imprint for Primary Bonding*
2. *The Imprint for Emotional Boundaries*
3. *The Imprint for Bridging Connections*
4. *The Imprint for Mature Dependence*

From birth onward, our interpersonal experiences shape our future ability to love and trust. Early experience leads us to predict from others either help or hindrance, harmony or conflict, when we attempt to get our needs met. This amazing correspondence between infant experience and adult behavior can be demonstrated graphically with Russian nesting dolls. For many years I collected these dolls without consciously realizing their significance to the work I was doing. Many dolls, each identical but in progressively smaller sizes, rest inside the largest doll. From the smallest to the largest, they are all based on the same pattern. Each is a slightly larger but similar version of the preceding one.

Mature Dependency and Interconnection
Development of Bridging Connections
Development of Emotional Boundaries
Primary Bonding
Inherited Potential

These dolls illustrate what I have experienced as a therapist. Inside each of us is the tiny newborn, the toddler, the adolescent, and the adult, re-created in larger and larger versions but basically shaped from the same mold. When we enter into adult relationships, the outermost layers of our development are the most visible, but our inner baby and child, filled with unique talents, strengths, needs, and wounds, is also a vibrant albeit invisible presence. Each of us carries the imprints of our earliest experiences, along with all of the same needs, met and unmet. As noted, these imprints do not merely govern our early years and then vanish into oblivion. They remain as vigorous psychological and emotional influences throughout our lives, connecting our earliest months with our last years, providing a cord of continuity that is remarkable in its consistency.

At every stage of development we learn a new way of connecting with others. We also learn how to protect ourselves from the emotional hurts that invariably occur in our attempts to make contact. The basic imprints of human development are formed during the years when we are totally dependent on others for physical and emotional survival. Each imprint, therefore, contains important information about our dependency needs. In adulthood, as in childhood, these needs are generally played out in our primary relationships.

In succeeding chapters we will examine each imprint in depth. For now, a brief sampling of each will provide an overview of what is to come.

Imprint for Primary Bonding

"If you loved me, you would automatically know what I need."

Warren, a tall, serious-looking man, was secretive about his therapy. He handed me the information form saying that although he had filled in his home number, he did not want me ever to call it. If I needed to reach him, Warren said I should contact him at work. I agreed to this, wondering what he was hiding or hiding from.

In response to my question "What brings you into therapy?" Warren said that he was surprised to be meeting with a therapist, that this was very unlike him, and that he had always seen himself as strong and able to handle whatever came up.

"Yes," I said, waiting for him to continue.

"I'm feeling very frustrated in my relationship with my wife," he went on. "Don't get me wrong, we have a very strong marriage. I wouldn't do anything to upset all the good things. I certainly wouldn't want to complain to her about it."

"What is it about the relationship that is frustrating you?"

"Well, I've got to tell you she is a terrific woman. In fact, everyone who knows us would say we have a pretty ideal relationship. Our son is a great boy. Carol and I have so many interests in common. We're active in politics, in charities, in our son's school. She went into business a few years ago and has been successful. I'm really proud of her."

"It sounds great. What's the problem?"

"Well, something is wrong and I tell her about it, and she listens and doesn't do anything to change it. I've decided that I can't change her, so I'll let it be. But I get very upset. I can't believe I'm talking about this to a therapist. It feels very strange."

"Can you tell me what it is that you have tried to explain to Carol about what is wrong?"

"Well, I go to work, and when I come home, she is often still at work. I like to cook, so I start the dinner. Carol often comes home very tired. Sometimes all she wants to do is take dinner up to the bedroom and eat alone. Even when we eat together, she goes up right after dinner and finishes things for her business or makes phone calls to friends to take care of the different activities she's involved in. I feel we don't relate with each other anymore. When I complain to her, nothing changes."

I said that he must be feeling pretty cut off from this important relationship, and he agreed. But when I suggested that this was a relationship problem, and that his wife should be there to discuss it with him, Warren appeared nervous about it. When I questioned him about this, he explained, "I have tried to get her to do more things with me, to spend more time with me in the evening. She should know what I need. If she loved me, she would know. If she doesn't take the time for me, it means she doesn't care."

I interjected, "Are you saying that if she doesn't know what you need, then she doesn't love you? She should understand you without words?"

"Right."

"What if you're wrong? What if she needs to hear what is going on inside of you?"

In the session that followed, we talked about his desire to be strong, successful, and competent in everything he did. He had difficulty understanding his reaction to his wife's increasingly busy and separate life. He did not want his need for her time, attention, and company to be seen by her because it might show how much he depended on her. She might see his vulnerability. By the end of the second session, Warren agreed to invite Carol to join him the next time we met.

Carol was surprised when Warren said he had seen a therapist. She, too, saw him as always strong, together, and perfectly capable of handling any problems. With some assistance, Warren told Carol that he was upset about her having time for everything and everyone but him. He went on to talk about his feeling of having lost an important person in his life.

Carol seemed surprised. "I know you complain about my being tired when I come home, and about you having to do most of the work for dinner."

"I don't mind preparing the dinner. You know I like to cook. It's a good way to relax from the pressures of work. That's not what's wrong. It's that you're hardly there. I need more of you. I need more and I don't feel comfortable asking."

"Why not? Why didn't you say so? You're more important to me than anyone. I've always thought we had a wonderful marriage. I had no idea why you seemed so upset lately."

We had one more session a month later and some follow-up correspondence several months later in which Warren said that things were going well.

It has been a year, and I just met with Warren to discuss what happened in therapy. There is no sign of the upset feelings, the need and the shame that went with being needy. With the relationship meeting his needs, he felt no need for therapy.

Warren's mind-reading fantasy derives from the very first bonding imprint, which is formed in infancy, the most dependent stage of our lives. When we are babies, our mothers do, in a sense, read our minds. Our needs are minimal and it's not difficult for a mother to know which form of nurturing her baby needs at a given moment. If our mothers give easily during this time, as adults we will feel that it is safe to be close. We reexperience this imprint each time we fall in love, and also during times of sexual passion.

If bonding needs are not met at any point in life, we may feel shame at our yearning and neediness for another. Indeed, whenever we feel needy in our adult lives, we can be fairly certain that some of our responses originate in this first Imprint for Bonding, which maps the wounds of our earliest needs for unconditional dependence on another.

When Bonding Needs Are Unfulfilled You May:

• Expect to be understood without words

• Yearn for more holding and touching

• Feel depressed and empty when alone

• Seek constant affirmation from others

• Want more emotional connection than others seem to

• Constantly try to control your partner's reactions

• Act as if you and your partner are "joined at the hip"

• Repeatedly test your partner for proof of love

• Expect your partner to be able to read your mind and know your needs

---

This first imprint for bonding develops before words, concepts, or symbols. The needs of the baby (and the "baby feelings" in the adult) center around bodily comforts, avoidance of physical pain, and feelings of safety and security. How our imprints develop is determined by how our needs are met at this time when our dependence on others is total and we have the least control over what happens to us. Wounds at this level are imprinted most intensely, and when there is a history of failure to meet primary needs for security, food, and comforting, feelings of fear and shame are usually attached to the reemergence of these needs.

Wounds originating in this imprint trigger highly emotional reactions that can feel overwhelming, uncontrollable, and "infantile." The solution, however, is not to label this behavior bad or immature, but to recognize that old unmet needs are part of our earliest imprint for love and will always be there. When our problems relate to our need to merge with another person, it is possible to find healthy ways to fulfill that need through loving relationships.

Imprint for Emotional Sharing

"Don't come too close—but don't go away either."
"If you love me, you would feel as I do and want what I want."
"If this is love, you would listen to me talk about my worries, my anger, my pain, and you would be able to tolerate whatever you hear."

These double-bind messages are the underlying themes of many relationships and derive from our Imprint for Emotional Sharing. Between the ages of six and eighteen months, we discover what differentiates us from others—the "boundaries" of who we are. We learn about these boundaries in interactions with our parents, through the feedback we receive when we express our needs. By watching how our parents react, we learn which feelings and responses are good and which are bad. When parents respond to our expression of need with anger, anxiety, disgust, or withdrawal, we learn about *negative dependency:* the message is experienced as if the need were shameful or destructive, insatiable or unfillable, because of something bad within. We may discover that, in order to get important needs met, we must alter those needs in whatever way evokes a tolerable response. In contrast, when we experience *healthy dependency,* our needs are easily and soothingly met and we learn to trust our experience, to trust others, and to expect favorable, safe responses.

I call this the Imprint for Emotional Sharing because it is the period in which we learn to read and be read by others. As adults, this imprint ultimately influences how open or closed we are emotionally, how willing we are to share the hidden parts of ourselves, and how willing we are to accept the hidden parts of our partners. Adults who have experienced healthy dependency during infancy are likely to be more open to relationships and less suspicious, fearful, or ashamed of their feelings. They will have a clearer sense of their boundaries—a clearer sense of selfhood—and show a willingness to risk intimate engagement with others.

Having imprints for healthy dependency helps us to distinguish in an interaction with a partner which feelings to "own" and which belong to the partner. Adults who experienced negative dependency early on will be more guarded, fearing a loss of self through engulfment in the other's needs. Often they mistake their own anger, hurt, and humiliation for their partners'. Often they are ashamed of their feelings because as infants their parents' response was disapproval.

The solution to problems stemming from this relational imprint arises from acknowledging the underlying need to be truly known and accepted no matter what feelings are expressed, to recognize feelings without acting them out in hurtful ways, and to accept each other no matter what secrets lurk within.

Imprint for Bridging Connections

"I have to start my day with the high that I get from running."
"Making deals is as exciting to me as making love."
"I must have a drink before I give a presentation or I become panicked."

The need for a crutch to help us engage in the *world of others* is the basis of Imprint for Bridging Connections. As toddlers, we learn to substitute things for people, to gain comfort from dolls, stuffed animals, and special blankets. These sources of comfort are called "transitional objects"[5] because they help us make the transition from living in a state of comfort and safety provided by the mother to developing a sense of boundaries and separateness. In this way, we learn quite early in life that we can use *things* to remind us of people, to recall the feelings of safety experienced when somebody is there for us, and to comfort us when we are alone. We can also learn how to quell the pain of unmet needs by depending on these substitutes.

Adults use a variety of transitional objects to give them a sense of connection to others—some positive, some very negative. Positive "objects" include shared activities, joint goals, common social, religious, and political participation. Negative "objects" include everything from the use of drugs, alcohol, and tobacco to computer and video addictions to workaholism and exercise mania. The problem with depending excessively on things instead of people for sustenance is that the underlying need for positive, dependent connections remains unaddressed and unfulfilled.

Imprint for Mature Dependence

"I love you, but I need my space."
"Be close, be interested, but let me be me."
"Don't tell me what to do and don't ask anything of me."

During the third year of life, the "terrible twos," children learn that they have minds of their own. "No!" becomes the catchword of the day as the child begins to create the fourth imprint, the one that contains instructions for independent functioning. This is the imprint we are most familiar with because it prescribes those qualities that are supposed to ensure "mature" adult behavior. The qualities of autonomy and independence contained in our Imprint for Mature Dependence are seen as prerequisites for being able to love. What we tend to overlook is that healthy independent behavior is actually the result of successfully meeting the *dependency needs* of the preceding imprints, which underlie what is commonly called independence. We can be independent only when we are sure that there are people in our lives whom we can depend upon. True independence is mature dependence.

In our current cultural climate, the independent capabilities generally equated with maturity reflect only one phase of development, but have been plucked out of context and deemed supreme in our society.

As a consequence, we are encouraged, ironically, to become increasingly detached. We are taught to banish or at least to be ashamed of traces of our normal human need to rely upon others or to be nurtured. We are supposed to be stronger than that. We have come to believe that we have to make a choice: be separate and self-sufficient or be connected and dependent. The truth is, we cannot be healthy if we utilize only the abilities developed in our imprint for mature dependence. Without exercising the life-giving qualities for relating contained within our earlier models for love, we can all too easily be seduced into the illusion of total independence and find ourselves living self-absorbed and ultimately lonely lives.

As adults, most of us have learned to repress or camouflage a whole range of what we consider "childish" needs. We struggle to turn a mature face to the world because that is what the world demands. Our relational imprints give us messages about how to handle interpersonal situations, particularly those that are emotionally laden. The result is that we respond not only in words but in waves of emotions and moods that we do not always understand. That is why I emphasize in Rule #2 how many levels of truths there can be in every statement until we know our partners very well. With each partner experiencing waves of moods and feelings that happen in a flash on an unconscious level, communication can easily break down. It pays to be patient and to listen more than talk. You might have had the experience, for example, of feeling angry and then paralyzed when arguing with your mate. You don't necessarily process these emotions at the time, and if you did, they would be mysterious unless you understood more about your models for love. The unmet needs contained within each of the imprints will always find some means of expression—be it through addiction, workaholism, depression, anxiety, self-imposed isolation, or failed relationships.

We cannot *pass through* our developmental imprints in the same way that we graduate from high school or college. Representing successive levels of development, they remain with us throughout our lives, one level nestled within the other, just like the Russian dolls. It is not "regressive" to experience our primary needs from time to time—it is healthy, as long as we know how to respect and respond to these needs. Contrary to the tenets of many modern pundits, I believe that *we must make a place for our basic dependency needs.* Unless we create such a place, we are virtually doomed to failure in relationships, to "relational conflict" characterized by some level of emotional breakdown. As healthy adults, we have the capacity to experience any of these needs at various times in our lives; each imprint plays a particular role in human relationships.

Instead of calling unwanted feelings "infantile," we can learn to recognize our normal human needs as resources that bind us together as a species. Our imprints contain the history of our needs and therefore shape the course of our adult relationships. Learning about our needs and those of our partner gives us clues about where we are most vulnerable, what basic needs we still yearn to fill, what emotions produce shame, guilt, or fear, what family patterns are being reenacted, and how to repair the wounds and become more accepting of all of our feelings and needs.

When Imprints Fail

Many of us feel wounded as a result of unmet dependency needs. We all have past injuries that make us fear the repercussions of dependence on others. The more we fear being close and vulnerable, the more unable we are to fill the needs that were not filled in the first place. Thus, our underlying need for love becomes the motivating force behind some very earnest but very wounded relationships. The resulting behavior is fueled by the invisible but ever-present imprints.

In the following description of a couple whose marriage was falling apart, we will see how the imprints of both partners influenced their marriage; how old wounds were initially healed by the relationship; and then, as the marriage deteriorated, how those wounds reappeared and ruptured their lives.

Dianne and Ernest were referred to me a few weeks after he had moved out of their home. When they came in, Ernest bombarded his wife with everything she had done wrong during more than twenty years of their marriage. He said that he couldn't come back home until

Independence vs Isolation

Positive Links

Imprint for Mature Dependence
•Couple has shared as well as separate experiences
•Couple has interconnection as well as interdependence
•Self-other needs compatible Oneness and twoness flow.
•Couple has true intimacy

Imprint for Bridging Connections
•Use of ideas, values, ideals, and experience as transition from oneness to twoness
•Shared activities— books, art, music, sports, work.
•Openess to play and creativity
•Emotional attunement— understanding, acceptance, healthy competition

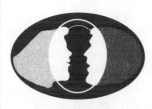

Imprint for Emotional Sharing
•Ability to experience each other's emotions
•Empathic attunement
•Holding and containing of frightening, even ugly feelings

Imprint for Primary Bonding
•Ecstasy of falling in love
•Experience the magic of feeling as one as one

Dangerous Liasons

Separateness but No Togetherness
•Driving need to prove self-sufficiency
•Fear of dependency
•Lack of connection to important others

Need for Security Object
•Use of objects to replace people
•Drugs, alcohol, food to ward off emotional injury
•Centering life on work or hobbies instead of family relations

Emotional Illiteracy or Emotional Invasion
•Can't let in or read the other's feelings
•Fear of being swallowed up by the other
•Inability to receive love from other
•Dumping toxic feelings into other

Merger or its Opposite, Isolation
•Lack of sense of existence as separate
•Regression to emptiness and isolation when alone
•Use of other to restore vitality and excitement
•Fear of commitment
•Inner chaos

Inborn Capacity for Connections

she changed. He insisted that she listen to how she never took care of him and was only interested in her needs and her position in the community. Whenever she spoke, challenged what he said, or cried, his anger increased. Working out his Imprint for Emotional Boundaries, Ernest wanted and indeed demanded that Dianne hear his complaints, understand his anger, and hold his intensely chaotic feelings. In short, he expected her to "read his child needs." Ernest could barely control his rage.

"I had to get out," he said, "or I might have picked up a chair and thrown it through the window. I can't live with her, but I am afraid she might kill herself if I divorce her. So we are here in therapy to see if you can help." What he didn't say at the beginning, but I learned later, was that Ernest was terrified of being abandoned and alone.

Dianne sat quietly during these diatribes. "We had a good marriage," she said, "until last year. I always felt loved and cared for by him. I knew I could depend upon him completely—I don't know what happened."

In fact, Ernest was so competent a caretaker that Dianne never had to arrange for plumbers, TV repairmen, car repairs—Ernest was in charge of everything around the house. He made a great deal of money and used his money, success, and power to provide a wonderful home and lifestyle for his wife and children. But he bought nothing for himself. He did not believe that he deserved things or that anyone could love him. He never could depend on anyone to stay with him. In fact, he was surprised that his marriage lasted twenty years. Furthermore, he still cannot believe he made it through law school. His self-image is that he is bad and unlovable. He felt unloved by his parents, and is "surprised I didn't end up in jail or in a psychotic ward."

As our work together progressed, Ernest related a history of failed relationships. He was a misfit in a family of high achievers. He had learning difficulties and was considered dumb at home and in school. Ernest felt inadequate, unloved, and not accepted by parents whom he saw as giving to everyone but him. He still resented his brothers, whom he felt got the love and acceptance that he missed. As long as he worked hard and achieved great financial success, he felt affirmed by colleagues and valued in his family. But he was doing work that sometimes pushed the boundaries of legality, and when he realized that he was being asked to do things that he considered dishonest, Ernest became increasingly anxious. He was always afraid of being unjustly accused of some wrongdoing, a residue of his early experiences. As a result he was scrupulously honest even when those around him were breaking the rules and violating laws. "I was so afraid of getting into trouble and being punished for something I didn't do that I avoided the trouble that my partners got into," he explained. He felt the pressure was making him ill and decided he had to quit.

Despite the awareness that he was giving up something that gave him financial security and social position, Ernest finally left the firm. Ernest's decision took place over a year in which he was increasingly agitated, and Dianne was terrified. Dianne did not understand his decision and repeatedly complained about his being home, doing nothing. The more panic Dianne experienced, the angrier Ernest became, until, ultimately, he said he had to get away from her.

Dianne had been an only child. She and her parents lived with her maternal grandparents. Her mother and grandparents were disappointed by her father's lack of financial success, and he was constantly humiliated by the grandmother. All the hope for the future was projected onto Dianne. The grandparents repeatedly gave messages to Dianne that she was so wonderful, beautiful, and talented that she would someday marry a "prince."

Unfortunately, there was a shortage of "princes" in her town. Ernest was the closest substitute she could find. He was tall, attractive, and by then a successful attorney. After they married, Dianne and Ernest shared a mutual illusion that he must be perfect. They moved to the right neighborhood, joined the right tennis club, took vacations in the right places, and had a wide range of the "right friends." Dianne idealized Ernest and for years counted on him to provide the security she never felt as a child. She totally depended on him.

It was through her marriage that she escaped her past and broke off her relationship with her parents. Through Ernest's legal acumen and her manipulations, she acquired the trappings of success, under which she hid her past, which she considered shameful. Dianne watched carefully and made it her life goal to learn the ways and manners of people who were born to good families. She learned to "pass." No one would ever know her shameful secret. Ernest gave her a home and a lifestyle that served as her bridge to connecting with people (a positive manifestation of the Imprint for Bridging). She loved Ernest for providing this although there was little emotional or sexual contact between them. This is where Dianne's negative residue from her bridging years came out, for she began to escape from the lonely marriage into a fantasy life—her "prince" whom she loved in her mind. As much as she tried to turn Ernest into her image of her prince, he remained what he was—a brilliant, quirky, difficult man. For years the relationship was good enough. Their imprints fit.

Until, that is, Ernest's father became ill and died after lingering for several months in pain. Ernest was suddenly faced with his own mortality. What if I became ill? he asked himself. Would she be there for me—or would she discard me? Would she put me in a convalescent home? He began a series of tests to see if his wife could accept him as he now saw himself, not omnipotent but human—a middle-aged man whose hearing was not so good, who needed glasses, whose back was giving him trouble. Their precarious balance began to change. When he talked about retirement, it frightened her.

What she heard were his constant complaints. He began to sound like her father, who was always too weak or tired to enjoy life. Dianne insisted that they maintain their busy lifestyle. She tried to cheer him up and mobilize him as she always had when he seemed upset. This made him angry, and in her hurt she withdrew, not understanding what was happening between them.

Ernest tried to explain to her that underneath his successful exterior he felt like a fake. He did not understand how he had achieved all that he had and believed that what the world saw was a sham. He felt like a failure and always expected to be found out for who he was. Sometimes, he said, he felt like a shell with nothing inside—just emptiness. When Dianne tried to challenge his view of himself, he became enraged.

"You want me to be a success to meet your needs," he shouted, "for your friends and your position. Think about me—take care of my needs for a change."

While Ernest's actions appeared to his wife as a self-centered acting out, his internal experience was one of a fragile self unable to maintain defenses that had worked for most of his life.

His father's death and his turning forty challenged his fantasy of invulnerability, and an earlier need, one that had been out of conscious awareness during most of his life, now emerged. This was a need for nurturing and affirmation by another—a need for a loved one on whom Ernest could depend. He wanted empathic responses to his needs, but got instead Dianne's hurts, her wounded self, and her tearful demand of "What about me? How can you do this to me? How can you break up our home and destroy our family?" He reacted to her tears with rage.

For years he had handled his dependency needs by becoming the caretaker for everyone around him. He tried to keep it all together while everyone saw him as powerful, successful, and someone who could solve all problems for everyone. But he couldn't hold it together, and Dianne would not listen to him when he tried to express his upset feelings. His anger, long bottled up, exploded—at his wife, his friends, his professional colleagues, and the male therapist he was seeing at the time. He was alone and frightened.

Both Ernest and Dianne had attempted to use their marital relationship to repair old wounds. When they were no longer able to maintain their precarious balance of providing needed functions to fill each other's dependency needs, the relationship began to fall apart. Like many of the problems that couples present to therapists, Dianne and Ernest's marital discord was the outward manifestation of deeply hidden childhood wounds.

Ernest and Dianne had each lived a life that covered up their extreme dependency needs and fragile selves. When Ernest left, Dianne could not turn to friends or to any group in the community. She felt intense shame and fear that the lie of her life would come out. Aloneness added to her pain. Like Dianne, Ernest felt that he had no one to talk to and no community, religious, or social organization other than the business that he had left. They were like atoms floating around in space, without connection to others to help them bear the intense inner turmoil of a difficult crisis in their lives. They had left behind the very things that family, community, and religion could offer them, that is, other people to depend on.

The past imprints of Dianne and Ernest were the underlying basis of many of their relational problems, and they both worked through some of their issues in therapy. For many people, however, the ability to grow and go on with their lives does not require that they analyze and understand every aspect of past traumas. While emotional wounds occurred in their past relationships, healing requires new ways of being in relationships that break the old patterns. Healing relationships provide the very things that were needed and, to a greater extent, available in the past. Among these things are love, affirmation, understanding, acceptance, respect, inclusion, and empowerment. When people enter new relationships, they hope for the very things missing in the past. In relationships in which they learn to trust one another and are able to lean on one another for strength, the wounds of the past can indeed be healed.

Signs of Positive Dependency

	Never	Sometimes	Often	Always
I enjoy taking care of my mate because I like the appreciation I get in return.	___	___	___	___
I can depend upon my partner to care about how I feel.	___	___	___	___
I like the feeling that we are a team.	___	___	___	___
My partner and I know each other's deepest core.	___	___	___	___
We are careful not to say and do things that cause each other emotional pain.	___	___	___	___
We depend on each other for the main things related to sexuality, nurturing, and communicating.	___	___	___	___
We have additional outlets, separate and together, for friendship, social, charitable, and spiritual connections.	___	___	___	___

I know from experience—my own, my patients, and my friends—how important such healing relationships can be. I know also, since I began asking people about their healing processes, that change and psychological cure occurs not only in good marriages and in good therapy, but also with loving friends, religious and community groups, or immersion with others in important causes (such as cancer treatment, AIDS, Mothers Against Drunk Driving, etc.).

Signs of Destructive Codependency

	Never	Sometimes	Often	Always
We have been involved in situations in which I or my partner have been physically pushed, hit, or forcibly held.	___	___	___	___
There have been times when I was forced to have sex against my will by my partner.	___	___	___	___
I am frightened that one of us may lose control when anger wells up.	___	___	___	___
I am constantly talking to friends and relatives about the pain that I continue to endure in this relationship.	___	___	___	___
I am always trying to fix defects in my partner's character.	___	___	___	___
I don't understand why I keep choosing the same kind of abusive partners.	___	___	___	___
I have low self-esteem and seek constant reassurance from my partner.	___	___	___	___
When someone loves me, I wonder what is wrong with him or her.	___	___	___	___

What we require for healing is the ability to develop relationships that feel trusting, in which we can be heard and understood, where painful feelings can be exposed and contained. These are relationships that we can indeed depend on. But this cannot be one-way. We must offer to those we care about our strength, our love, our resources. This, too, is part of our growth. A hug goes two ways. We get when we provide for others; we give when we appreciate what we receive. Of course, we must know when a relationship is one in which positive dependency, giving and receiving, is possible, and when it is a destructive codependent relationship.

If you have the capacity for positive dependency, you are able to develop relationships that meet the dependency needs of both partners. However, it is also possible to become involved in relationships with people who take but cannot give.

Check your current and past relationships for signs of destructive codependency using the chart on page 69.

When you are repeating old dysfunctional family patterns of interaction in your current relationship, you are experiencing destructive dependency. When a relationship is damaging to your emotional well-being, or to your physical health and safety, it is destructive dependency.

Knowing When Your Imprints Lead to Codependent Relationships

- You are prone to repeatedly selecting dysfunctional partners.

- You believe that your goal is to change the other to become the person you need.

- You are giving what you believe your partner needs rather than understanding his or her true needs.

- Your self-esteem is low and you do not believe others care about you.

- You demand constant reassurance of your partner's love.

- Your idealized images of a relationship are much more important than the relationship you are in.

When enduring the pain of the relationship becomes a major preoccupation and a constant subject of conversation with family, friends, and therapists, it is a relationship permeated by destructive dependency. When you are drawn repeatedly to people with problems, you are in danger of becoming involved in destructive dependency.

Part 2 Imprints for Relating: Patterns of Intimacy

The Ten Rules for Positive Dependency

1. Remember that your partner needs love as much as you do. Give signs of love generously with your praise, compliments, hugs, gifts, passion, prayer. When the truth includes words of love, speak freely. Feel free to address your partner with a special name and talk often about why you feel such deep love. Note things that are simple and often forgotten that will enhance the ego of the one you love.

2. There are many levels of "truth" from the surface message to the deepest core emotions. In every adult there is a wide range of dependency needs stemming from childhood. Listen for the imprinted messages of childhood to help you understand the true meaning of your partner's words.

3. Money, work, family, and sex are often the battlegrounds upon which the deepest bonding needs are fought. These battles are substitutes for emotions beyond words. Be aware of the underlying dependency issues around love, understanding, and acceptance.

4. There is no rule of relationships that requires the truth, the whole truth, and nothing but the truth. Do not say things that cause pain or shame.

5. Choose your battles carefully. A spotless house and gourmet meals can be a gift of love or a battleground over which unmet dependency needs are fought. Evaluate which issues are so important to you that they are not negotiable. Everything else should be open for discussion and compromise.

6. Do not depend on your partner to meet all of your needs. Develop interests together but also be sure to develop separate interests. Share your excitement of life with others outside of the relationship and you will see it come back to you in many ways. The more you give, the more you will get.

7. Be generous with your body; not only in sexual intimacy, but also in offering a gentle stroke, a foot massage, a back rub; touch gently or hold firmly depending upon your partner's response. Touch is a basic means of bonding, sharing, and connecting. Remember that a hug goes two ways.

8. Validate your partner's feelings and actions often. Notice his or her positive qualities as if using a magnifying mirror. Comment on what you like. Be free with your compliments. Use selective inattention for the negative qualities. Your partner will think that you are wonderfully perceptive.

9. There will be times when you fail each other, hurt each other, and do things that may feel unforgivable. If you need to register a criticism or complaint, make sure you do it in private. Be generous with forgiveness. To forgive is to begin again, to touch a place of internal transformation, to re-create the relationship.

10. Accept the fact that your partner will probably not do all of the things you hope for. Most of us have too many obligations and too little time. Agree on what is essential for both of you. Use your energy for the important things—like loving each other.

3 Imprint for Primary Bonding

> *And did you get what*
> *you wanted from this life, even so?*
> *I did.*
> *And what did you want?*
> *To call myself beloved, to feel myself*
> *beloved on the earth.*

—Raymond Carver

Rule #3 for Positive Dependency:

Money, work, family, and sex are often the battlegrounds upon which the deepest bonding needs are fought. These battles are substitutes for emotions beyond words. Be aware of the underlying dependency issues around love, understanding, and acceptance.

Romantic Love

You might wonder why I launch into a discussion of romantic love when describing an early-developmental period of infancy. The reason is that my intent in this book, as in my sessions with couples, is to help adults become aware of how early wounds may affect their current relationships and to clarify how to use relationships as a source of healing rather than add additional injury. We downgrade relationships in which feelings are intense, buttons are pushed, partners seem on a roller coaster of wild passion that bleeds seemingly inexplicably into rage, pain, name-calling, even the occasional "street scene." Those relationships are toxic, we are told, the feelings are immature. Sometimes romantic love is codependency masquerading under another name.

Well, I disagree. After studying in depth many couples with just such a demeanor, a few of which we will meet in these pages, I have come to understand relationships that operate at the level of the Imprint for Primary Bonding. In order for such a relationship to offer the potential of healing, it must reach deeply within. Each partner needs to be emotionally transparent to the other so that the individuals can touch each other emotionally, can "get under each other's skin," to heal—and grow. If we lack passion for our partner, we cannot hope to touch the unresolved bonding issues that need to emerge in order to be resolved. Without intense feelings it is likely to be harder to access these deep dependency needs. In short, intensity may mean that the relationship provides an opportunity to learn, to change, to grow together.

Each person's Imprint for Primary Bonding contains the history of the earliest needs: what those needs were, how he or she responded as a baby when those needs were met and when they were not met, and how the primary caretaker responded or failed to respond. Although the extent of these needs diminishes as we grow older, the core bonding need to be taken care of and to be united with another human being remains with us as part of our makeup. This first imprint contains our strongest emotional "pull." We cannot escape it because the need is both psychological and biological. The most basic human need, to be touched by another, is a need that lasts throughout life.

Instead of calling the basic bonding need "infantile" because it originates in infancy, we must learn to recognize it as a shared resource that helps to bind us together as a species. It is not childish or immature to desire in adulthood the comfort reminiscent of early bonding experiences. Indeed, "to think of growing out of dependence on others into a realm of independence," said psychoanalyst Heinz Kohut, "is no more possible, let alone desirable, than a corresponding move from a life dependent on oxygen to a life independent of it."[6]

Human beings are not meant to be alone. We develop the capacity for healthy aloneness only when we know we are loved and that someone is there for us. Considerable evidence indicates that there is an innate need for connection and bonding from the time we are born to the time that we die. Those who do not feel loved and affirmed in a secure, bonded relationship from the beginning of life suffer emotional injury and may spend the rest of their lives trying to repair the damage.

Lawrence: Lifelong Fears

Lawrence, twice married and now living with a woman, cannot sleep at night without his partner next to him. If alone, he experiences body tremors, has trouble breathing, and feels as if he were going to die. His overwhelming fear and need, often experienced by his partner as smothering, was the cause of his previous failed marriages and is affecting his current relationship. The wounds Lawrence experienced during his first year of life have haunted and handicapped him for four and a half decades.

When something goes wrong in the early bonding experience and the infant's needs are not met, wounds develop and protective defenses arise to soothe the pain. When such early wounds are present, the adult will unknowingly feel the effects in every relationship he or she attempts. Amazingly, the infant's early fears *do* coexist with the adult's current interpersonal problems. If these feelings are available in the relationship, they can be met and potentially healed.

Lawrence was born in London during a blitzkrieg in World War II. He recalls stories his mother told him about sirens and bombs, fear, and buildings completely destroyed. His mother's parents were killed in an air raid in 1943. When he was a year old, his mother took him and an older sister to the countryside, where they lived in a rebuilt barn for the duration of the war. Lawrence's father, who enlisted before Lawrence was born, was killed when his ship was torpedoed. Despite her many losses, Lawrence's mother kept her family together and after the war moved back to London, where she reestablished her family's jewelry business and eventually remarried.

From the time he was six, Lawrence's life was a relatively stable one of school, sports, family outings, and trips abroad with his mother and sister as the jewelry business expanded. We uncovered and retrieved the remnants of Lawrence's early history from his questions to those who were there with him. They described the explosive noise, the fear, and the sense of danger during his first year of life. It seemed clear that, although he has no conscious recall of his first year, his sense memory and body reactions are the cause of his night terrors and lifelong sense of danger.

Resurgence of the danger mode causes Lawrence's clinging behavior. When his girlfriend, Cassie, thought of the tight hold he had on her, she first saw it as love, then as control, and finally as pathological. Her tendency was to pull back, to move away, which caused a resurgence of his terror. He wanted her to reach out, take him in her arms, and hold him tightly. When he was able to share this with her in a therapy session, she decided to try something different to help their relationship. She moved closer, held him, and didn't let him go. She overdosed him, enveloping him in her space. Lawrence knew that she was doing this as a conscious attempt to heal a bonding wound. Despite this, he was surprised that it still seemed to calm and comfort him.

They have been married for ten years now and, the last I heard, are still sleeping locked in each other's arms all night—a regular dose of the medicine he needs. His dependency needs met, he is rarely bothered by the deeply buried memory of terror and danger.

Back to Basics

Without our Imprint for Bonding, with its prescription for intimate dependence and its illusion of merger, we would be unable to fall in love. The driving passion of new love overcomes reason, logic, and any semblance of separateness from the loved one. In each other's gaze, lovers re-create the primary bonding experience of being special, appreciated, accepted, and enjoyed simply for being. New love is experienced as a fusion in which "two become one" (often entwining like pretzels for long periods of time), and each sees an idealized version of the other. Love is perfection, timeless, and forever. Love exalts and enhances the value of each partner. Each shines in the light of the other.

The metamorphosis that lovers feel is not simply an illusion. We *are* enhanced by the experience of merger and idealization. Our joy, vitality, and vigor are there for all to see. It is no wonder that we wish to continue this experience "eternally." In real life, alas, it is a place to visit, not to live in.

Eventually, the romance of lovers must make way for the realities of living in a family and a community. For some the special world of merger and idealization yields in a healthy way to more realistic experiences of acceptance, understanding, and mutual dependency that are essential to growing relationships. The intensity is relieved by the necessary routines of life. Nevertheless, some people feel alive only when they are experiencing the feeling of being intensely connected at this peak level. When not feeling the blinding bliss of new love, they may feel empty and deflated or may become angry and provoke arguments and fights—battles royal that may be followed by passionate lovemaking; another way, however painful, to return to the feeling of intense bonded connection.

To me this is always an indication that bonding issues have reared their heads. I know when a couple is constantly merging and then breaking abruptly apart that somewhere in either one or both partner's Imprint for Primary Bonding, needs as basic as nurturing and acceptance have not been met, and the battles that seem to be about money or sex are smoke screens for primary feelings crying to be heard. Such painful and unfulfilling forms of bonding are often based on unacknowledged and inexpressible wounds from infancy. Relationships operating in this way may require therapeutic intervention, because the needs and fears underlying the problem re-create emotions that began before language was acquired. Needs that cannot be expressed in words are often acted out dysfunctionally.

Because the early failure causes such profound wounds, and because the vulnerable self erects protections against the pain of dependency needs that are unmet, new relationships are always balanced between hope and fear. The fear causes exquisite sensitivity to even minor slights and often a painful feeling reminiscent of the original wound. In every relationship subsequent to the one of the infant with its primary caretaker, the unmet need for a safe, secure connection reemerges and is relived—always with the hope that the need for loving attachment will be fulfilled.

The hope in this new relationship is that someone who resembles, in some way, your primary love will be capable of giving you what you always needed—emotionally attuned, understanding, holding love that accepts you just as you are, more loving and accepting of you than you are yourself, an idealized version of perfect mother love.

Thus, the purpose of new love for many who suffered early bonding failures is to heal the inner pain. What often happens is that we select a partner to love who bears a striking resemblance to the needed parent. The early pattern for relating then reemerges, as if old and new relationships are one and the same.

Like rubbing on a painful area of the body, the psychological wound is touched repeatedly. It hurts too much to put it aside. We want the wound to be touched, a salve rubbed on by gentle hands and a loving heart. But all too often, we get a re-creation of the old failure—a reaffirmation that relationships hurt—and a reemergence of the defenses learned early. This is the painful dance of despair that so often occurs in intimate relationships.

The Origins of Codependency

Newborns come into the world "prewired" for a wide range of emotional responses and emotionally prepared to relate to and connect with those around them. Sensitive and receptive to their surroundings, infants develop a wordless language of "primary emotions" that expresses their basic sense of existence long before they can think or speak in words. Primary emotions such as excitement, joy, anger, or fear are part of our inborn repertoire. Babies are capable of a wealth of emotion, and since they do not censor responses, what they feel is what they show.

The parents' responses label the baby's emotions good or bad. This is how a baby begins socialization. A benign caretaker who arrives at a crying baby's crib, warmly scoops up the infant, rocks it, and speaks soothingly will evoke feelings of comfort, safety, and warmth. This entire package of responses remains with the baby as a memory later identified as positive. If, on the other hand, the baby experiences being yanked out of the crib by an anxious or angry parent, spoken to tersely, bobbed up and down for a few minutes, and then redeposited in the crib, the package of responses remains as a negative memory. If the negative experience is not repeated, it will shortly be forgotten. If similar interactions occur over a period of days, weeks, or months, however, the infant learns to expect a negative experience whenever needs arise. In this way a developing baby learns to experience needs as "bad" because having a need seems to lead to unpleasant consequences. This can have dire effects later as an adult's ability to bond in a positive way is negatively colored by the early experience, which may produce a pattern of destructive codependency.

Passion and Chaos

When Peter and Mary came to see me, they agreed that their relationship was in trouble. "But it feels so good when it's good," they explained, that they wanted to find a way to make it work. Although their arguments were ostensibly about money, work, and living arrangements, they were really battling about deep conflicts over the basic bonding issues of trust and dependency. Their relationship was an example of the important of Rule #3 for healthy interdependence. Being aware of the underlying issues around love, understanding, forgiveness, and acceptance can keep couples together if they are willing to be there for each other's unmet bonding needs, or pull them apart if they are not.

The relationship of Peter and Mary was both passionate and chaotic, alternating between times of intense togetherness and total alienation. When a couple presents this pattern in therapy, I am immediately aware that the relationship is suffering from early-experienced bonding failures—both yearn for love; neither can depend on others for love. Mary, a very attractive successful designer, is militantly self-sufficient and prone to ending intimate relationships abruptly. Peter is a businessman who works long hours and travels frequently. Despite having grown up in dysfunctional families, Peter and Mary both function as highly successful adults, seemingly having overcome their traumas—at least on the surface. But their relationship brought these wound issues to the fore.

Since being introduced by a mutual friend fourteen months ago, Peter and Mary have been inseparable—except for the times when one or the other insists that their relationship is over! At times, Mary feels emotionally abused when they are together and abandoned by Peter when apart. As we examined each of their early histories, some of their volatile interactions that had made no sense to them began to be understandable seen in light of experiences that occurred so early that there were no words to describe the pain and chaos.

Mary related how her parents abused her repeatedly. Whenever she didn't listen or do exactly as her mother demanded, Mary was beaten or locked in a closet. Mary turned to her father for safety from the always enraged, possibly psychotic mother. Sometimes he offered comfort, while at other times he, too, would beat her, saying, "I don't want to do this, but I have to because Mom wants me to and I don't want her to be upset with me." Hence, Mary grew up in a painful double bind of both needing and hating her parents. As a young adult she moved to a city far from her parents' home, but continued to visit occasionally and to talk to them by telephone.

Despite her genuine efforts to salvage something positive from her periodic contacts with her parents, she always ended up feeling detached and debased. Once, when they visited and brought her a present, she felt that she had a chance to tell them of her feelings, and they acted as if they understood. The next day they called, demanding an apology, and insisted that she return the gift. Once again she had been "betrayed." Ultimately Mary gave up the possibility of getting the love she wanted from them and broke off all contact with her parents.

It is no wonder that when she feels intensely about someone, as she feels about Peter, the old needs and fears arise. Peter triggered in her old memories of a strong, successful father whose love was withdrawn as soon as more important matters caught his attention. She yearns to win Peter's love, hates herself when she feels "not good enough" as she felt with her parents, and wants him to treat her consistently with love and tenderness.

For Mary, in this relationship, past and present are merging. What is going on between her and Peter is short-circuiting her adult censor and cutting right to the heart of the child within her who was not given the opportunity to safely bond.

In Peter's family, his father was abusive to his mother. As far back as he could remember, Peter recalls hearing the warning sound of his father's footsteps as he came home drunk on weekend nights, before he physically brutalized his wife. Terrified of the beatings, Peter would throw himself between his parents to ward off the attack. If this failed, he would go to his mother afterward and hold her bloody face, fantasizing that it was all a dream and that it had not happened at all, desperately trying to reassure his mother that he could make things better. His job as a very young child was to take care of his victimized mother, to be the man to save her.

Peter worries about being used, demanded of, forced to take care of an overly dependent woman, as he had to with his mother. When Mary showed her needy, vulnerable sides, he ignored her and kept referring to the strong, competent woman he sees in her. Peter's reaction, coming from his past, intensified their problem.

When they were together, Peter did things that re-created in Mary feelings of abandonment and rejection. When he left her alone at social events where she knew no one, he could not understand why she became upset. "He makes me feel diminished, closeted," she would try to explain. "When some other pursuit interests him, he forgets about me." (Just like her successful father, who would turn his love away from her for his work or his wife.) If Mary persisted in trying to talk about her needs or fears, Peter became angry. And his anger grew rapidly.

Sometimes his reaction was so volatile that it frightened both of them. Once during an argument Mary, backing away from Peter, tripped and gashed her hand, requiring a trip to the emergency hospital. "I never laid a hand on her," he said, frightened that he was turning into his father. Peter was aware of his violent feelings and was determined not to let them get out of control. Always he carried the image of his severely beaten mother around with him.

Mary and Peter are experiencing a relationship in which their intense emotional interactions sometimes override their more "civilized" adult selves. By the time they came to see me, this couple was stumbling into the danger zone. And yet they hoped this relationship would be the "corrective emotional experience"[7] they each might use to heal their wounds.

For a long time their relationship was in constant danger of ending abruptly. Because so many emotions were being set off in them, their arguments escalated quickly. Mary's tendency to withdraw and threaten a breakup when upset or afraid would cause Peter to feel rejected and enraged. When Mary turned her back to him and walked away, Peter felt a surge of rage, but resisted his urge to strike out. I suggested a ground rule: rather than threatening breakups or intense fights as a part of every argument, the decision to end their relationship should be made in my office, where we could begin to think together about the feelings of each. After an argument that almost destroyed their relationship, we had an opportunity to test this ground rule.

Peter was hosting an elaborate business dinner for more than fifty people at a restaurant. Mary had agreed to meet him there. She was looking forward to seeing and being with him. But he was expecting her to circulate and talk to the guests. She looked for someone she knew, but felt herself in a room full of strangers, with Peter only a distant image across the room. "It felt the way I used to feel whenever my mother punished me by locking me in a closet—alone and ashamed." Desperately wanting to be loved, confused about why she was rejected and locked away, Mary reexperienced these old bonding failures whenever she felt isolated or alone. The neglected, rejected child in Mary kept looking to Peter for reassurance, and not finding it.

Mary sat through the dinner trying to contain her uncomfortable feelings. When it was finally over, Peter was expected to take the top executives to a supper club for dancing. As the group piled into the rented limousines, Peter said he had to detour to pick up one of the guests. He asked Mary to go ahead to the club and make sure everything was okay, again pushing her childhood fears to the foreground, making her feel abandoned. Feeling overwhelmed with anger and humiliation for Peter's inconsiderate treatment, Mary could not bring herself to walk alone into a club full of strangers. So she went home.

The next day in my office Mary began talking about her feelings, what she could have done differently, and about what they both could learn from the incident to help them in the future. Peter looked at her and said, "There will be no future. I'm just here today to say that we are finished." With this surprise tactic, Peter had replicated Mary's humiliating rejection of him in front of his business associates by his rejection of her in front of the therapist. In fact, they were using each other to replay old patterns of interacting. The imprints of long ago reemerged in ways that endangered their current relationship. But it was not yet over. The fragile bonds of their on-again, off-again relationship continued.

The next day, Peter called to schedule another joint appointment. When he and Mary arrived, he said that he had not meant to end the relationship. He was just very angry at Mary at that moment, and wanted to hurt her. "Help me to understand why I mess up my relationships," he pleaded. Mary added, "This relationship is very impor tant to us. If it wasn't Peter I'd find someone just like him. Help us understand what goes wrong and how to fix it."

The Hope for Repair

The bonding experience between infants and parents is the arena in which primary emotions develop. When the experiences of bonding are negative, the infant-as-adult will have expectations of harm connected with intimate interactions. But alongside the negative legacy is a deep longing for the experience of positive dependency and the hope for repair. This hope propels us to search for people who feel familiar—people who express some or many of the negative imprinted emotions—and then attempt to make things right. Ultimately, we all search for someone with whom we can bond, who won't cause fear, anguish, anger, or trigger feelings of shame and humiliation. We want someone who will make us feel safe, secure, and cared for, and who will not leave us feeling alone when we are dependent on them.

Whether the Imprint for Bonding is dominated by positive or negative emotions, dependency needs remain throughout life. As adults, Peter and Mary were trying hard to get their infant needs met without acknowledging their unconscious fear, anger, and dependence on one another. As a consequence, they each automatically replayed the same destructive scenarios that had characterized their earliest relationships.

Emotional defenses arise when needs are not met and feelings become intolerable. Unfortunately, experience soon teaches infants who do not receive the kind of attention they need that they should be ashamed of having the needs. Need, vulnerability, and shame soon lead to strong defenses against feeling or showing needs around others.

One defense is *withdrawal*. In extreme cases of deprivation, babies are completely unable to respond to their environments because they have never been responded to. Infant researcher Daniel Stern tells of visiting Rumanian orphanages, where babies in the first months of life are left without human contact and do not learn to respond at all to others.

Stern shows videotapes of his wife, Nadya, attempting to engage six-to-twelve-month-old babies in a game of "got ya," trying, unsuccessfully, to make hand and eye contact with them.[8] The kinds of connections that normally developing babies easily respond to were already beyond the capacity of these youngsters. These children had missed out on some primary bonding tools and were apparently unable to connect when the stimulation from others was offered. Some of these children who were adopted after severely delayed bonding opportunities remain physically and intellectually regressed. Psychologist Renee Spitz, who studied infants many years ago, described a similar failure to thrive produced by institutionalized social isolation.[9]

The infant whose needs are not met can also react by *denying needs and feelings*. If the parent cannot or will not bring relief and the infant cannot get the parent's attention, from the infant's point of view it is best simply not to need and not have to experience the painful reaction.

Some people, when asked what they are feeling, invariably answer "nothing." They have become emotionally disconnected and have no words for feelings. The adult who identifies needs as bad may simply deny having any needs. For such people to desire anything from others is a cause of discomfort or insecurity. They are marked by emotional deadness, stilted connections, and lack of appropriate affect.

Trauma during infancy is particularly injurious because we are so powerless to deal with it. In adult life, we have many resources to draw upon when we need to defend ourselves psychologically. Our brains are fully developed and we have a storehouse of information that we can retrieve when necessary. As infants, by contrast, our experiences occurred before the development of language, which means that what we felt during those times has no connection to words or thoughts. When situations later in life trigger some kind of upsetting preverbal memory, we feel overwhelmed, powerless, and desolate—just as the infant did—and are just as unable to articulate the reasons.

These preverbal memories manifest in various ways. There may be a feeling of fragmentation ("I feel like I'm cracking up"), a loss of control ("I don't know what came over me—I just lost it!"), or a strong sense of being out of touch with daily life ("I'm in such a *fog*"). At this threatening juncture, the adult typically reacts by defending against the buried primary emotions. Often what emerges are "irrational" out-bursts or periods of sullen withdrawal, for example, Peter's wrathful pronouncement that "there will be no future" for this relationship.

For people like Peter and Mary, whose early bonding experiences were ruptured, love can be terrifying. These two wounded people were able to bond at a primary level, which intensified their passion for each other. But the blissful feelings were always threatened by the fear and pain of old wounds being re-created.

Perhaps, like Peter, you have sometimes felt claustrophobic or afraid of "losing yourself" if you became dependent in a relationship. Or like Mary, when a relationship draws close and then seems to abruptly distance, you may have felt dismissed, abandoned, lost, or disjointed. You may wonder why you are so easily overcome with such feelings. "I look like I am very strong," Peter once said in therapy, "but I feel as if I am just patched together. People look up to me. I play the role well. But it's not really me."

Many of my patients with early bonding ruptures express this feeling. They never totally trust themselves and worry that they are im-postors. Like Peter, these people are always searching for a safe haven—someone stronger than they are—whom they can turn to for caring and comfort. Yet, when they find it, they are apt to distrust it, test it repeatedly, and turn away at the first sign of disappointment.

Through hard work and the willingness to accommodate and un-derstand each other's needs and fears, couples like Peter and Mary may be able to use their relationship as a healing experience. If they cannot meet each other's needs and grow together, the relationship will con-tinually touch old wounds and may end in a re-creation of defensive distancing or emotional outbursts.

The Courage to Love and Heal

Because of the great pain I see in people who have had very early bonding failures, and because healing of early wounds is so difficult in therapy, we have focused many of the mental health training programs at UCLA on the implications of early development on psychological illness in adults. We have studied the profound effects of the early interactional experiences as they are re-created throughout life. What I have learned has changed the way that I work and live.

Four years ago I became a grandmother. Having spent so many years studying infancy and the effect of early bonding on relationships, I now had a chance to try something new (for me) in the care of a special newborn. Instead of hiring a baby nurse, my daughter invited me to visit with her and her husband for the first three weeks after my grandson was born. She welcomed the help and support, and I welcomed the opportunity on many counts.

Whenever my grandson was not with one of his parents, I held him. He and I hid out in the baby's room, where I kept the heat high so he needed no shirt. I wore no shirt, either, so that we could bond, skin to skin. In one sense we were two strangers. He knew nothing about me—I, along with the rest of the world, was new to him—and what I knew about him was a fantasy of my hopes and wishes for the person he would one day become. But at night as he slept on my chest, his tiny body molding itself to the form of my body, readjusting as I occasionally moved, I knew the feeling of two being one. For three weeks, we were in perfect harmony, each of us filled with pleasure and contentment as I held him in my arms. My daughter described similar feelings. I welcomed and enjoyed the deep bodily pleasure that comes from holding an infant—a pleasure I had not thought about since my children were babies.

In those days—the days of my own childbearing and child rearing—I lacked the understanding of how profoundly important it is to depend on another for physical and emotional connection. I thought the goal of child rearing was to help children become independent as soon as possible. Now I know that the best way to nurture independence is first to meet an infant's most basic need to depend on someone. Moreover, after listening to adults in therapy, I know that this same truth operates *throughout life*. Independence can flourish only when dependency needs are met.

Like it or not, the normal feelings babies experience being picked up and fed—a craving for close contact, a sense of oneness, a blissful surrender—remain with us throughout life, surfacing periodically whether we recognize them or not. Underneath the harmful distortions concerning our core need to depend on another is an unstated desire, felt by many "normal," successful adults, to overcome the anxiety of separateness by becoming "one with" an intimate other—the same need the infant experiences.

We all have times when we want to curl up in a safe place and be totally taken care of. Out of shame at appearing too "needy," we rarely act on this impulse in a straightforward way. Instead, we may behave manipulatively, feigning incompetence or developing physical problems.

That dependency needs are inescapable is evidenced in the symptoms that patients routinely bring into therapy. One patient complains that her husband, a highly competent surgeon, cannot balance his checkbook, forgets to pay bills, cannot pick out his own clothes—in fact, cannot manage his life without her. A woman who used to travel throughout the country as a buyer for a major retail chain now has to be driven to my office by her husband because she has become agoraphobic. Unable to leave the house without her husband, she is *totally* dependent on him. Meanwhile, he is assured by her disability that she will always be there and available to him when he gets home. When normal dependency needs are ignored or disallowed, they often surface in extreme, incapacitating forms. I see these extremes in my practice every day. My hope is to help my patients and readers to experience and reveal these needs in ways that can avoid the pain and shame, and to help them grow toward mature dependence.

4 Imprint for Emotional Sharing

> *Feelings are "entertained": love comes to pass.*
> *Feelings dwell in man; but man dwells in his love.*
> *That is no metaphor, but the actual truth. Love*
> *does not cling to the I in such a way as to have the*
> *Thou only for its "content," its object; but love is*
> *between I and Thou.*
> *Love is responsibility of an "I" for a "thou."*
>
> —Martin Buber, *I and Thou*

Rule #4 for Positive Dependency:
There is no rule of relationships that requires the truth, the whole truth, and nothing but the truth. Do not say things that cause pain or shame.

Last week I visited a hospital nursery to see the new daughter of a friend. It was late in the evening and everything was quiet . . . until one baby began to cry. Moments later a second baby began to cry . . . then a third. Within a few minutes, the nursery was a resounding wail.

Emotions are contagious; it is hard not to be pulled into the orbit of intense emotional reactions. The cry of a baby cannot help but affect the feelings of nearby adults. We are predisposed to respond to such a cry of distress; it "cuts to the core" and "pulls at our hearts."

We respond not only to distressing emotions, but also to positive ones—excitement, joy, pleasure, laughter. Anyone who has been to a sporting event or concert knows about the "electricity" of the crowd. Children who exude delight and vitality with each new adventure typically make the people around them smile. Shy, anxious children evoke concern and watchfulness. Similarly, the emotional states of parents invite complementary responses from their children. Mothers and fathers who are comfortable with a baby's explorations are inviting their children to share the excitement of interacting with the world. Overly vigilant parents who see danger everywhere transmit a climate of fear.

I am thinking about these things as I watch my grandson play. He is still learning to distinguish his emotions from his mother's. He falls down, and before he decides whether to cry, he looks to his mother to see how she is reacting. If she treats his fall as a minor event, so does he. If her face has a frightened look, he cries. If she becomes upset, runs over, and picks him up, he cries louder at first and then calms down as she comforts him. He sees her as a mirror and a determiner of his responses.

The sending and receiving of emotional messages is the basis of communication in early childhood. During the first year of life we move from the sense of oneness that comes from our Imprint for Primary Bonding into a growing awareness of twoness that emerges during the formation of our Imprint for Emotional Sharing. Emotional messages flow back and forth between parent and child, as separate beings. We discover what differentiates us from others: the difference between our needs and preferences and those of our caretakers.

Our boundaries of identity—our sense of self—are slowly shaped through our interactions with others. For the first three to five years of our lives, these boundaries are tentative and permeable. This is the time when *shared* empathy between mother and baby first blossoms. Dysfunctional family members show little respect for one another's boundaries—which is to say they invade one another's emotional terrain without caring how hurtful this can be. That is why it is so important for the parent to know what *not* to say—when to pull punches to spare the child's sense of identity. Unfortunately, some parents, in the name of honesty, fail to subscribe to Rule #4—they believe that they are just "telling it like it is," while causing great shame. They cross the line in word or action, oblivious to the ways that they invade their child's boundaries. The child then grows up bruised and, more often than not, riddled by shameful feelings he or she doesn't understand.

This bruised child, who is now an adult, can be repaired in a healing love relationship with a partner who knows when to give feedback and when to keep quiet. Alternatively, such an adult may be further bruised by a partner who believes too much in some variation of "letting it all hang out"—verbal aggression masquerading as honesty. Empathy is not something one person provides and another receives. It is a two-way street, with parent and child, husband and wife, intimate friends, sharing each other's emotional life.

It is widely acknowledged that mothers can recognize the precise meanings of different distress signals given by their babies, despite a complete absence of words. Most mothers know the difference between cries of hunger, discomfort, boredom, and fussiness. As I observe my daughter and her child, my daughter seems to know her baby's needs moments before he signals in a way that I can understand. "That cry means 'pick me up,' but this cry means he needs to cry a little before he falls off to sleep," she tells me when I come to visit. "He'll wake up in a minute," she says as I observe him sound asleep. What does she hear and see that I don't? I wonder.

What is less recognized is the degree to which a baby perceives the feelings of the mother as well as the emotional tone of the household. Every interaction for the baby is a heartfelt experience of some kind. Emotions are broadcast like radio waves, and babies are not equipped to tune them out. If household tension is intermittent and there are many calm times, the developing child feels safe in the home.

In well-functioning families, parents recognize and respect the child's expression of both positive and negative emotions; conversely, the child is able to recognize the moods of others in the home and have safe ways to respond to them. In dysfunctional families, however, respect for the emotions of others is absent and the child does not learn healthy responses.

The most extreme examples of this are in homes in which there is physical or sexual abuse of a very young child. A baby who feels attacked, penetrated, and used for the pathological needs of a relative has difficulty trusting or depending on anyone, even him/herself.

With the current dis-ease of society, many families that suffer illness, job loss, poverty, and homelessness lack the wherewithal to pay attention and respond to the needs of young children. It is a sad paradox that the more we know about the emotional needs of children and adults, the less time, energy, and resources we have to meet the needs.

Because empathy, or "emotional attunement," develops during the first year of life, it is unaccompanied by words. We depend upon this nonverbal communication to meet two basic human needs: the need for *mirroring* and the need for the *safe containment or holding of our emotions*. Later in this chapter we will see how these two needs are as integral to the adult experience of positive dependency as they are to the child's developing sense of self. Both of these needs must be met in a positive way if we are to be able to form a healthy dependence on another person.

The need for mirroring is a primary need; it is a desire to see ourselves reflected in a favorable light in the eyes of another. A second basic reflective need is to share distressing emotions with someone who makes us feel safe. Good mirroring helps us to know and be known, and to form the rudiments of a positive self-image. When mothers smile back at their babies or imitate their little noises, they are helping their babies to see themselves in a positive light. As adults, we still need mirroring; we want our jokes to be laughed at, our profound thoughts to be appreciated, and our unique qualities to be acknowledged.

Children who do not receive adequate mirroring will have difficulty developing a solid sense of self. Throughout life they will seek, through relationships, the attention and affirmation they yearn for, and their self-images will depend entirely upon how they see themselves reflected in the eyes of others. *So they will continue to seek out mirroring relationships for reassurance*. However, distortions from the past will often be reflected back.

A second basic human need is to be able to share distressing emotions with a person who makes us feel safe. Sharing our responses with someone willing to listen—someone willing to "hold" or "contain" our feelings without passing judgment on them—provides temporary respite from overwhelming experiences. When a child comes home from school, distraught with humiliation and anger over some incident, the "good" mother is able to listen fully without trying to fix it. Rather than telling the child "not to be a baby" about some small hurt, this mother can allow the little boy to cry, the little girl to vent her rage, offering comfort in the form of accepting the child's feelings.

In the early years, when our boundaries are just being formed, mothers ideally act as safe "containers" for their infants' emotions by detoxifying frightening feelings. Each time the mother responds to her baby's distress with a soothing and comforting expression, the baby learns that, although it may be uncomfortable, it is also safe to be upset.

When the Imprint for Emotional Sharing functions optimally, this is how it operates. By contrast, when the mother responds with tension, anger, or anxiety, however subtly, the baby's emotions remain frightening to the baby because no message of safe containment has been given. In either of these cases, the baby's emotional responses are ingested by the mother, blended with hers, then returned to the baby altered for better or worse. This "emotional soup" is a mysterious commingling of the parent's and child's emotions.

The Transfer of Emotions

Lynn is a new mother who immigrated to America quite recently. She is shy, insecure, and lonely so far away from her parents. She turns to Beth, her one-year-old daughter, for company. Beth is a curious, cuddly, responsive child. Taking care of Beth makes Lynn feel competent. She knows that she is doing it right. Beth's pink cheeks and curly blond hair make Lynn proud to be with her. People often stop to comment on mother and daughter as a beautiful pair.

But when Lynn's husband Burt must go away for weeks at a time, Lynn's loneliness increases. "Can't he do something that will keep him nearer to home?" she complains. But Burt's answer is that he must do his job, and he cannot earn this kind of money doing any other job. So Lynn is alone, depressed, and considering an affair with a man who pays her a lot of attention.

She drives with Beth in the backseat and her mind is not on driving. She almost gets into an accident. Beth is frightened by the screeching brakes and begins crying. Upset herself, Lynn cannot comfort Beth, who cries even louder. Lynn screams, "Shut up!" and Beth, more frightened, cries even louder. Lynn tells me the next day how Beth's crying made her feel enraged and how close she came to hitting Beth. "I feel like I went a little crazy and it scares me," Lynn admits.

When a baby and mother are together, their moods can play off each other's. The fear and anger passing back and forth between Lynn and Beth is the basis of the emotional soup between them. Each caught the tension of the other and acted in response to the other. If this occurs only once, it is not a problem. But if, as may happen, it is part of a pattern, the dependent child will develop a way of relating in reaction to the mother that may distort reality. The child's imprint for relating will be one of "catching" upset feelings and trying to find some way of dealing/coping with them. In Beth's case, she might be forced to pay close attention to her mother's moods, watching for any signs of upset, trying to be extra cheerful, to entertain her mother in order to turn her "bad" mood into a "happy" mood. Beth will have developed an imprint for interacting that says, "To get love, you must keep others happy no matter what you feel."

Whose Life Is It Anyway?

Somewhere between the ages of six and eighteen months, we learn to watch for feedback when we express our needs. Are our needs positively mirrored in the faces of our caretakers? By observing how our parents react to us—if they accept or reject our failures—we learn which emotional expressions are good and which are bad. We learn whether our behavior brings joy or displeasure, if the expression of our emotions and needs is acceptable, and how we can become "good" in the eyes of our caretakers. When our needs are met easily and soothingly in a consistent way, we learn to trust our experience, to trust others, and to expect favorable, safe responses—in other words, we experience *healthy dependency.*

When early attempts at self-expression are responded to with fear or criticism, we experience *emotional contamination.* Rather than containing feelings in a comforting way that helps to detoxify them, parents may add their own emotional toxins to the experience by being critical, fearful, or punishing. When parents respond to our expressions of need with anger, anxiety, or withdrawal, we learn about negative or *destructive dependency.* We discover that, in order to get important needs met, we must alter those needs in whatever way evokes a tolerable response. We learn how to get the love we depend on by modifying ourselves to become acceptable to the conscious and unconscious expectations of other family members.

The toddler whose questions about his body are rebuffed as sinful, the sensitive boy who is told to stop being a "sissy," the girl who is told that she is bad for doing the same things allowed her brother—each is being contaminated by the parent's emotional state. The child now learns to hide or distort a part of himself or herself. This is when the flow of emotions in the soup cooked up between parent and child works to the child's disadvantage. Whether positive or negative, our Imprint for Emotional Sharing records and preserves this transfer of emotions between child and parent that characterizes the boundary-building years.

Breaking a Codependent Pattern Is Difficult

The child with a distorted boundary imprint might develop a pattern that I have come to call *boundary busting.* A person with such an interactional pattern may actually get you to feel what he or she is feeling. In another mysterious comingling of feeling, in that invisible space between two people across which emotions ebb and flow, the *boundary buster* has learned to transfer unacceptable feelings to others, and to let others take the rap for them.

Carrie and Jim:
When Feelings Are Like Hot Potatoes

Carrie and Jim have been married six years. He is a high-level executive in a major reality company. He says that people think of him as very successful. "What they don't know is that I wake up every morning in a state of high anxiety. I feel so anxious that I can hardly function." He goes on to explain that what he needs from Carrie is for her to "be a wife." Asked to explain what that means, he says that he needs her to keep things calm at home, to take care of their children, arrange their social schedule, etc. Carrie explains that she really does want to do the things Jim wants, but there is so much going on in their lives that she gets scattered.

"Give me an example," I suggest.

Carrie describes her day, doing things for her own work, for the children, arranging social events with friends, running the house. By evening she is tired. Jim comes home and looks around the house. "Why are all these papers in the den?" he asks. "When do you clean up the children's toys? Why is the telephone ringing so much? Get a baby-sitter, and let's go out to dinner."

"Jim is so upset about everything, I get upset myself," Carrie says. "I can't do everything. No matter what I do, he will find something else that I should have done. Our house is cleaner than most. But it's not enough for Jim."

Jim says. "I feel so harassed at work. My boss is demanding and critical. I feel the pressure constantly. When I come home, I need things to be calm. But I can't get calm. It's a mess in the house. So I tell Carrie what I need her to do, and she blows up."

"And what do you do when Carrie blows?" I asked him.

"Usually I calm down. I have to, because we can't both be upset or the house will be crazy."

"So you are anxious most of the time, Jim, and at work the pressure is so high that your anxiety level goes even higher," I observed. "You come home upset and say things to Carrie that aren't so different from what your boss does to you. Carrie feels criticized and gets very upset— then you calm down. It sounds like a setup for ongoing problems."

Jim agreed. "I know that happens, and I know Carrie does a lot of wonderful things. But when I come home, I can hardly control myself when I see what is going on in the house."

"I wonder if you know what you really are wishing for, Jim," I said.

"I guess some time alone with Carrie. I'd like her to welcome me, not be sitting and talking on the telephone, or greeting me with her current crisis of the day."

"You want her to be available to you when you first come home. Instead you feel bombarded with her business, the house, the things that upset her, and you can't hold any more anxiety. So you put out to her the upset feelings you have, and she gets your message of the upset feelings," I said. "Your emotions are like a hot potato that each of you throws back and forth. "But Carrie feels bombarded by your feelings—so then she explodes, and you calm down. Carrie, you need to learn what to do when Jim's feelings come at you.

In this game of hot potato, Carrie is unable to contain Jim's feelings, so she explodes—and the couple is "off to the races." What has to happen to break this pattern for Carrie is to learn to just hear Jim's feelings without reacting, keep a level head even though a lot of chaotic feelings are floating around. If she can expand her ability to stay rational even when there are all these confusing feelings floating around, she won't be hooked into his anxiety." Jim will have to find better outlets for his emotions.

Are You Stuck in the
Imprint for Emotional Sharing?

Do you

• Feel unknown to your partner?

• Feel misunderstood by the world at large?

• Wish to pull your partner into your feelings of anger, depression, and anxiety?

• Know how to provoke anger or other bad feelings in your partner in a passive-aggressive manner?

• Feel compelled to argue constantly about trivial points and insist that your partner agree with you before stopping?

• Encourage your partner to open up and share his/her emotions and then use the revelations to attack when you are angry or hurt?

• Expect those around you to accept and tolerate behavior that rational judgment would deem unacceptable—such as acting out rages, etc.?

• Refuse to meet your partner's needs unless your needs are met first?

Finding a way to think about intense emotions is the way people can learn to deal with the kinds of toxic feelings that otherwise get dumped into each other. Jim and Carrie have been learning to expand their emotional repertoire in order to meet each other's needs in their relationship.

Emotional Scenario

Did you ever have this experience?

Your relationship has been going through a difficult time. You are feeling distant from your partner. There's a lot of other stress in your life, but you haven't wanted to discuss it because you are not feeling close. You look at your partner and wonder why he is feeling so remote. Then you start to scrutinize his every word and gesture, asking "Is everything okay?" and "What's on your mind?" and so on. Soon, of course, this gets taxing and he might answer you in a terse manner, or, caught up in his own thoughts, he might not answer you at all. Your attempt to discuss this quickly turns into an argument because you are feeling vulnerable and needy to begin with. This has happened before, so what your partner says pushes your buttons.

What is happening here?

You are transferring your stress and feelings of aloneness and distance across the boundaries of your relationship and into your partner's container of deep feeling. Your partner can be operating at any of his imprints. He may be doing a crossword puzzle, reading the financial pages, writing a proposal for work, or doing nothing at all, just resting. You pull him into awareness of the relationship through your projection of stress and distant feelings, knowing that the interaction will be an argument, but that's okay because you want some contact—any contact—to relieve your tension. In essence, you transfer your tension to him.

If this is the general tone of your relationship, you are heading into turbulent waters. But if it is an occasional interaction between you, there are ways to avoid turning it into a more serious problem.

What you can do:

- Don't push your partner to talk if he/she is not ready.
- Take responsibility for your feelings and needs.
- Respect boundaries.
- Pay attention to what your partner needs.
- Call a friend to talk about your stress if you see your mate is not emotionally available.
- Talk about your feeling of distance when your partner is receptive, e.g. over dinner or on a walk together.
- Send clear, nonblaming messages.

The capacity to read another's feelings can be either a positive or a negative trait depending on how it is manifested. If you can choose to be open and receive your partner's feelings, you may have a great capacity for emotional attunement or empathy. But if you do not have control of your psychological boundaries, you may feel invaded, may be invasive, and your relationship may feel out of control. This is when it's important to remember Rule #4. The ability to read your partner, that is, being able to penetrate his or her emotional boundaries, is a powerful tool—be careful how you use it.

We Are All "Adult Children"

The face that we show to the world is only one part of ourselves. Within the boundaries of the entity that we call "I" are many parts. In this way we are all multiple personalities. The scared child hides inside the corporate tycoon . . . the wealthy charitable donor vicariously fills the emotional hunger of her needy baby within . . . the calm scientist keeps in check his rageful "monster." We all have the wish to be known, understood, and accepted; we all share a fear that, should our hidden parts be revealed, we would be judged as weak, inferior, disturbed, sick, or even criminal. And we all need someone we can depend on to love even our weak and fragile parts.

In loving partnerships that endure, a mutual dependency evolves in which the partners know and accept each other beyond the partial portrayals the world sees. They mirror, share, contain, and understand the many-shaded facets of one another's inner worlds.

In unhappy relationships, by contrast, each has an inkling of the partner's needs, desires, and dreams, but does not accept the other's feelings and so does not respond in ways that allow for dependency or for the relationship and the partners in it to grow. Each may find in the other an unwanted mirror of disowned and frightening feelings. Attempts to share feelings only produce escalating, negative reactions. Neither feels understood, accepted, or loved. Each must be on guard against future hurts that open past wounds.

No one has a perfect childhood. We are all trying to repair our childhood wounds, open our emotional boundaries, and share our deepest feelings and fears with someone we can trust. As adults, we remain the children of our early caretakers, however competent or inept they may have been. To a great extent, each of us attempts to relive aspects of the relationships that failed us. Our early experiences determine our capacities for sharing our true feelings, for moving back and forth between times of loving merger and times of separateness, for allowing our boundaries to loosen and expand rather than erecting "walls" to protect ourselves. Our boundaries open to others only when we feel safe and can allow ourselves to be vulnerable. Indeed, what we allow ourselves to share in a new love relationship is often those emotions that have been hidden the longest. There is good reason for this. The window to our deeper emotions opens only to the extent that we feel safe. Looking at it in the early days of love makes everything seem magical and perfect. The full mosaic of our emotions looks like a window with four quadrants.

At any given time we unconsciously open or close any or all of these quadrants. We each have the ability to share these different aspects of ourselves. But some people are more adept at transmitting and/or receiving the "unthought emotional truths" of another.

In recent years psychological theorists have attempted to identify those processes by which emotions are transferred between people. The "reading" of emotional states that takes place nonverbally seems like magic at times. Somehow, we learn to attune to the feelings of others by decoding nonverbal and nonconscious messages. When it occurs, it almost seems to be telepathic. Is this telepathy? It may be that

The Emotional Quadrant

1	2
The things of which I am consciously aware and share with acquaintances, my façade, my best foot forward.	These things that I know and share with close friends, my hopes and dreams, my fears and complaints about my mate, my job, my life.
3	4
That which I am ashamed of and share only with people who I know will not judge me. Things I would tell a therapist, or a lover in a moment of complete candor.	Things I cut off from awareness, for-which I do not even have words. Feelings given to someone who is willing to receive transmissions of my unthought or unvoiced emotions.

telepathic communication was actually an evolutionary forerunner to our present style of direct verbal expression.

In 1933, Freud expressed this view:

> The telepathic act is supposed to consist of a mental act in one person instigating the same mental act in another person. . . . One is led to the suspicion that this is the original archaic method of communication between individuals and that, in the course of phylogenetic evolution, it has been replaced by the better method of giving information . . . but the older method might have persisted in the background and still be able to put itself into effect under certain conditions.[10]

This sounds suspiciously like mind reading. The ability to receive messages across the boundaries that first develop in the early years of life can be used to translate another's feelings into conscious thought and words. The more disturbing element in this "talent" is the possibility of receiving unthought emotions, with such force that the emotional state is received directly, without thoughts or words. These feelings are then experienced by the receiver with all of the painful emotions that the sender is trying to cast off.

The positive side of this is what new lovers experience in blissful merger. The boundaries of one overlap with the other's. Two share as one for the moment. Both imagine they can depend on the other to understand them through and through. This phenomenon, when mirrored back in a positive, nonjudgmental way, is the basis of empathy. What may be wished for is described by Virginia Woolf in *A Room of One's Own;* it is the ability to mirror back another person at twice the normal size.

With the deepest sense of relief, we find someone with whom to share everything. *"Finally* there is someone who wants to know *all* of me." But often the other can no more tolerate these emotions than we can. Like a hot potato, the emotions are passed back and forth between the boundaries that are the edges of each of us. But when the "hot potato" can be held, accepted, and understood, it is a most healing part of a relationship, a corrective emotional experience that repairs the hurt of messages we received in our past.

That is why the openness to receive each other's emotions is such an important part of positive dependency and mutual empowerment. People can provide for each other an arena within which each can reveal inner feelings without fear. In fact, this capacity is a crucial component of a healthy dependency. The ability to hold the emotions of another person depends upon an inner sense of solidness, a sense that if we open our boundaries to another, we will not be damaged by the emotions that flow between us. For some, any emotion, even love, is too frightening to hold for long. For others, emotional exchanges of all kinds are part of the excitement of life.

Our Imprint for Emotional Sharing ultimately influences how open or closed we are emotionally as adults, and how willing we are to accept the unknown secrets in our partners. Adults who had predominantly safe experiences of sharing their feelings in their early years will be more open to relationships and less suspicious, fearful, or ashamed of their feelings. These lucky people have a firm foundation on which to build intimate relationships; they innately believe that it is safe to send and receive emotional messages—they will be willing to risk intimate engagement with others. In contrast, adults whose frightening feelings were not consistently detoxified by parental soothing tend to be far more guarded and fearful. To these people intimacy threatens a loss of self through engulfment in the partner's needs, and dependency means weakness and neediness.

Relationship problems that originate during the creation of the first two imprints for primary bonding and emotional sharing are the most formidable for couples to resolve because these problems incorporate patterns of response that were fixed solidly in place at a preverbal level—responses that can feel frightening, revolting, chaotic, even mindless or crazy. These volatile areas are invariably triggered when our dependency needs go unmet or are critically rebuffed.

When our personal boundaries are weak, and when we don't feel safe with our hidden feelings, we are inclined to project or transfer those feelings onto a partner. If we feel shame, we will find something shameful in the partner; if we feel mean or ugly or otherwise deficient, the boundary buster throws that feeling onto the partner—so he or she is the shameful, mean, stupid, ugly one. This kind of boundary busting is the attempt of the needy infant in the adult to shore up its defense system. The closer the partner gets, the more the boundary buster feels it is necessary to protect or hide weak, dependent feelings by "giving" them to the partner.

As we shall see in the story of Alice and Eric, this projection or dumping of unwanted intolerable emotions only causes more pain.

Alice and Eric: Taming the Monster

It is eleven at night. Eric restlessly rolls over in bed. His right foot slightly brushes Alice's thigh. She makes no move. He puts his leg over her leg. Alice, who sleeps precariously at the edge of their bed, moves even farther toward the edge. Although no words are being spoken, they are having a profound conversation. Words are not used because words would cause shame. Alice and Eric do not even consciously register the thoughts that momentarily sear through each of their minds.

In therapy the next day we take a moment to examine and consider the meaning of this brief but powerful interaction. Eric recalls the painful feelings that passed through him and were immediately put out of his mind. He now puts words to the humiliation of Alice's rejection, describing it as feeling like "scorching flame." "It wasn't sex I wanted," he explained.

"Just some contact, some touching, a positive response to your reaching out," I ventured. Eric needed mirroring far more than he needed sex.

"It's hard to explain," he said as he nodded in agreement.

"And when Eric was searching for the physical touch of connection, what did it feel like to you, Alice?" I asked.

"I felt like he wanted me to put my arms around him and hold him. I felt bad that I didn't want to, but I wanted to get away. I felt smothered."

"I can feel it," Eric said. "She sleeps as far toward the edge of the bed as she can. If she moves any further away, she'll fall off."

"So *you* try to get closer to make contact," I said, "and you feel rejected. But you go to sleep, saying nothing. Where do the feelings of rejection and shame go?"

"Nowhere," Eric replied.

But intense feelings are hard to contain. Although Eric thinks they go nowhere, they are likely to be "dumped" on Alice.

As though she were reading my thoughts, Alice interjected, "They show up the next day. He's cross; he picks on me and finds ways to criticize, or he deprives me of something I want."

"Buried emotions always come out in some way," I said. "If Eric feels a need for contact he can get only from you, he will feel rejected when you withdraw. His protection, as always, is to hide from the pain and find a way to dump the hurtful feelings onto you." I was referring to Eric's issues concerning his Imprint for Emotional Sharing.

As the child of an alcoholic mother, Eric was thrust early into the role of caretaker. When he was seven, his parents divorced. Eric learned early to draw on his resources and talents to give him the strength he was called upon to provide. Any weakness or anxiety that was unacceptable to him, he "gave" to women, to his mother specifically, later to other women in his life.

Eric is always in search of a container for his unsafe emotions, a lifelong pattern of boundary busting. Alice's attuning nature makes her a good receiver. In his own way Eric is also a good receiver. His permeable boundaries make him able to attune to and *utilize* information he receives about the emotions of others. It serves him well in negotiating high-level business deals, but not so well in his family relationship.

Turning to Eric, I said, "Part of your power and success in business is that you understand the needs and moods of others. You don't let things hurt you. You keep an emotional shield around yourself to protect against feeling things that may become too painful or uncomfortable. You can sense the vulnerable areas in others and use that skill to negotiate your deals. You know how to make everyone look like they have won." Eric nodded and I continued.

"So when you are in charge, you succeed by helping others get what they want. It's only at home with your family that you fail to create win-win situations. At home you feel vulnerable.

"Your dependent side comes out at home and you are afraid it makes you appear weak and vulnerable to being hurt. If you do feel a stab of pain or touch an old wound, you have a way to get rid of whatever is hurting, by making others feel hurt instead, which gives you the illusion of control and renders you safe from emotional injury. I guess we will have to figure out how Alice fits into this pattern and how you fit into hers."

Despite the serious problems that had brought them into therapy two years before, a tumultuous period that might have led another couple to a divorce lawyer rather than to a marital therapist, they were determined to make their marriage work. They respected one another, they both had been married before, and they each knew that trading in one partner for another would simply be trading one set of problems for another. While they wanted things to be better, they didn't expect perfect bliss. When Eric and Alice first came to therapy, Eric calmly reported that, in an angry outburst, he had told Alice to "get out!" Although she had moved to her sister's, neither wanted a divorce. Together, they made a commitment to make their marriage work.

Alice, who looked strained and fragile, spoke haltingly about the beginning of their relationship. When she first met Eric, he was charming, bright, successful, and attentive. She readily married this "wonderful man" after a six-month courtship. Shortly after their wedding, however, he turned into a different person—one who could get extremely angry, who was emotionally abusive about things that didn't seem important, and who frightened her.

At the same time, Eric's good qualities continued to surface. Alice dutifully ticked off the items on the positive side of Eric's ledger. "In the evenings, he always wants to be with me. He doesn't get involved with other women. He provides a very nice home, a very nice lifestyle. There's a lot of excitement in our lives. We do a lot of traveling and entertaining, which I enjoy."

I commented on her looking tired. "I've gone downhill for three years," she admitted. "Sometimes I get so depressed, I literally can't move. I don't know how to cope with Eric's mood swings—his dark side. My family life growing up was fairly harmonious—I'm not prepared for all these upheavals. What I don't understand is how Eric could change so drastically."

I ventured an explanation. "There is something about intimacy that brings out the true person. The Eric who courted you was not living a lie, but he was revealing only a part of himself. These other parts may be only dark shadows, as dangerous and foreign to him as they are to you. But they are things he has had to learn to deal with to survive the traumas of his childhood."

I asked Eric how he saw his pattern affecting their marriage. He launched into a complicated but impeccably concise summary of the underlying dynamics of their last three arguments. Alice sat silently as Eric's persuasive tones filled the room. I mentally noted that the dangerous emotions, which erupted so frequently at home, were nowhere to be found in this session. By presenting his behavior in a positive light, and feeling heard and understood from his perspective, Eric felt safe. My goal was to free him to open the pathway between his thoughts and the underlying feelings. However, he was not yet ready to touch the emotional underside.

The topic of their last three arguments was how to care for Joel, Alice's seven-year-old son from her previous marriage. Eric repeatedly complained that Alice sabotaged his attempts to be a father to this boy. "That's because you're always reproaching him for minor infractions," Alice told him accusingly.

"That's ridiculous!" Eric spat back. "You *know* I've always wanted to be a father to him. I'm just trying to help him grow up and *not* be a sissy. You baby him."

"I need you to accept who he is. He needs a male figure with whom to identify. He does *not* need to be bullied."

"But you interfere."

"Why do you criticize him so much?" Alice shot back angrily.

At first I wondered if we were looking at issues of rivalry and jealousy so common in stepfamilies. I waited to hear more about how each saw the problems in their marriage. As I listened, I realized that the issues being debated were but a thin veneer covering deep emotional wounds and unfulfilled needs.

Eric's dependency needs were unacceptable to him. They made him feel small, inadequate, weak. He found a way to release himself of these feelings by criticizing Joel and transferring wounded feelings to his stepson. It is not so difficult to behave in ways that project uncomfortable feelings like fear or anger onto another person. Screaming loudly causes anxiety. Constant criticism causes feelings of inadequacy. It takes great self-confidence and solid self-boundaries, or a strong support system of others who confirm worth, to ward off the boundary-busting behavior of a person who is close to you or in a power position.

Alice complained that she was in an impossible double bind. If she doesn't take a stand against Eric's hurtful behavior, she feels "steamrollered"; if she does oppose him, he can become so angry she fears for her physical safety.

In Eric's version of their problems, Alice was emotionally unavailable and judgmental of him: "She acts as though she is perfect and that *I'm* the one with all the problems." Eric explained quite "logically" that he simply wanted Alice to acknowledge that she, too, was part of their marital problems.

This did not seem an unreasonable point, since marital problems are a two-person process. Alice seemed sincere in her bafflement about what she might be doing to justify his unpredictable and sometimes explosive behavior. When I suggested that there might be some less visible issues fueling their problems, Alice continued to look bewildered while Eric authoritatively retorted, "There are no underlying dynamics to this; I know exactly what I'm doing and why I'm doing it. In each argument, I'm very aware of what I'm doing that upsets Alice. In fact, when things reach that kind of a boiling point, it's my *intention* to upset her."

Eric knew his power to reach into and break through her boundaries. It is his intention. But no one *always* knows why they are doing whatever it is they are doing. We each develop personal stories that organize and explain to ourselves the deep layers of emotions that are out of conscious awareness. We would have to understand why Eric needed to "rattle Alice's cage" in order to begin to peel away to the deeper layers of dependency and defense.

I came to understand more as Eric related something of the earlier relationships in his life. After his parents divorced, Eric's father remarried. His new stepmother resisted Eric's attempts to maintain a relationship with his father, although they lived in the same neighborhood. She quickly had two children, who received all of his father's attention. Eric desperately wanted to be accepted by his father and be included in his father's family, but his stepmother remained an unmovable barrier. Barred from one family and enmeshed in another as a child caretaker with his mother, Eric had no one he could depend on for safety and comfort, and no safe place to express his hurt, confusion, and anger. Instead, he adjusted and accommodated on the surface and found ways to siphon off the unwelcome emotions, projecting them onto others, particularly his dependent, alcoholic mother. If he was lonely, he might ask his mother why she was so sad. If he was angry, he would set up an argument with her so as to be able to deal with the anger. Eric was performing classic boundary-busting behavior, throwing his unmanageable, "unacceptable" emotions onto his mother in order to tuck them away, to deal with them safely if not completely.

Throughout his growing-up years, only the talented, powerful side of Eric was allowed to surface and to develop. Any needy, dependent, vulnerable feelings were "given" to others. He didn't allow himself to need the love and attention of his unavailable father.

Only when Eric graduated from college and entered the family business did he finally have a chance to build a close relationship with his father. As Eric described it, the renewed relationship began amicably enough, but slowly, over a number of years, they began to compete openly and destructively.

Eric contended that his father was aggressive toward him: "There was nothing I would have liked better than to continue working in my father's business and ultimately take it over when he retired. But he made that impossible." Finally, Eric left and, joined by several employees from his father's business, started his own version of his father's business. Eric believed his judgment had been vindicated as his father's business foundered and disintegrated while his own company grew and thrived. Eric's father did not talk to him for ten years.

"My father and I finally started talking and seeing each other again two years ago. I'm glad we've had a chance to talk to each other, especially because he is quite ill now and not expected to live much longer."

After this session, Eric seemed more willing to talk. Several weeks later, Eric's father died. This loss was followed by a period in which Eric began to focus all his energy and attention on his work, scarcely paying attention to Alice except to give her long lists of chores to do for him and his business clients. Alice described how fatigued she was feeling and complained that Eric remained oblivious. She was left to do all the work fixing up a new home that they had bought. Worse, the day they had moved across town, Eric invited friends to dinner without consulting her. Alice said that she was too exhausted to entertain. He persisted, saying that it would not be much trouble. He was pushing at her boundaries. She resisted, but complied wearily to avoid an argument.

At the end of the evening, as soon as the guests had left, Eric provoked an argument. Again the boundary-busting behavior emerged. He wanted her upset. He did this despite Alice's protest that she was exhausted and wanted to postpone the discussion until the next day. Eric persisted, following her from room to room as she tried to walk away from him. "You can see your method of breaking through to her," I said to Eric. "What did you do, Alice?" I asked.

"I was exhausted. Finally I said I was leaving and got my keys to go to stay with my sister. Eric blocked the door. At that point I just stopped and slumped down on the floor. I couldn't move."

"Alice became catatonic," Eric jumped in.

"He's right. I felt paralyzed. He picked me up and carried me into the bedroom. I couldn't move. I had this awful feeling that if I moved, he would want sex. So, I didn't move. I was afraid of him, and something monstrous was happening. He seemed as if he was sadistic. There was a part of me that knew what was happening, and I just wanted him to leave me alone."

Eric yearned for his father's love, hated his father for his emotional abandonment, revenged himself in the fierce business struggle and was still the child who wanted his father's love, admiration, inclusion, and respect. When his father died, Eric lost his last chance to get what he needed. He was bereft, but had so strong a shield around him that these feelings were not allowed to emerge. He was emotionally paralyzed. He could come back to life only by finding a way to rid himself of these untenable feelings. By pushing Alice beyond her emotional limits, he made her his "dumping ground." She was now holding his chaotic and paralyzing feelings.

We were touching dangerous emotional territory. Either their patterns of relating had to change or the relationship would end. Although new patterns do not require a complete modification of the underlying imprints for relating, they do require learning a different way to interact in stressful situations. I said to Alice, "I think he was trying to reach you in the deepest way, and your only defense was to totally immobilize yourself."

Turning to Eric, I said, "I assume that you were trying to connect to her, you wanted her to hold and contain some important feelings that were perhaps too much for you to bear." He nodded but could not talk. After a silence he said, "It's scary."

After another silence Eric went on, "It's like the movie *Who's Afraid of Virginia Woolf?* There is a sexual energy in that kind of fight."

"Perhaps there is for you," I said, "but not for your wife. Alice only deadened herself further. I know that's not what you wanted. Can you tell me more about what it is you need from Alice?"

Eric quietly admitted, "I was hoping to find the monster in her."

"What monster?" I asked softly.

"No one is so perfect that they don't have a monster somewhere inside."

"What does it mean to you to find that Alice has a monster deep inside?"

"She has to have a monster. If she can't face her own monster, there is no way for her to accept mine."

Now I was beginning to understand. "You want her to accept you, monster and all. You want her to accept the part of you that you have not yet accepted, a part that has been buried for a long time."

"Right."

"Maybe that's why you always try to be so logical," I suggested. "As long as you are in a thinking mode, the emotional monster can be kept hidden."

"Not hidden. I just throw him into a corner," Eric explained emphatically, pointing to the corner of my office behind him. He was describing how he temporarily got rid of his shameful feelings by projecting them onto his "monster." By searching for Alice's dark side, he was trying to project his demons onto her. He did not want to be alone with these feelings. Thus Alice had to have a monster or she could never understand him. He had to elicit one from her through torment, even violent behavior. What shows on the surface may be contained, but as a therapist what I see is the child, Eric, struggling to find someone to contain his dark feelings and make them safe enough for him to reown.

"And when the emotional monster nudges you, what do you want from Alice?" I asked.

"Just that she be there."

"But you push me away," she protested tearfully. "You are so mean to me."

"I'm just trying to find your monster, to connect, so we can be together," he said calmly.

"So, you want Alice to come closer when you are upset," I began, "but the actions you take to bring her closer just push her away. Then you continue to push, harder and harder. If you keep doing it this way, her walls will get higher and higher until she locks you out permanently. You will have re-created your relationship with your father."

The next time we met, Eric returned to this comment immediately. He said that he had thought a lot about his monster all week, and that he wanted Alice to meet his monster.

"You want Alice to know and understand and maybe feel some of the same emotions you feel," I commented. "That way, you won't be alone."

"Yes. If she knows, and accepts that she also has a monster of her own, then I will know that she understands and accepts me."

What was happening between this couple was a classic demonstration of a potentially toxic dependency, but we were on the brink of helping it become a healing one. If Eric could get what he needed from Alice in a more direct way, if she was willing to give it, I recognized that there was a chance for them to use the dependency creatively. If Alice could acknowledge, for example, that everyone has unacceptable feelings inside—his or her personal monster—then she would be able to understand Eric's experiences and he would feel mirrored by a non-judging, accepting partner. Eric was desperately seeking a way to tolerate his feelings without being overwhelmed by shame. He was asking Alice to tolerate and contain feelings that he had always dealt with alone.

Little by little, as Eric accepted and integrated the vulnerable facet of his personality, which he referred to as "the monster," he became gentler and less provocative to Alice and her son. At times Eric still reverted to controlling, hurtful behavior, when he seemed to be testing Alice, making sure she really knew his monster. But he no longer had an unending supply of emotional contamination to "dump." Alice, in turn, became increasingly accepting and responsive. She learned ways to deal with Eric when he provoked. Instead of feeling weakened and paralyzed, she stood her ground. Eric seemed to enjoy this "strong" Alice, who differed so much from all of the other women in his life.

Despite the inauspicious beginning, the marriage has grown increasingly solid and there is no further talk of divorce. Both are getting more of what they want from each other. In therapy together we continue to explore the early injuries that impact their current relationship and the many ways that they enhance each others' lives.

The interchange of emotions and the crossing over of feelings from parents to infant, and then from one lover to another, that characterizes our boundary-building years is a powerful part of our development. This alchemical miracle can be used to channel either love or ill will. Most of us do not intend to inflict harm. Because of buried, vulnerable areas, however, we may misread the intent of others and react in ways that are hurtful to those we care about most. A cycle of misunderstanding and emotional injury is perpetuated, passed on from husband to wife, parent to child to grandchild, down through generations of wounded people. The only way to break this cycle is through the willingness to attune to one another's inner experience. To care enough to hold in one's heart the pain that each has lived, to love even while aware of the other's deepest vulnerabilities and needs, is a true test of love. This is the gift of our Imprint for Emotional Sharing.

5 Imprint for Bridging Connections

For, after all, I have been happy. I have made the films I wanted to make, I have made them with people who were more than my collaborators; they were my accomplices. This, I believe, is one recipe for happiness: to work with people you love and who love you.

—Jean Renoir

Rule #5 for Positive Dependency:

Choose your battles carefully. A spotless house and gourmet meals can be a gift of love or a battleground over which unmet dependency needs are fought. Evaluate which issues are so important to you that they are not negotiable. Everything else should be open for discussion and compromise.

From the time he was two, my grandson knew about sharing. He would hand me one of his toys whenever I came to visit. The moment I walked in, Ari would begin looking over his possessions, selecting one to give to me. As I reached to accept his "gift," he would visibly relax, as if to say, "I did it!" This was an important transaction. We had made a new kind of contact, one in which he had exercised choice and experienced a sense of his power. The toy was a message without words that allowed Ari to connect to me in a way that retained the desire for closeness while adding a dash of distance and a pinch of "I-ness." The toy was a bridge of his choosing that linked him to me.

Between the ages of two and three, most children form devoted attachments to special things—blankets, dolls, teddy bears—that they will not allow to be replaced or taken away for any reason, no matter how worn-out and dirty they may become. Linus's blanket, which has been a running joke in the *Peanuts* comic series for decades, demonstrates an important truth about our third imprint for relating: sometimes, we must use *things* to temporarily replace the people in our lives on whom we depend. While it's true that we all need someone to love, someone to meet our basic needs for emotional and physical comfort, sometimes that person can't be there. In that case, a healthy baby might learn to use the thing to which he feels attached to assuage needy feelings until mom comes home. When the object being used has become more important than the person's attachment to a loved one, it is a sign that bridging problems are being exhibited. Where a baby might use a blanket as a bridging object, an adult might use anything from work to other lovers—even shopping, collecting, sports, alcohol, or drugs.

Babies achieve major developmental shifts as they move from the state of merger and oneness (Imprint for Primary Bonding) into an increased perception of being separate and distinct from others (Imprint for Emotional Sharing). As these shifts occur, the presence of the parents continues to be associated with the need for security. During times when their parents are not present, babies look for ways to soothe themselves.

Learning to substitute things for people is a necessary part of maturing. The needs of a growing child are forever changing and may not always be perceived accurately by family members. Caregivers may be unavailable at the moment the baby becomes aware of a need to be close; or perhaps the parents are immersed in their own problems. A parent who is ill may not be able to provide the amount of care a baby wants or needs. Whatever the reason, serious or mundane, all children go through times when mother isn't available, when security is not ever-present.

In the course of normal development, children typically select a symbol of security to reassure themselves and provide a sense of positive dependence during these tenuous moments. An inanimate object—a fuzzy stuffed animal or a special blanket—now becomes a reminder of the loved one, a bridge from baby to mother and from feelings of fear and insecurity to those of comfort and safety.[11] This security object helps the baby recall the mother's image and, in fact, the entire caretaking environment. Growing up, children internalize the feeling of safety provided by these precious possessions. In time, external symbols of security are no longer necessary, and the stuffed animal or blanket is relegated to the attic.

These security blankets and special animals and toys are technically called *transitional objects*.[12] In part, this term captures the ability of these things to bridge the empty spaces between mother and child. The term also conveys the function of the blanket or toy in helping the child make the *transition* from being a baby to being a youngster. Although we eventually internalize the functions of our transitional objects, we never entirely lose the need for symbols that help us connect with others, for a "security blanket" that can act as a temporary replacement for love and attention. That need, together with our original means of meeting it, forms the basis of our third imprint for relating.

Our Imprint for Bridging Connections can also be used to help us quell the pain of unmet needs by depending on these substitutes. In other words, security objects can be used as a positive bridge that leads toward safe feelings of connection, or a negative bridge that leads away from our feelings and needs. The child who awakens from a nap while her mother is outside hanging up laundry might cuddle her teddy bear for comfort until her mother returns. This is different from the baby who clings to her doll all night long, trying *not* to feel terror as her parents wage their private war in the next room.

Does Gender Affect Imprints?

When patterns of interaction develop and become fixed during the formation of our first two imprints for bonding and sharing across emotional boundaries, gender is not yet part of our awareness. But the Imprint for Bridging Connections emerges around the time that a child begins to acquire a sense of maleness or femaleness—a gender identity. The differing characteristics of male and female identities result in the selection of different categories of security objects—different bridges to connection—in childhood as well as adulthood.

Considerable research describes the different ways male and female children develop a self-image and learn to relate. One important finding is that a girl's perception of herself does not require the degree of separation from the mother needed by a male child.[13] The objects of a young girl's play re-create the role she has observed her mother perform. In order for the young boy to begin creating his identity, however, he must first identify with his father—which means that he must separate from his mother, giving up some of his sources of security, long before his sister might.[14] Since most fathers are less available as sources of comfort and security, the male child is more likely to turn to security objects to provide the needed sense of dependable connection.

Despite all the efforts of the women's movement to "degenderize" child-rearing attitudes, boys and girls are generally taught very different, gender-related values and behaviors. Boys are taught to *not* express what they feel; even as children they must be "strong." They are shamed by peers for being sensitive or emotional, for showing dependency or a need for intimacy. A little boy is allowed to wrestle with his father for physical contact but is teased and called a "sissy" if he wants to sit on his mother's lap. As he grows older, he learns to throw a football or play basketball as part of male camaraderie.

Growing up as a male requires early separation from the nurturing comfort offered by the mother. *To be male is to be taught how to use security objects as substitutes for intimate connections with people.* Because many of the substitutes used to compensate for renouncing the need for the mother come in the form of competitive activities, boys are reinforced for winning and achieving rather than for connecting with people.

Since girls tend to use language skills at an earlier age than boys, they typically use these skills to bond with others. Even in childhood games, girls choose maintenance of relationships over competitive values. Carole Gilligan, author of *In a Different Voice,* described how boys typically argue over the rules of a game, whereas girls will select another game to play if conflict arises.[15] Thus, *to be female is to maintain connections with people*—in essence, to re-create the nurturance

and comforting experiences offered by the mother. When family problems disrupt the developing relationship between mother and daughter, girls learn to replace people with things.

So, in addition to all the personal and family variables that influence
our preferences, we also experience cultural reinforcements for one
relational mode or another influenced by gender. Men are typically
more comfortable operating from the Imprint for Bridging Connections
or from the Imprint for Mature Dependence, which will be described
in the next chapter. Women, having less need for separation, are more
often comfortable with closeness, connection, and the open flow of
emotions that characterize the Imprint for Bonding and the Imprint for
Emotional Sharing.

Adult Bridges

Relationships that work make use of many kinds of bridges that help
partners connect in nurturing, caring ways. In loving relationships,
both partners can depend upon the consistency of these connecting
links. When people do not feel accepted, understood, and cared about,
however, the bridges lead *away from* the pain, away from the relationship. Positive adult bridges provide direct ways of relating to others
through shared activities, joint goals, common social, religious, or political projects, not to mention gifts, letters, a poem, flowers. Negative
bridges, by contrast, act as *substitutes* for these needed but unobtain-
able connections and may include drugs, alcohol, tobacco, computer
and video addictions, workaholism, even exercise mania.

Larry, for example, used his successful career as a Wall Street merg-
ers and acquisitions specialist as a bridge. He believed that his mania
for money and his constant conversation about it connected him to
others. Certainly it seemed to get the attention of people in his social
circle. In fact, investments and finance were his sole topics of conversation. His wife complained that all he ever talked about were his stock
deals.

"They *want* to talk to me," he answered defensively. "Because of
what I do, they want my advice."

"You're boring," she retorted. "It's as though nothing else has any meaning to you. You never talk to me about what you feel. I have no idea what our relationship means to you. I feel all alone when I'm with you."

Larry knew she was right, that something was wrong with his relationships, that he felt connected to no one. But he was terrified to change. As we worked together, we learned that beneath his persona and the buffer of his expertise, Larry had many anxious feelings. Vague fears of being unwanted, unloved, and emotionally abandoned fueled Larry's compulsive need to be an expert. The middle child in a large, boisterous, and bickering family, he had never excelled at school and was labeled a "behavior problem."

Only when he discovered his niche in the world of high finance after graduating from college did he finally stop feeling like a failure. As a stockbroker throughout the booming 1980s, he acquired a small fortune. When the market fell, Larry took the money he had earned and moved from New York to California. But without his position in a leading firm, unable to replenish his fragile self-esteem with the accolades from his investment acumen, Larry felt lost and deflated. This is when he sought out therapy. He had gone from busy workaholic to virtual isolate. He had not learned how to interact with people except in his role as a financial genius. He had few friends. Retirement at the age of forty-two was no pleasure for him; working excessively has been his way of relating to the world.

Larry's behavior was seen by others as workaholism. For him, however, it was a passport to attention and acceptance. Without this bridge between himself and others, he felt the terror of aloneness, disconnection, and abandonment that was buried in his early imprints.

For people like Larry, work is both a substitute for bonded connections and a bargaining chip—a means of exchanging successful talents for emotional support. In essence, the bargain states: "I will provide a certain style of living if you will be there for me, understand me, accept me with my imperfections, acknowledge my strong points, love me." Such people attempt to meet their dependency needs for love and belonging without openly acknowledging any needs whatsoever.

The result, almost invariably, is a string of failed relationships offset by enormous success in business or creative endeavors. When stripped of his successful business challenges, Larry was finally confronted by the other half of his life scale: his failed relationships. When he returned to work, he made a conscious effort to do it differently this time: he worked fewer hours and he made an unexpected commitment to marital therapy. To make these major changes, he realized, was an acknowledgment that he did, indeed, have needs, that he desperately wanted to be loved, that he did not want to live as a totally self-absorbed person.

The problem with negative bridges—with focusing on things instead of people for our emotional sustenance is that the underlying need for positive, dependent connections with others remains unaddressed and unfulfilled. *Positive bridges support positive dependency.* The accurate perception by one partner of what the other wants, and the appreciation of the other partner for what is given (another aspect of positive dependency), nurture both. The flowers sent after an argument, making birthdays special events, cooking a special dinner, writing a love letter—all represent love and strengthen the link between partners. However, it should be noted that what makes a bridge positive is not *what* it is, but the degree to which it is a product of accurate perception, and the degree to which it is received with appreciation.

Gifts can easily be used as negative bridges that exacerbate distance and misunderstanding between a couple, which is why Rule #5 specifies that a gift can be a positive or a negative bridge depending on the source of its inspiration. Give to your partner what will work for her/him—not something to assuage your own unfulfilled needs.

For Alice and Eric (in chapter 4), the exchange of gifts was a point of contention. His complaint was that Alice showed little appreciation for the expensive presents he bought for her. Her experience was that Eric gave her presents that showed little understanding or concern about what was important to her. In a recent session, Alice described her differing experiences of receiving gifts from Eric. Last year's expensive gift was still sitting in the closet, brand-new yet irrevocably discarded. "The gift had nothing to do with me," Alice said, explaining to Eric why she ignored his gifts. "This year you made my birthday a special day and you gave me a gift that had care and thought behind it. You knew I was studying art history, and the book of Georgia O'Keeffe artwork that you gave me was perfect. I was really touched. It felt like you truly *cared.* You were paying attention to what matters to *me."*

Many couples have difficulty selecting gifts for each other because a meaningful gift requires attunement to the desires of the other and the willingness to respond to those desires. This means responding at two relational levels: with empathic awareness of the other (Imprint for Emotional Sharing) and through an outward manifestation of that empathy through a gift (Imprint for Bridging Connections). Feeling known and responded to through giving and receiving gifts enhances the feeling that we are part of something larger, a "team" feeling of reciprocal, positive dependency.

Turning Differences Into Resources

Gift-giving is one kind of bridge connecting two people. There are many others. As mentioned, shared activities and involvement in one another's special concerns can be important bridges to positive dependency and love. Even *differences* in interests can work to the couples' advantage. Matt and I have been involved in two very different fields during our lives together—he in the world of business and finance, I in the field of psychology. I don't read books about finance and he doesn't read psychology books. But we do share a mutual interest in history, philosophy, and ethics, and so we read and discuss these kinds of books. He has encouraged me to write about my work; I have encouraged him to actualize his dream of obtaining a Ph.D. and developing programs for lifelong learning. It is not so much a specific contribution that I can offer Matt in his pursuits, or that he can give me. It is an enthusiasm for each other's goals that allows us to depend on one another for support and encouragement as we each build different bridges to the world outside.

This ability to participate in one another's outside interests is not automatic; it requires care and willingness from both partners. The work and play rhythms of my husband and I are quite different, for example. When he undertakes a project, he is careful, meticulous, and methodical. He sets aside a certain time for work and adheres to his schedule rigidly. I know that any change in plans feels like a disruption to him.

Unlike Matt, I have no particular schedule. Since I am busy with my psychotherapy practice during the week, I use weekends and vacations for writing. I may fill up every spare moment, even working through the night. Matt had to adjust to my total immersion in my work at times when he was most ready to play and relax; I had to adjust to his need for scheduling when I have no such need myself.

Matt could complain about my compulsive working; I might demand that he learn to be more flexible. He could have pointed out that I had no experience writing when I began my first book, that taking on such a project was a bit presumptuous, and that it would require a lot of time that could be spent traveling and enjoying the freedom of being "empty-nesters." In which case, I might have pointed out that his ideas for changing the education system of our country are quite grandiose and should perhaps be left to national leaders; and that getting a Ph.D. when he was well into his retirement years would certainly curtail our freedom to travel. But, in fact, we both preferred to support what might be possible in one another rather than making assumptions about what was not.

Turning Similarities Into Weapons

I have long attempted to understand the difference between couples who accept each other's habits, eccentricities, offbeat behaviors, unusual hobbies and pursuits, and those who react to such things as intolerable infringements. I think the difference comes from the simple fact that, when our dependency needs are *not* being met in the relationship, we are more inclined to focus on limitations and flaws.

Couples need to be aware that their bridges can either strengthen or help each of them avoid intimacy in their relationship. The same bridges can be connectors or disconnectors depending from where they emanate and to where they lead.

When Carl and Anna first married, he was a fledgling actor hoping to become a writer. She was an executive assistant at a major film studio. Anna supported and encouraged her husband's career, and he became a successful television writer. She encouraged him during the long lean years, sometimes offering creative suggestions for his projects. Anna was gifted in these areas and Carl frequently used her suggestions, always giving her credit for her contributions. She felt a part of his accomplishments and shared in his success.

Over the years Anna began to think about writing herself. She freely discussed her ideas with Carl. Later, she was shocked to find those very ideas incorporated into his work. Carl didn't understand why that should upset her. Because he always gave her credit for her ideas, Carl didn't think he had done anything wrong. "Her ideas are helpful, but Anna has never completed a single project," he said.

Anna was deeply hurt and lost her enthusiasm for assisting him. "Nothing I do counts for anything," she said to him in an early marital therapy session. "You push me into the corner, ignore me, and then you think I shouldn't mind you waking me up in the middle of the night to talk to me about a problem with your work."

Carl became angry and got up as if to walk out of the room. "This marriage isn't working," he stated. "I work my butt off. I've given you more than I ever promised when we got married; you've gotten everything you asked for—marriage, house, kids—and what do I get?"

"What do you need, Carl?" I asked, focusing, as I often do, on the unmet underlying needs and the resulting emotional hurts that might precipitate his anger.

"I need a wife who cares that I am upset in the middle of the night, who doesn't mind waking up to talk and *listen,* or to make love. With Anna, I feel alone. It's depressing. Sometimes it's so bad, I feel suicidal," he replied despairingly.

"You're being overdramatic; you're not going to kill yourself," Anna said quickly, seeming anxious to minimize what he was saying and avoid the subject.

"I believe he is telling you how he feels right now, Anna, desperately depressed. It may be that he can hide his awful feelings by being creative. He has always turned to you when he needs input, either your creative ideas that unblock him or your encouragement and support so he wouldn't be alone." After saying this to Anna, I watched Carl sit back in his chair and seem to relax somewhat. He then turned to his wife, watching her for a challenge to his claim of being suicidal, but she said nothing.

I asked her if it frightened her, and she said that she, too, had periods of deep grief, perhaps depression, but she tries to keep her spirits up and her thoughts away from such negative thinking. "I try to cheer him up, and he becomes angry. He doesn't believe that I want to help him," she said.

"And you feel you are with a man who gives you his upset feelings and doesn't give you the good things he has to offer," I observed.

When Carl was given an opportunity to direct a television movie of a script that he had written, Anna decided she could offer the talents that she had developed when she had worked in films many years before. She came to the set of the film, but when she began to offer suggestions, Carl ignored and insulted her. "You think you know film editing! You have the audacity to tell people who have been doing this for years how to do their job!" he growled derisively. Defending herself, Anna explained in caustic tones that *some* people in the film industry exchange ideas and draw upon each other for support. Others, she added embitteredly, were too insecure to collaborate on anything.

Instead of using their mutual interest in screenwriting and filmmaking as a positive bridge to support and encourage one another, Carl and Anna use it as a weapon. As a result, each feels disconnected and discouraged, each feels alone and angry, and both believe they are married to an uncaring and unavailable mate who gives too little in return. They have lost their bridge to each other, and if they do not find new ways to relate, their marriage will continue to be painful to both. Carl needs to be listened to, understood, not left in the isolation he has built for himself as one of the prominent men in his field. Anna, on her side, needs to be affirmed as a valued partner, respected for her talents and abilities. On the surface, each functions independently, and underneath each feels terribly distressed and alone.

When Bridging Needs Create Problems

Check descriptions that fit:

Partner	You	
_____	_____	Put so much energy into work (or hobbies) that there is little left for the relationship
_____	_____	Rely on things or people outside the relationship to make up for what is missing between the two of you
_____	_____	Feel affirmed only when you get messages that you are attractive and sexually desirable
_____	_____	Show more interest in acquiring things than in relating to people
_____	_____	Feel empty and long for something to fill the void
_____	_____	Misuse food by binge-eating or starvation dieting to maintain a sense of control
_____	_____	Like the high that comes from exercise so much that you often overdo it
_____	_____	Deny or become angry when others confront your abuse of alcohol, drugs, or other

---

These are signs of problems in using bridges to fill the space between people. Emotional or physical separation may be experienced as traumatic loss and opens feelings of emptiness, depletion, or even terrifying chaos. To avoid these unacceptable emotions, security is reestablished by the use of transitional or bridging objects.

We all use such bridges to fill the space between the reality of connection with others and the security found in making connections through things. Music, art, and rituals are generally nondamaging, nonaddictive bridges. Alcohol, drugs, and food may be misused as ways to calm the fragile psyche when intimate connections are unavailable or feel unsafe. It is not use but overuse to make up for what is missing inside that is so damaging to you and to the relationship.

If you checked anything on the preceding list, ask yourself:

- What would your life be like without this bridging connection?
- Who would you blame for the problems?
- What would the problems be?
- What would you like to ask from each other?

Emotional Scenario

Have you ever had this experience?

You come home from a stressful day at work. You look forward to sharing your day and talking over some frustrations that keep upsetting you. When you get home, your partner is already there, ensconced on the couch with the TV on and reading a newspaper. You try to talk, but he won't take his nose out of the paper. You can feel the tension building between the two of you and know from experience that if you say anything about time together, there will be an argument.

What is happening here?

This interaction is a conflict between bonding and bridging needs. One partner deals with the stress of the day by turning to a transitional bridging object, a newspaper, magazine, or TV, and has some control of how much need, demand, or stress is allowed in. The other partner wants the security of a bonding experience, even a conversation together about the events of the day.

What you can do:

1. Attune to the specific needs of each of you and determine how they might be met.
2. Recognize how important it is to have a time of quiet withdrawal, an opportunity to interact with a totally nondemanding object—for some a drink, others a television program. There is a time for bridging with things, not bonding with people.
3. Say nothing at this point if previous experience tells you that your interactions will lead to a fight.

4. Offer something positive if you do talk. Avoid discussing usual problem areas.
5. Understand when your partner needs you to listen and simply reflect back without criticizing or offering a solution.
6. Agree to bring up the subject in a later meeting between you and your partner to discuss whose needs get met in these situations. Make sure it's fifty-fifty.
7. Choose your battles. Evaluate which issues are so important to you that they are not negotiable. Everything else should be open for discussion and compromise.

Bridges to the World

Because no relationship can be sustained solely between two people without bridges to the outside, you may need to develop positive bridges that take care of the emotional needs of both partners. The issues you must negotiate have to do with how much bridging you can do separately and how much you and your partner can do jointly in order for each to continue to depend on the relationship for emotional support.

The feelings of isolation and loneliness that so many experience today make us turn to personal, sometimes destructive, bridges. Turning outward, bridging to others, takes away many of the demands for fulfillment that partners otherwise impose on each other. Rejoin the world, and when you feel you belong, become aware of new feelings of autonomy that emerge.

Independence without connection to something larger than yourself is isolation or narcissism. Independence with bridges that connect is mature dependence, which will be considered in the next chapter.

Turning Tragedy Into a Positive Bridge

All couples must discover their own ways of bridging connections between themselves, their marriage, and the world (community) in which they live. Oftentimes, life circumstances (unusual career opportunities, natural disasters, illness) provide the raw materials for bridge building, and the couple's capacity for connection and healthy dependency determines whether the bridge leads toward or away from deeper intimacy. For example, sometimes the bridge of common interest is based upon traumatic or even tragic events. A child with a severe behavioral or neurological problem might motivate one parent to immerse herself in finding solutions to the problem, while another parent turns away, investing energy in work and numbing his pain with alcohol or drugs. Some couples whose foundation for relating is firmly grounded in successful bonding and boundary building can rally tremendous emotional resources and are successful at bridging together. The shared activities required to cope with the tragedy can become the center of their lives together.

Matt and I belong to a charitable organization called the Lita Dirschwitz Cancer Fund, which is affiliated with the City of Hope Hospital in Arcadia, California. Lita Dirschwitz was a little girl who was afflicted with childhood cancer. During her illness and after her death, her parents funneled their grief into the accomplishment of a goal that would hold some sense of redemption for their great loss: they started a fund for research at the City of Hope. Hundreds of people are currently involved in this endeavor, which has raised millions of dollars for cancer research. The Dirschwitzes' lives were filled with friendship and purpose by making cancer research a bridge to connecting with the meaning of their child's death.

A similar story is told in the film *Lorenzo's Oil*, a true account of two parents who refused to succumb to the hopeless diagnosis doctors had given their child. Here, the tragedy of the illness becomes the bridge to what may be a phenomenal medical discovery. In a worldwide search for new answers to their son's disease, they opened an investigation into a completely unknown treatment that became a bridge to others and an impetus for lifelong work.

More typically, tragic events trigger whatever emotional chaos is buried in the couple's respective histories. Fear, anger, and blame are flung back and forth as husband and wife struggle to cope. Emotional resources are quickly depleted as partners turn away from, rather than lean on, one another. The two couples described above were able to deepen their intimate connection. Catastrophic illness became the bridge for each partner to the other and to their communities as they found meaningful ways of responding to the challenge.

Surrogate Connections

In today's world, children grow up surrounded by technological advances that have made surrogate connections as easy as turning a dial. Television, which is used as a surrogate for social contact by millions of children and adults, is probably the clearest example of how a basic human need for connection can be redirected toward an object that conveys an illusion of connection and belonging. Television stars receive huge salaries to become characters who can compensate for our lack of genuine closeness with people. Instead of relating with one *another*, we relate to the folks in *Cheers, Murphy Brown,* our entertaining "friends" on *Saturday Night Live,* our idealized family on *The Cosby Show,* even to fantasized humans and nonhumans of the twenty-third century on *Star Trek.*

Television screens are in our view more than ever since the advent of the personal computer—a new form of security object. Want a chess partner, a bridge lesson, a chance to explore other parts of the world? Want to converse with a brain that is not (yet) as smart as you are and that always obeys your commands? Want to spend time with an always available companion? Computers are tailor-made surrogates for those with the suitable abilities and temperaments. Indeed, I have worked with patients who, given the choice, preferred computers to people.

With the growth of satellites, of VCRs, compact discs, and "virtual reality" computer programs, we have yet another phenomenon: videotapes simulating life and relationships are under our (remote) control, safe and available on demand. In the late 1980s we called it *cocooning*: two people, alone but together, with preprepared dinners and the latest release. Nothing comes between them and their "entertainment center," as they immerse themselves in stories of other people's lives, loves, and emotions.

"I'm tired when I get home from work," said Myra, my thirty-something cousin, seven months after her second marriage. "We both give our *all* at the office. At night, we just want to conk out, turn off all of the telephones, and watch videos. I don't want my mother to call, and I certainly don't want his mother or his impossible kids to call. We never go out anymore. It's too much of a bother."

She tells me they are perfectly happy with this lifestyle. Who am I to argue with this? They weren't asking for advice. I can't help thinking, though, that some of our latest inventions are serving as negative bridges that create a pseudo-experience of being connected, without the bother and energy of actually relating to one another.

Ed: Bridging Away

Ed did not come for help with a relationship. But his relationship problems relate to his failed dependency needs. Therapy was suggested by his parents and his dermatologist, who believed that his chronic psoriasis was caused by the stress of his isolated life. At age twenty-seven he still lived at home, although he rarely spoke to his parents. His life revolved around his work. He was a self-taught computer programmer with grandiose ideas: he firmly believed that one day, like Bill Gates at Microsoft, he would become a multimillionaire by designing a program no one could do without. His anger that this great day had not yet come was palpable. He was envious that others had succeeded while he had not, and he was bitter that no one seemed to care about this personal injustice.

Ed got back at "the system" by finding ways to break into the codes of large corporations and infecting their computers with data-erasing viruses. He also entertained himself with a computer game called Playmate, in which the image of a woman can be manipulated into various stages of undress and sexual positions. He even disseminated this program by modem, unrequested, to several staid corporations. This was his idea of "having fun."

As I tried to understand his current behavior, Ed described his attempts as a child to "fit in," even as he felt himself to be a socially inept "misfit." Ed's parents were social isolates—loners who often fought with each other, ignoring their son unless they wanted him to do something. From the time he was very young, Ed recalled, his mother expected him to respond exactly as she wished. When she needed company, she wanted him to entertain her; when she was busy, he was expected to play quietly and alone. She also expected him to take her side in arguments with her husband, to be angry at his father when the parents separated, and to seek comfort at night by climbing into her bed and filling the void left by her husband's absence. Whenever Ed failed to meet her expectations, she would withdraw, barely speaking to him and "freezing him out" for days. By adolescence, immersion into the world of computers had become Ed's bridge to emotional survival. Once this bridge was in place, Ed never sought any others. Growing up, he had no model for relating, but he *did* have the need to love and be loved—and a burning anger that he had never had the chance.

Throughout his teen and college years, Ed was extremely shy. The few times he tried to go out with women, he became embarrassingly tongue-tied. He increasingly turned to his computer whenever he felt lonely, withdrawing from the world of relationships just as his mother had withdrawn from him. But, although his relational life was limited to the computer games over which he had full control, his emotional disappointments and hurts erupted in a skin condition that he could not control any better now than when he was an infant.

When babies experience conflicts or trauma, they react solely and automatically through their bodies. Their somatic reactions can become part of their lifelong patterns of relating. As we explored the childhood roots of his psychosomatic symptom, Ed realized that his skin condition was a "protective shield" to keep out his demanding, intrusive, but emotionally unresponsive mother. Because he was in such discomfort, she had to be careful not to touch him in ways that caused him further pain. In this indirect way, Ed's skin condition actually gave him a reassuring feeling, amidst the physical discomfort, that his body belonged to him and not to his mother.

It took many sessions of intense work before Ed could identify the connection between his mother's behavior, his need for safe, noninvasive relationships, his devotion to his computer, and the skin condition that plagued him. I would like to be able to say that Ed became a healthier, happier young man, finally able to relate to humans instead of computer surrogates. He is relating to humans now, but I don't know if he is healthier or happier.

Quite suddenly, Ed broke away from the confinement of his parents' home by joining a religious group that was, in fact, a cult. I listened to his early excitement with some trepidation, recognizing that the more he immersed himself in his new "adventure," the more he seemed to distance himself from our work together. Not long afterward, he stopped coming to therapy and moved in with a group of fellow cult members. As they bombarded him with "love" messages, he became increasingly enmeshed in the group's lifestyle. Throughout his life, Ed had used his Imprint for Bridging Connections as a way of separating from the fused attachment his mother had offered. Nonetheless, he still yearned for bonded closeness and emotional sharing, just as he had as a child. Perhaps Ed felt the cult offered him a way to meet these primary needs on his own terms.

I do not hear from Ed, so I have no way of knowing if he has been damaged by cult life. I doubt his unhappiness is any greater now than before. Ed had never been able to depend upon people for safe, secure relationships. The cult he joined offered a pseudorelationship with others and the promise of a "higher power" on which he felt he could depend. In exchange, he had to pledge obedience and sever all outside connections. How much he lost is hard to say, since he had always had such limited relationships with people.

In the final case of this chapter, we will see how a husband learned to use sports to bridge the loss of love first experienced as the unfavored son, and how his wife uses her home as a substitute for genuine relating, having learned from her father that she could not trust men. Their Imprints for Bridging Connections became love substitutes for both of them. With little access to their healthy dependency needs, Betty and Gary were standing on a weak foundation that could not support the true intimacy they both yearn for.

Betty and Gary: Building Separate Bridges

Betty and Gary had been married for almost twenty years when Betty called for an appointment. It was Gary, however, who began our first session by voicing his dissatisfaction with their marriage. "I do all the adjusting, all the accommodating to Betty's needs. I feel like I'm 'on call' twenty-four hours a day. She even phones me at work to come home and help her with some minor problems, like telling an electrician what needs to be fixed. Then, when I get home after a long day at work, I'm supposed to 'relieve' Betty. I want to be there for her and the kids, but I also want someone to be there for me. I'm not getting enough in return. We've tried therapy twice before, but nothing really changed. If this doesn't work, maybe it's time to call it quits."

Ironically, Gary had been the one to insist each time that they see a therapist—yet Betty got the attention. Twice before when they had tried marital therapy, the therapist had focused on Betty's problem. She soon ended up in individual therapy, while Gary glided out of the process altogether. Betty acknowledged being plagued by lifelong anxieties that often made her feel inadequate, unable to manage the home, the children, and a career as a teacher of learning-disabled children. With two advanced degrees, Betty is seen as very capable by others, but her surface persona does not match her underlying anxieties. Gary, meanwhile, presented himself as hardworking, doing what was necessary to provide for his family, long-suffering, tolerant of the foibles and weaknesses of his wife, but by now fed up. At first he gave no admission of feeling any dependence on this relationship or any need related to its continuance, except to acknowledge that he did not "look forward" to going through a divorce. His discussion of himself was in keeping with his image of what it means to be a man—controlled, emotionally isolated, capable of handling the problems that arise.

The work of therapy was to discover what might change their long-term relational pattern, that of using various bridges to avoid intimacy between them while maintaining the facade of a "functioning" marriage. Gary used sports to fill his unmet needs and to make up for what was missing with his wife. He not only played tennis in every free moment, but also attended every baseball, basketball, and soccer match he could get tickets to attend. Betty ostensibly encouraged Gary to engage in his sports pastimes, but, in actuality, sabotaged his efforts to do so by finding chores or creating "crises" that forced him to choose between these activities and what Betty called "family responsibilities." Work and sports were sturdy bridges for Gary that safely and reliably connected him to the outer world.

Betty lacked these sturdy outer supports. She spoke about her fantasies of other men and how Gary never lived up to the idealized men of her fantasy world. It was clear these fantasies served as a bridge for her. No matter how hard he tried or how good he was to her, Gary couldn't break through: "I always thought, 'If I get through one more hurdle, then I would have her.' But there is always something more I must do." "I never really have you, do I?" he asked once, and Betty acknowledged that it was true.

Gary knew that his wife appeared to others as a loving confidante and nurturing friend. But she lived in a world filled with anxiety. Gary seemed unable to give her what she needed to have a full emotional and sexual relationship. The one anchor of stability in her life was her home, where she felt safe, contained, and protected. It was *her* domain. She was always thinking of ways to expand and improve the house and, when she finally exhausted every redecorating possibility, convinced Gary that they needed to move to a larger home.

The house was a security object for Betty. Decorating it and entertaining in it was her bridge to the outer world. Gary's failure to understand the importance of the home to Betty was a source of conflict between them. "I don't know why she wants a bigger house," Gary said condescendingly.

After listening to their complaints, I commented on how easily they found ammunition to use against each other and suggested we examine where they learned to fight so well. With little encouragement, they began to talk about how they had met, their respective parents, and the homes in which each had grown up.

Betty's accusatory tone suddenly vanished as she recalled her early impressions of Gary. Animatedly, she described how Gary was the opposite of her "crazy," abusive father. Gary was strong, stable, and goal-directed, qualities quite foreign to young Betty. When they first met, Gary had pursued her openly and vigorously. At first, frightened by his intense interest in her, she was reluctant to accept his advances and kept a distance. Gary remained unwaveringly attentive, however, frequently asserting how much he wanted to marry her. Despite misgivings about whether she loved him "enough," Betty felt safe with him, a feeling she didn't have with most men. She had dated a lot, but had never made a commitment to anyone. Because of early, damaging experiences first with her father and then with other men during her adolescent years, Betty did not feel safe relating to men. She had learned to treat men as objects, as bridges to momentary love. "I tried to separate men into categories: schoolmates, friends, lovers, sports partners," she said. "I liked Gary when I met him and wanted him to be a friend, but he wouldn't have it that way. He wanted it to be all or nothing. I didn't want to lose him, so we got married."

Gary said that he fell in love with Betty, a beautiful blond freshman, when they met during his last year of business school. She had a lot of boyfriends and was different from anyone else he had ever dated. "Besides, I thought she was rich," he said, kidding. But his tone and her reaction said that money was indeed an issue for them.

"Not really," she responded. "We weren't as rich as we looked. We just lived as if we were as rich as some of our relatives. The truth is, I came from a pretty disturbed family," Betty added tentatively.

When I asked her to tell me more, Betty described a family that presented a facade of normalcy but, in reality, concealed two dysfunctional parents—an alcoholic, volatile father and a passive, frightened mother. Betty recalled having had only one happy relationship, with a warm, loving nanny who took care of her until she was three and was then abruptly fired. When I asked how she coped with her unhappy family life, Betty said that she focused on her intellectual abilities; early on, she made school into a haven, a safe place to which she escaped, immersing herself in her studies.

Left to fend for herself in a chaotic family, Betty tried to model herself after her father, whom she perceived as stronger than her inadequate mother. Betty's excellent grades made him proud of her, and she felt favored by him. But as she reached adolescence and became interested in boys, her father's behavior changed markedly. He became increasingly suspicious of her and physically abusive. Betty recalled being restricted for minor infringements on numerous occasions, and she was almost never allowed to go out with friends. When she finally challenged her father's authority by attempting to run away, hoping to get her parents' attention to her plight, her father's rage was so great that, when he caught her, he "tried to kill me." Her voice quavering, Betty described how he had picked her up and thrown her into the swimming pool. Stunned and terrified, she had swum to the edge, her fingers grasping the tile of the pool. When he stomped his foot on them, the last vestige of hope that she could have love and protection from her father vanished.

Betty had to go through a turbulent adolescent sexual awakening alone. On an unconscious level, she knew that her emerging sexuality was extremely threatening to her father. Deepening her confusion was the fact that she seemed to attract boys as well as older men in ways that were beyond her capacity to handle. There was no one at home with whom she could talk, so she went to a therapist—but he also responded to her sexually. Frightened, she discontinued therapy.

As Betty described her history of emotional and physical abuse with strong sexual undercurrents, Gary listened and then enthusiastically added information he recalled about her "crazy" family. I could see how easy it had been for both of them to identify Betty as the "patient" with her various obsessions, sexual fears, and occasional confused states. Together they had orchestrated a scenario in which Betty harbored all the problems. Gary could remain the strong one as long as Betty carried the emotionally wounded part for both of them. He expected therapy to repair her toxic history and thereby transform her into a healthy, loving wife.

I questioned the fixed portraits they jointly presented of Gary as the supercompetent partner and Betty as the unstable, overly emotional wife. Deciding it was time to focus on Gary's half of their relationship, I asked him to tell me something about his history.

As he described it, Gary's early life was much less traumatic than his wife's. He was from an "assimilated Jewish family," the older of two sons of an autocratic, intellectual, unemotional father and a distant, unavailable mother. As Gary proceeded to describe his family further, however, it became apparent that he alone had been ignored by his parents. Because he was a sports enthusiast from a very young age (to his parents, sports were a waste of time), Gary got much less of his parents' time, attention, and concern than his more scholarly brother.

Clearly, Gary was something of a misfit in his family. To numb the pain of his second-best status, Gary increased his immersion into sports at a young age. But, although he played on every team in school, competing and winning, his parents never came to watch. Gary convinced himself that he didn't care. He had found a bridge to success and approval from others, if not from his parents.

In college, Gary had been forced to face the fact that, although he excelled in sports, he was not good enough for a professional career. In considering what career he could pursue, he decided that law and business would provide the same kind of competitive spirit, challenges, and opportunities to win that sports had offered. After graduating from business school, he set about building a career that would meet his needs for affirmation and success while allowing him to live in a style and a community that pleased his wife.

"I Just Want to Be Wanted"

I asked Gary how he thought Betty felt about him. He said that he didn't really know. I wasn't convinced. Most partners have a clear picture of how they are experienced by their mates. I believed that Gary knew, but didn't want to admit, how Betty viewed him. It is humiliating to recognize that you are not valued or admired by your mate, and Betty conveyed that disparaging message to Gary in many subtle ways. I shared my thoughts with both of them together, and he quietly acknowledged that Betty seemed to have time for everyone but him.

"Her friends tell me how wonderful, understanding, and supportive she is, but she never has a good word for *me* or even a kind gesture. For years, she refused to kiss me, saying that she didn't like the taste of cigarettes on my breath. Then I gave up smoking. Instead of being pleased, she said that she didn't like the weight I gained when I quit smoking. She still won't kiss me!"

"How do you handle your feelings of rejection?" I asked, noting that Betty was hardly moving a muscle during these revelations.

"I used to just go out and murder the tennis balls. But I can't do that anymore," Gary answered dejectedly.

For two decades, Gary had directed all his energy and talent toward solidifying his career. His one luxury was tennis. By his own admission, tennis was more than a pastime—it was an addiction. He regularly pushed his body to play through the pain of injuries. "I stopped last month only because my back gave out and my legs gave out—in fact, my whole body began giving out," Gary added, a little too lightly, once again using his humor to lighten the pain of his feelings.

Betty interjected forcefully, "He was hospitalized with a perforated ulcer. He came close to destroying himself, but he refused to pay attention. I told him that he should have seen a different doctor."

Gary clearly resented this criticism. "She didn't like the doctors I consulted because they were friends and tennis partners."

"They didn't take your discomfort very seriously—and you were trying to ignore it, too," said Betty in an I-told-you-so tone. Gary bristled. He didn't like to be told that he'd done something dumb that could have damaged his health, especially when Betty thinly disguised it as concern.

Perhaps this was why he kept focusing on what was wrong with Betty, I thought to myself. Perhaps it was retaliation for Betty's subtle way of undermining him. Nonetheless, Gary had indeed been wrong to ignore his ulcer. As we talked about why he had ignored the warning signs, Gary said that he didn't like to be incapacitated in any way, and that he had done the same thing in response to stomach pain as he had done with injuries from tennis—he "fought through the pain." He was used to taking care of himself, he asserted a little too confidently, adding that he had always done so as a child.

As we continued to work together, Gary talked more freely about his disappointment in his marriage, about how he didn't feel he could depend on Betty to know what he needed or to want to take care of him in any way. "I try to talk about the frustrations I have to put up with at work," Gary said. "Instead of listening in a supportive way, she tells me I'm stupid to keep working there, that I ought to quit my job. The last thing I want to hear at that point is that I'm *stupid!*"

"I just think you're too good for that company. They obviously don't appreciate all your abilities," Betty replied in a superior tone.

"So who do you think will pay the bills for the new house we bought?" Gary retorted. Turning to me, his face finally showing some anger, Gary continued, "Betty thinks she is showing concern for me when she tells me I shouldn't work at a job that aggravates me—or when she says that I shouldn't listen to the doctors *I* chose. But all she is really doing is *criticizing* me." After a long pause, Gary added, almost inaudibly, "She doesn't give me what I want."

"What is that?" I asked.

"I want to be with someone who cares about me, about who I am, as I am—who responds sexually—who appreciates me instead of telling me who I *should* be," Gary responded quietly. "I want someone who *wants* me, not someone who just puts up with me." Gary had reached the needs that lie below his "bridging" defenses. As a tennis player and as a businessman, he thrived on competition and achieving—ways of declaring he needed only to win. But as his body let him down, as his surrogates failed him, there was no way left for him to disguise his need for belonging and love, his yearning to depend on Betty to accept him, once and for all.

"In work and in sports you have won whatever you set out to achieve," I reflected, "but you still haven't gotten what you really want—acceptance, approval, and love. You want more in your marriage, but Betty is not responsive to your needs."

"Yeah," he said sadly, "I've always got to be perfect or she lets me know what a jerk I am."

"And you get even by letting her know how incompetent she is," I suggested. "The two of you have a way of operating together that doesn't meet either of your needs. You keep repeating the same pattern of interaction, perhaps in the hope that if you do the same thing often enough, you will somehow get a different response. But you never get those different responses. What you need to understand is, if you want different responses, you have to *be* different."

New Beginnings

Neither responded for several moments. Then Betty spoke. "I *do* keep expecting Gary to be perfect, it's true. Even now, when he talks about feeling weak, it scares me."

"What is scary?" I asked.

"I think of Gary as being very strong. I don't feel strong, but Gary can do anything. Whether it's playing tennis or making money, he's the best. He keeps it all together. He never seems to let things get out of hand."

"Not like your father?" I asked.

"That's right. I never knew when something would upset my father. When it was time for him to come home from work, my mother would get very tense, worrying if she had prepared the right food for him, was the house clean enough, were his shirts ironed, was there anything that would upset him? He would go into a rampage over nothing. I was so scared of him. Gary was never like that—he never came apart. I need him to be strong."

"Even if it requires you to appear weak?" I asked. She didn't answer. To Gary I said, "Betty feels as though you see her as somehow defective—overly emotional, confused, and always in need of therapy." Turning to Betty, I said, "I think Gary feels as though you think very little of him, even as you expect him to be strong. He has tried to stay strong at a very high cost. Both his business and his sports skills confirm his competencies, yet he has compulsively pushed himself to the limit. He has used tennis as a vehicle to discharge unexpressed emotions, stopping only when his body made it impossible to continue. I think his ulcer was a message that murdering the tennis ball was no longer working.

"Betty, your husband has been trying to tell you that the old way of relating isn't working for him—and it isn't so good for you, either. You've played the part of the dysfunctional spouse your whole marriage, and Gary has colluded in assigning you this role. But it is killing him physically and keeping you from becoming the fully functioning person you can be.

"Gary, you have had ulcers, a bad back, and are frequently depressed. Your body is definitely telling you that it's time for a change."

Gary said he agreed, but that he didn't know how to change.

Addressing me, Betty said, "I had no idea that Gary felt like this. I just thought he didn't like me very much, so I found other things to keep me going. I guess I just didn't want to see his weak side."

Both Gary and Betty have unfulfilled dependency needs. Each used their relationship to defend against, rather than to heal, the disappointment of these unmet needs. In the end, they got the opposite of what they both needed.

"Do you understand that for Gary to have and express feelings doesn't make him weak?" I asked. Gary was staring at the floor, not yet comfortable with his emotional visibility.

"Yes," Betty responded softly. She was looking at Gary with intense curiosity. "In fact," she continued, searching for the words to articulate her feelings, "there's a lot about him I don't know—that I've been afraid to know. It was unfair of me to require him to be Superman. I was just so afraid that anything less would mean the worst."

Gary's eyes glistened. Quietly, without a trace of glibness, he said, "This is not so bad to take."

"You might find it's better for you than tennis," I said. As they learned to understand, accept, and respond to each other, the need for surrogates for intimacy diminished and therapy became less necessary. Each has experienced the strengthening of the relationship and each feels stronger individually.

In the next chapter we will see how our fourth developmental imprint, for mature dependence, can lead couples into isolation and lonely self-sufficiency—or into lifelong mutual positive dependency.

6 Imprint for Mature Dependence

The romance of new love, the romance of solitude, the romance of objecthood, the romance of ancient pyramids and distant stars are means of making contact with the mystery. When it comes to perpetuating it, however, I got no advice. But I can and will remind you of two of the most important facts I know:

1. Everything is part of it.

2. It's never too late to have a happy childhood.

—Tom Robbins, *Still Life with Woodpecker*

Rule #6 for Positive Dependency:

Do not depend on your partner to meet all of your needs. Develop interests together but also be sure to develop separate interests. Share your excitement of life with others outside of the relationship and you will see it come back to you in many ways. The more you give, the more you will get.

Becoming an independent person who is also capable of depending on another is not simply a stage of development that has a definite finishing point. Rather, it is a process of incorporating previous stages, culminating in far-reaching emotional changes that reverberate throughout all our subsequent experiences. Throughout early childhood our "emotional vocabulary" continually expands as we learn how to handle the increasingly complex responses, impulses, needs, and desires that emerge as our imprints for love unfold.

The Imprint for Mature Dependence adds to this repertoire, but does not replace it. Although our fourth imprint refines and solidifies our sense of self so that we can function autonomously when we need or choose to, that is *not* the sole achievement of this last stage of early development. Independence represents only one-half of this developmental goal. The other half is to equip us to connect intimately with others, while keeping our emotional integrity intact as a result of a solid sense of self.

No other developmental stage has become more entangled with mixed messages and incompatible values than has this fourth Imprint for Mature Dependence. The changes in women's roles conflict with the unaltered gender expectations that women are to be nurturing yet dependent, while men are supposed to be strong and hide their dependent needs. Furthermore, the new cultural ideal of independence and self-sufficiency conflicts with our inherited, biological need for connection and *inter* dependence.

This fourth imprint has nothing to do with current changes in the roles of men and women. For both boys and girls, the purpose of independence in development is simply to cultivate an inner sense of solidity, a feeling of cohesion. In childhood, this is the time after you have solidified your sense of personal boundaries so that the emotions of others cannot overwhelm you. If you successfully navigated this stage of development as a child, now as an adult you know your values and beliefs, likes and dislikes, who you are, what you believe and don't believe.

As an independent being, you are in touch with your feelings and have the strength to act in accordance with them. You listen, you temporarily "hold" the feelings, you know who you are, where you end, and where your partner begins. You do not lose yourself in the interaction; you remain *you.* Once your sense of yourself is solid, it is safe to loosen your boundaries at times, allowing a permeability that no longer threatens your sense of self-cohesion. If you have a strong sense of self, you can open your boundaries temporarily to another through empathy and allow bonding, because you know how to hold both your feelings and another's.

Paradoxically, mature dependence, which underlies and fosters *in-dependent* functioning, is actually the product of successfully meeting the *dependency* needs contained in the preceding imprints. Some people feel vulnerable and do not know how to remain open to the emotional dangers of depending on others. They cover up a sensitive, fragile core and build around it the structure that is the "pseudo" independent adult. But this grown-up isn't built on a solid foundation. There is a lifelong struggle between the vulnerable inner self that constantly yearns to reemerge and be healed and the facade of self-sufficiency, which keeps tight control on these yearnings.

Thus, for those without the healthy, solidifying aspects of an Imprint for Mature Dependence, adult relationships actually operate from more primary imprints for relating. Those people seek intimate connection but are unable to maintain a sense of separateness and autonomy. On the other hand, when independence emerges from the healthy soil of previous imprints, *positive dependency* becomes possible. We have "emotional literacy," we can merge, we can bond temporarily, we can give and receive—all without losing or compromising our own identities.

Strides Toward Independence

During the second, third, and fourth years of life, we develop an increasingly consolidated sense of self distinct from our parents. This is the time for emerging claims of selfhood. In the play of young children, we hear, *"My* toy, *my* game, *my* jacket, *my* mommy." I have spent a lot of time in the park watching children play over the last few years. The two-and-a-half-year-old runs ahead of mom, no longer needing her constant presence, but looks back frequently to make sure she is there.[16] The three- and four-year-olds play with other children, hardly casting a glance in their mothers' direction. From past experience, they are secure in the knowledge that their mothers will be waiting when they are ready. Others constantly check, needing reassurance that they will not be left. A large body of research confirms my anecdotal observations: each of these patterns of separating and reconnecting first develop in the early bonds between parents and children. The time during which the fourth imprint unfolds follows the last phase of total dependence, when one's survival depends on the caretaker.

Psychologist Margaret Mahler has characterized this period as the "psychological birth of the human infant" because it is a time of increasing separation and independence. It is a time of growing ability to express wishes in words and to recognize the difference between *mine* and *yours*. Many psychological researchers have mistakenly concluded that this level of development supersedes the previous levels to create a "mature" person. This erroneous view, reinforced by our cultural heritage of individualism, has disseminated and virtually enshrined the ideal of independent functioning.

When Your Imprint for Mature Dependence Is Impaired . . .

- You always question your decisions

- You judge yourself harshly

- You don't feel "real"

- You feel a sense of emptiness or lethargy

- You often feel that you are performing for others—people don't see what is under your façade

- You have ideas that you want to convey to others but are afraid to express in words

- You are anxious when you do not have plans for the weekend

- You worry about how others see you because your sense of power is outside of yourself

- Alternatively, you are militantly independent, professing no concern about the reaction of others

- You are surprised at how people perceive you because you see yourself so differently

---

When Your Imprint for Mature Dependence Is Operative . . .

* You take responsibility for your thoughts, feelings, and actions

* You recognize the effect you have on others

* You are aware of how others affect you

* You can adapt to a variety of situations without being false to yourself

* You have your own life without having to push others out of your life

* You can trust others

* The people you care about know you well

* You trust yourself

Fearing entrapment of overdependence and the dreaded burdens of obligation and commitment, many of us have lost the ability to recognize deep needs that are met through relating. Having sanctified individualism and independence, we have labeled dependence as negative and even pathological. We confuse healthy dependency with dysfunctional codependency.

Gender and Mature Dependence

Our cultural definition of maturity is based on the supposedly masculine ideal of autonomy, separating from the mother (which means separating from the need to depend on another), and moving out of primary relationships into the goal-oriented world of action and achievement. Female development, by contrast, is characterized by maintaining primary bonds with the mother (which means being allowed to depend on another), identifying with her nurturing functions, and choosing the maintenance of relationships over activities and external goals. The net result of this dichotomy on intimate relationships is that men and women are conditioned to think they have different needs—but is it so?

We have made great strides in changing society's messages about "what little boys and little girls are made of." Some messages are so deeply ingrained, however, that consciously changed attitudes have little effect on the unconscious gender expectations of parents and teachers. Dr. Lee Hausner, a colleague who is a school psychologist in the Beverly Hills School District, expressed her concerns about these hidden expectations. One of the kindergarten teachers was worried about Russell, who cried and refused to let his mother leave when she brought him to school; another first-grade teacher was concerned about Barry, who cried when some of the children teased him and again when he fell down on the playground. "I've never had a teacher come to me worried about *Ellen* because she cried when her feelings were hurt or when she fell down," Dr. Hausner says.

When teachers respond to boys as if they have a problem when their emotions surface, the implicit message to boys remains what it has been for centuries: "Hide your wounds and be more independent." Girls are still allowed to be dependent (sensitive and vulnerable) longer than boys are. This early indoctrination is solidly ingrained as the children grow up.

Although we continue to expect boys to be independent from early on, the need for nurturing attachment, bonding, and emotional attunement is not gender specific. Boys require a positive response to their dependency needs just as much as girls do. Men and women *both* thrive when they are in relationships in which positive dependence is allowed and responded to without shame or guilt.

In my work with couples, I have found no gender differences in dependency needs, but I have noticed differences in the way these needs are expressed and experienced. Men, having learned the importance of presenting themselves as strong, resourceful, and independent, have years of practice and peer reinforcement for appearing self-contained and invulnerable. They come into intimate relationships with all their dependency needs well hidden *but nevertheless quite present.* Women, on the other hand, accustomed to being seen as more dependent and allowed to be more emotionally needy, are expected to be the caretakers in their relationships.

Until recently, and even to some extent now, boys have been trained in their families that it is normal to expect needs to be responded to by a nurturing woman. Girls are socialized to be the nurturers. These gender-oriented behavior patterns become ingrained, along with the imprinted messages for interacting in family relationships. Ironically, in these circumstances there is little opportunity for women to experience a range of dependency needs in their relationships with men, because men are simply not expected to meet them. Consequently, both men's and women's dependency needs remain unaddressed. Women have become angry about this and men have responded to the new expectations by withdrawing.

The Shift in Women's Roles

With the movement of women into the workforce, independence, wanted or unwanted, has become a reality for millions. Living the myth that we should all be able to function as independent centers of initiative has only intensified the emotional and physical exhaustion many experience. Meanwhile, our dependency needs, acknowledged or unacknowledged, remain underground.

One of the most important messages I ever received about my future came from a colleague, Dr. Robert Anderson, during a casual conversation almost three decades ago. I had decided to go into private practice half-time, had just opened an office, and was still learning to juggle the competing demands of home, family, and career. He asked me if I was limiting my practice because of a fear of becoming too successful. "Of course not" was my instant reply. But he went on anyway, telling me that many of his women patients had expressed a fear that if they became too successful, their husbands might leave them.

Although I had harbored no such fears consciously, his remark forced me to think about my efforts to integrate a career and marriage. Although I considered myself quite independent, the women's movement was just beginning to emerge. Looking back, I realize that, despite my liberated self-image, I was living the traditional marital myth: I was in a solid relationship in which my husband was a little older, a little taller, and considerably more successful. I was comfortable under his wing, never thinking much about what my full potential might be.

Now I began to wonder. Would he continue to encourage me if I continued to push toward goals that took me further out of the home? At the time, I didn't know. Nor did I know how to discuss it with him. What would I say? "Honey, could you handle it if I became as successful as you? Or more?" However he answered, would I believe him? What if I tried to have a career and failed? That would be humiliating. What if I became a success and it caused us to take very different paths? Would he see me as competing with him? Would *I* see me as competing with him?

In the last few decades of the second half of the twentieth century, a major shift in women's roles has produced a challenging dilemma for both men and women. As women have sought or been forced into increasingly independent functioning, often working full-time as they raise their children, the ground rules for intimate relationships have also shifted. Independence is a relatively new role for many women; responding to independent women is an equally new role for men. Confusion, misunderstanding, bitterness, and anger are frequent by-products of these jolting changes.

Pitfalls of the Imprint for Mature Dependence

Many children today are encouraged to become prematurely independent. Often this precocity is prompted by employed parents. Sometimes, the emotional problems of one or both parents catalyze premature development in the child. In such situations, *the child becomes the caretaker*. Scott, whose story follows, was such a child. For much of his early life he learned to control his needs, to ask little of his mother, and to give his parents the overachieving, successful child they desired. He learned to accomplish through *action* instead of expressing *needs*. He remembers wondering why his achievements always felt so hollow and why he didn't feel better when he won awards. "It was always a letdown, and I could never figure out why."

Scott and Rhea:
A Marriage of Approach and Avoidance

Rhea and Scott had been married eighteen years when they made an appointment with me for marital counseling. As their stories emerged, it was evident that their surface problems were small but their underlying issues were immense, destroying the fabric of the relationship. They once had the ability to lean on each other, but it was long gone. Rhea described having major problems together, yet said that ninety-five percent of their relationship was good. Scott added, "But we spend ninety-five percent of our time on the five percent that is not good."

After talking about what was good, what they had in common, what they saw as common goals, I asked why they spent so much of their energy focusing on the unsatisfying aspects of their relationship.

"I feel emotionally battered," Rhea answered quickly, "and I have to do something to feel better. I try to keep Scott from getting upset with me, but no matter how hard I try to do what he wants, it's never enough. His list is always so long that I never get it all done. He can waltz into the house after a week away on business, and I have everything perfect—candles are lit for our dinner, the meal is ready, our son has all A's on his report card. What does Scott do? He reaches for a book on a high shelf and tells me that the dust is building up. So what if it's building up? I'll never be enough for him. I can't cook well enough, I don't entertain well enough, I'm not in good enough shape physically. I used to think of myself as pretty competent, but I've lost all confidence. I tell him if he's not happy with me, that he should get a divorce—he should find someone he likes. It's obvious he doesn't like me."

"You said that ninety-five percent of your relationship is good. What is the good part?"

Rhea proceeded to describe a husband who from the outside seems like Prince Charming. Scott is successful, handsome, and intelligent; he's a loving if imperfect father. He loves to take long walks with Rhea and talk about his plans, aspirations, and feelings. Scott, in turn, described Rhea as a woman who is warm, clever, a good listener, and nurturing to her friends and their son. She had a career before they met. She continued her education after they married, raised a son whom any parent would be proud of, and she had made Scott truly happy for the first five years of their marriage.

On paper they sounded too good to be true. In fact, they were each terrific people. The problem was they were miserable together. Rhea had become increasingly depressed, and Scott was chronically disappointed and upset. I wondered how their early imprints might be operating to create disappointment and hopelessness in their marriage. I asked them to tell me what they remembered about the beginning of their relationship, as well as their memories of their childhoods.

Rhea's Story

The child of Hungarian immigrants, Rhea was an eczema baby. As a newborn, her skin was raw and she cried at every touch. She recalled her mother's stories about how she cried "incessantly" during her first months of life. Her parents were preoccupied with their plans to escape from their native land in postwar Europe, and we can well imagine that Rhea's constantly agitated state only exacerbated the problems of these already anxious parents.

Once in America, her parents could finally direct their efforts toward providing a secure, comfortable home for themselves and the children. With a doctor's assistance, Rhea's eczema was brought under control by the age of one year, but it had left its mark on her. As a young child, she remained extremely sensitive to her physical as well as emotional environment. She learned to control her environment through her accomplishments and carefully chose friends who were nonabusive.

Living with a mother whom she experienced as constantly critical, she learned to protect herself from the wounds of rebuke. She remembered her father as being passive, willing to do anything to please his wife and avoid a fight. Rhea spent a lot of her energy keeping her mother's responses as benign as possible. Imprinted with her early experience of living constantly with a chronic rash, during childhood she tried to create a calm and soothing environment. Whenever emotional discord surfaced, Rhea would protect herself by withdrawing from the situation as quickly as possible. School was a haven for her and she continued to be a high achiever. As an adolescent, she started to challenge her mother's attempts to control her, and once she went away to college, she began to build a life of her own.

Now a successful biographer of peoples' lives, the adult Rhea appears quite capable of intimacy. She is attuned to the emotions of others and is giving and loving with friends, but she experiences Scott as constantly critical and in their relationship she feels that she is always "being rubbed the wrong way." It is the cause of serious marital problems.

Scott's Story

Scott recalled that his mother proudly talked about him as always being "so grown-up." Even as he grew into a toddler and young child, Scott remembered that he rarely cried or complained, and he never threw tantrums, as his sister did. His role in the family had been set and he continued to fulfill it. The problem was, in being such an ideal child, Scott's dependency needs were shoved aside. Instead of being a normally demanding, occasionally self-centered child, Scott was turned into a premature caretaker whose needs were implicitly less important than those of his parents, particularly his mother. His reward, of course, was his parents' adoration of him. Scott's sense of the earliest phase of his life, his first bonding experience, was that it had been nurturing and positive. His movement into the developmental phase in which he would learn to distinguish between his emotions and those of his parents, however, was short-circuited by his mother's dependency. Instead of learning to identify his own needs and desires during this time, he learned how to take care of his parents' needs.

The Story of Their Relationship

By the time Scott and Rhea met, they had buried the remnants of their early experiences, and both functioned as highly successful adults, independent in their careers and nurturing with each other. With her friends and early in her marriage with Scott, Rhea's most soothing self came out. She gave what she wanted, gentleness and love. She described Scott as a "pleaser" who attached like "Super Glue." He was almost obsessive in his pursuit of her. She wonders sometimes why she married him, but added that it was hard to resist him. She felt that no one would ever love her as he did. Besides, Scott usually got what he went after.

For the first five years, they had a relationship that they described as "almost perfect." It was the first time in his life that Scott had let his guard down and allowed himself to be taken care of emotionally. He had come to depend on Rhea to be there for him. He loved to come home from work and share stories of his day and listen to her stories as well.

"We blissed out," Scott said with a smile.

Rhea agreed, explaining, "It was a little more closeness than I wanted, but it felt so good to be loved by such a wonderful man that I didn't mind."

"What happened to upset this perfect harmony?" I asked.

"Rhea went back to school to study journalism," Scott offered. "I didn't think her going to school would bother me—I'm a modern man—but it did. I was no longer the center of her attention. Then I got a cross-country job offer and it only made sense to take it."

"Which meant that I had to leave school if I wanted to stay married," Rhea interjected. "I felt that I could lose him. Very soon afterward, I got pregnant. Throughout my pregnancy and even after the birth, Scott was totally unsupportive. He expected me to take care of myself. We lived in a new city, far from everyone I knew, and Scott just wasn't there for me. He threw himself into his work and I was alone with a new baby. That's when I took up writing and actively sought new friendships. Our relationship was disintegrating. It never got back to being good. I kept trying, but Scott always seemed angry and upset. No matter what I did, it was never enough."

"It wasn't what she did or didn't do," Scott countered. "She just wasn't there for *me* in the same way either! So I got more involved in my work, where I felt needed and appreciated, and Rhea got involved with her life, her work, her friends, our son."

"Since your emotional needs were not being met by one another," I suggested, "you found other outlets?"

"Yes," Rhea agreed, "and I had to pick up my career and meet new friends in a new location. I adjusted to all that, but I couldn't adjust to Scott being constantly upset with me. He had long lists of things for me to do, and no matter how much I tried to get done, he would walk in the door and notice the one thing I hadn't done right. I would have left if we had not had a baby."

"She's right," Scott added. "I *was* upset, but not because of the things she did or didn't do. Even though I was working tremendously hard, I was worried about work. I was stressed a lot, and Rhea couldn't stand my being upset about *anything,* so I tried to hold it in. I could do it for a week or two and then it all came out at once."

"He was like a bubbling volcano," Rhea interjected. "Always ready to erupt. Even when he didn't say anything, I could tell when he was enraged. Sometimes he got so upset doing chores around the house, I told him to hire someone! I couldn't stand how angry he got."

"But I like to do chores," Scott protested. "I could let out my agitated feelings when I was doing physical work. I didn't want you to stop me."

"It was a way to let out the feelings inside you," I reflected.

Scott agreed. "It was a way to release some of the demons," he said, smiling as if we shouldn't take what he was saying seriously.

But I knew what he was describing. Scott had learned at a very young age to control his emotions and perform well. As a toddler, he was praised for being his mother's "little man." He was praised for behaving in a manner that pleased his parents.

With this kind of training, a child never learns to distinguish clearly between what he wants and what the parents want. The boundaries between child and parent remain blurred because the "mature" child is rewarded for behaving in ways that make parents feel good about themselves. Love then becomes synonymous with pleasing others.

Scott found a good way to compensate for his chronic feeling of agitation by becoming a successful, action-oriented businessman. But his strongly imprinted model of action and achievement, which had the additional benefit of helping him to obtain the love of his parents, left him unable to feel happy about the accomplishments for which he worked so hard. It was not until he met and married Rhea that he felt he could depend upon another person to be there for *him.*

In Rhea, Scott found someone who was gentle, nurturing, and almost always calm—the opposite of Scott's mother. Rhea, in marriage, appeared to be a lot like her father, seeking peace and harmony above all else. For five years, there was only the two of them; their boundaries were completely down with each other. Both worked and came home to share a small apartment. "We were like two peas in a pod," Scott said.

This should have been a danger sign. The couple was avoiding Rule

#6 to develop interests together and to also have separate interests. Living blissfully in the "pea pod," they were depending on each other to meet all of their needs for emotional contact. It is a fragile paradise because reality so easily invades.

Still, they both recall it as the happiest time in their lives. Rhea had the tranquil setting so important to her, and Scott allowed himself to relax and be taken care of by Rhea. He felt almost "blissful" the first five years. There was no anger at Rhea. He would get angry about things at work, and Rhea was an excellent listener. She talked to him about her frustrations and difficulties at work, and he offered lots of ideas. Both were independent but also met needs for bonding and emotional attunement with each other—the dependency needs of each were being met.

When she decided to return to school and Scott decided to take a job in New York without carefully planning the move with Rhea, the "perfect" twosome began to move in opposite directions for the first time. Their "fusion illusion," the denial of separateness, could no longer ward off old wounds and current pain. Rhea felt discounted and upset. She disliked New York, and when she complained, Scott said that he would only work there a few months and then find a way to get back to California. But a few months turned into a year, then two and five and ten. By the second year, Rhea pulled away from Scott; she didn't want to listen to him talk about his job. Since he could not depend on her to be there for him, he also turned away, focusing all of his energy on work. Feeling that no one was there for her, Rhea became emotionally involved with another man who "looked me in the eyes when he talked to me." Although there was no sexual involvement, it made Rhea see what she was missing in her connection with Scott. Her dissatisfaction was obvious to him.

As she had in the past, Rhea erected a shield to distance herself from hurt. The shield became a "Plexiglas barrier" and finally a "stone wall" that went up as soon as Scott's feelings emerged. Scott similarly used his old way of dealing with too many emotions: he put them into his projects, and in the last few years, he dumped his agitation onto Rhea, who was particularly vulnerable to "negative" emotions. Both Scott and Rhea turned away from each other, and the positive dependency that had characterized their early years was lost. Scott responded by being "superfunctional," extraordinarily successful, and Rhea became depressed and closed down. They stopped giving to each other, and each stopped getting sustenance back.

Each had moved from a mutual, positive dependence on the other into feelings of loneliness and isolation. The memory of five happy years gave them some hope, but they had no idea how to recapture the spirit of collaborative intimacy and healthy dependency.

Adultified Children

Many of the patients I counsel recall early lives in which they were unusually attuned to the needs of others while appearing to need little in comparison with other children. Like Scott, they are "adultified" children, appearing to function independently and successfully, while their unacknowledged dependency needs languish. Eric, in chapter 4, was also mature for his age because he learned early that he had to be strong or he would be devastated by the pain he felt as an unnoticed child. He had no other choice, as his parent's unhappy relationship and his mother's drinking gave him no opportunity for safe dependence. Peter, in chapter 3, took on a "lifesaving job" at the age of four: jumping between his parents when they were about to fight. As children, each had achieved a kind of independence, but they had to sacrifice access to their own needs and feelings. A child pretending to be strong for ill or needy parents can only do so by shutting off his or her needs and feelings. In effect, the child is walking through life playing a role. Precocious maturity requires the child to conceal vulnerability in order to win approval and love.

On the other hand, when a child is allowed to grow up without the parents imposing their own needs, independent behavior will emerge as the child develops and is ready to express it—not as a defensive maneuver. Then the child, the child-as-adult, and the people in that person's life can depend on this independence—because it's real.

Adultified children who serve as parental caretakers are not the only ones who suffer distortions in their fourth imprint. "Superbaby" children are also pressured into premature functioning. Well-meaning parents, wanting to give their children "everything," can exert such enormous pressure that a four-year-old can feel like a failure. I work with a pediatrician who, much to his distress, has listened to four-and five-year-olds tell him that they feel "burnt-out"—their words, not his. Expected to excel, these children learn early that their needs only stand in the way of pleasing their parents.

Children have a large investment in meeting the demands they perceive as emanating from their parents. The caretaking child denies his needs by transferring them onto his parents and then attempting to meet the parents' needs. Superbaby children learn to squash their dependency needs in exchange for the parental approval that comes with achievement. The child who becomes a powerful caretaker learns to maintain acceptable behaviors, in exchange for both the accolades of success and the safety of the earlier imprints, by keeping an otherwise unavailable parent close by. In both cases, the child appears to be high-functioning and independent. Because the "independence" is founded on the denial of basic needs, it is false, unreal. What *is* real is the buried need to be cared for, adored, and loved, *not* for caretaking and *not* for accomplishing, but just for being.

Mature Dependence—The Pathway to Intimacy

Peter, in chapter 3, expressed the painful pretense of independent functioning when he said to me, "People see me as very strong. They look to me for leadership and I can provide it. I do it well. But underneath, I feel like I'm just patched together." Peter is speaking for many adults today. Appearing strong and accomplished, functioning as capable citizens, they lack connection to their earlier imprints, which, in conjunction with the Imprint for Mature Dependence, would allow a balanced, secure experience of both separateness *and* togetherness. Truly loving relationships include a wide range of interactional patterns in work and play, in joyful and stressful situations, in times of aloneness and togetherness. Access to the entire *spectrum* of relational imprints makes intimate relationships mutually collaborative. In a real relationship each partner feels connected and each can depend on the other when necessary. Also they can totally function and bring their entire presence to an activity when they are apart.

At its healthiest, the Imprint for Mature Dependence imparts the ability to feel both autonomous and connected. It includes the capacity to experience the needs and ways of relating taught by earlier imprints. Because the Imprint for Mature Dependence links preverbal patterns of relating, those of the bonding and boundary-building years, with the ability to communicate needs developed in part during the years of building bridging connections, it opens the pathway to true intimacy.

Until we have the capacity for firm, separate boundaries, the temporary sharing of emotions with another may be fraught with danger. "Can I allow myself to merge? Will I lose myself in the other's needs? Will I want so much that I will be pushed away? Can I control my needs, emotions, and fears?" Once we feel sure of ourselves, we do not fear times of loving merger—sexual or emotional. Clearly we need the ability to be independent, but it is not a "place" we must live in all the time. On the contrary it is only a station from which we can depart and to which we can choose to return, just as a child can return to receive mothering after a session in the sandbox.

The Imprint for Mature Dependence is the basis of what is called a cohesive self—the ability to share relatedness while maintaining separateness. When partners connect at this level, there is a functional flow between oneness and twoness, between merging and differentiating. Each can trust the other's goodwill. The result is an interdependent and collaborative relationship. For most of us, this does not simply happen. It takes a working partnership in which we make conscious choices to understand our partner's needs. When one partner's needs consistently supersede another's, the couple may achieve independence, but not interdependence; separateness but not togetherness; emotional acting out but never the solution of any problems.

Emotional Scenario

Have you ever had an experience like this?

You have worked hard to plan things to do together, but increasingly your partner wants to do things separately. He wants new adventures that feel uncomfortable to you (mountain climbing, skiing, etc.). You try to talk about it, to compromise, but your partner uses words like needing "space," needing "excitement," "being bored." You are not certain of what it means and what you should do.

What is happening here?

It may be that your relationship is in trouble. Alternatively, it may be that there has been so much togetherness that the relationship needs input from the outside. The need may be met through separate friends or new joint interests.

As needs are met, new, sometimes opposite, needs arise.

I want safety	and/or	I want exciting adventure
I want to idealize you	and/or	I want to know the real you
I want a successful career	and/or	I want more time to play
I want more closeness	and/or	I need to be alone

Isolation Man

There really are some people who do not need intimate relationships in their lives. It is important to know this in case you are trying to develop a closer relationship with such a self-contained person. They find fulfillment in their commitment to some cause, not in love relationships. Seth is one of the few people I know who is totally self-contained. He has a mission to which he devotes himself with single-minded focus—to find a cure for cystic fibrosis, an illness that killed two of his brothers when he was still a young child. He keeps himself apart, devoting himself wholeheartedly to his cause.

Seth recalls being different as far back as he can remember. He was not shy, but he steadfastly resisted his parents' pressure to play with other children; he always felt that the other children were too young. Because of his intellect and precocity, his parents spoke to his school about advancing him, but it was a time when schools encouraged children to stay with their class in order to avoid the social-adjustment problems associated with "skipping." So Seth remained with his class, but he also remained emotionally isolated. He compensated for his disinterest or discomfort in relating to people by immersing himself in his studies and learning to entertain himself without any stimulation from others.

Seth followed this pattern of intellectual self-absorption and emotional isolation through high school, college, and graduate school. His temperament made him an excellent scientist, but a poor candidate for an intimate relationship. Human beings are social animals. Most of us have known loners, but they rarely look happy in their placid solitude. To remain alone is usually to remain walled off from parts of ourselves as much as it is to remain walled off from other people. Taken to an extreme, complete autonomy can be a trap. For a very few it is the freedom to be totally absorbed in a passionate project.

Marie and Tony: Keepers of the Family Secret

The years spent developing independence can teach children how to ward off intimacy if the developmental years are fraught with family problems—particularly those revolving around family secrets. The adultified child, in an effort to keep the family secret safe, might become isolated, withdrawn—what might appear to be a healthy, self-sufficient, independent child might grow up to be an adult with major problems maintaining intimacy. Uncovering those secrets can unravel a lifetime of defenses and trigger major disruptions in a marital relationship.

After twenty-one years of marriage and two children, Marie had decided to "do something more" with her life. She returned to school, went into therapy, and informed her husband, Tony, that she wanted a divorce.

Tony was a soft-spoken, gentle man whose successful career as a violinist had provided his family with a comfortable lifestyle. Although his career required that he travel a lot, Tony was always pleased to return home to the warmth of his family and their many friends. He relied on Marie's social skills, energy, and nurturing abilities—qualities he lacked himself. Together, he thought, they were a great team. From his point of view, they were. Knowing that he could depend on his wife to manage their home, their family, and their social life, he could

dedicate himself to his work, which gave him a great deal of fulfillment.

When they first arrived for therapy, Marie said that she wanted to
develop herself, to grow as a person, but Tony was holding her back.
He was "clingy, like a puppy who'll never leave my side."

"I'm not trying to be clingy," Tony said softly. "I'm trying not to pull
on you. I'm managing my life. I'm doing things on my own. If I'm
bothering you too much, I'll hang back—I can give you as much space
as you want."

"You say that, but you can't do it!" Marie retorted. "First you move
out of the bedroom, which is what I wanted, but then in the evenings,
you hang over me as I'm trying to work at my art table, saying things
like, 'Hey, we're doing really well, aren't we?' I can't *stand* how needy
you are—how much reassurance you try to pull out of me. I don't want
to hurt you. It's all very painful, but I don't know if we'll make it
together. I feel that there is so much more of me that hasn't come out.
I know I have talents and abilities inside that I've never touched. I want
to *do* things with my life," she said determinedly, as if anticipating the
protestations of her husband.

I wondered to myself if this was the classic conflict of the woman
who is ready to blossom and grow and be independent now that her
children are all finally in school, but whose husband is threatened by
the change.

"Is Tony's behavior markedly different from the way it was a few
years ago?" I asked.

"Yes," Marie answered emphatically. "Everything started to change
when his mother died a little over a year ago. Until then, Tony seemed
quite different. I mean, he was very devoted to the kids and me, but he
certainly wasn't clingy. How could he be? He traveled five months of
the year, depending on his bookings. We both liked having time to
ourselves."

"How did your mother's death affect you, Tony?" I asked.

I saw light red flush marks quickly appear on Tony's cheeks. Marie
glared at him sideways, her face immobilized by her clenched expression. Avoiding eye contact, Tony mumbled, "I guess her death made me
realize how much I had missed as a kid." Gaining conviction, he continued with some vehemence. "I didn't have a normal life, you know,

what with five hours of practice a day. When she died, I felt flooded with sadness. I guess I realized I'd *never* get to be just a normal little boy who wanted to sit on his mother's lap once in a while. I was always a prodigy—and it's damn hard to be a prodigy when you're a little kid."

I glanced at Marie, expecting her expression to have softened. If anything, she was more walled off than she had been before Tony spoke. I was puzzled, indeed. Was there another woman involved? Another man? I didn't know the secrets of this relationship yet. When I work with couples together rather than in individual therapy, I do not always get the full picture—partners can conceal affairs for as long as they wish—but it is hard to miss the repercussions. People who feel frustrated in their attempts to connect with each other, who feel alone when they are together, often turn outside the relationship to fill their needs. But that was jumping ahead, and I did not know at this point whether this was the secret of Marie and Tony. It was time to find out more about each of them.

"Marie," I began, "do you disagree with anything Tony has said?"

"Not exactly. Let's just say he's leaving out a lot."

"And you disapprove of what he's leaving out?"

"*Yes,* I disapprove! What he's leaving out is the whole point! It's why we're here!"

I looked at Tony, who had a tortured look on his face. He stared at the floor for several seconds, then spoke in a choked voice. "I thought we came here to talk about *us.* I'm not ready to talk about my family. All I want to know is how to keep our marriage together and still give you the space you want."

"You can't keep our marriage intact unless you talk about your family," Marie stated firmly. "It all goes back to them and you know it!"

They were at a stalemate, it was obvious. I tried a compromise. "Tony, do you think you'll be able to talk about your family at some point . . . at a time of your choosing? Maybe that's all Marie needs to hear—that you know it's important to talk about these things and you will, when you feel up to it."

I looked over at Marie, who nodded in a resigned sort of way.

"Yeah, sure, I know. . . . I will, Marie, I will. Just give me a little more time to get used to all of this," Tony said, gesturing with his arm, indicating my office.

Marie's Childhood

I began our next session by asking Marie to tell me a little about her history. I wanted to draw the focus away from Tony so that he would feel comfortable enough to volunteer information. I also needed to gain some sense of the determined woman sitting before me.

As Marie talked, she revealed a bright and perceptive woman who had made decisions for herself since she was a young child. Growing up in a large Eastern European immigrant family in San Francisco with little money but much love, Marie had veered toward independence as early as she could remember. "From the beginning," she said, "I was a free spirit. I was determined to do things my own way. I fought against being put in the traditional role of wife and mother expected of all the women in my family." She was accustomed to close family ties and had a rich model for nurturing mothers in her mother and the mothers of extended-family members who lived close by in the neighborhood. Nevertheless, nurturing relationships often felt smothering to Marie. She knew that she had to get out of this closed environment to live her own life. I noted that her feelings of being smothered seemed to be kicking up again because of whatever was going on in her marriage.

Marie constantly had to defend her independence against the pressure from her family and the pull of her cultural heritage. To her, dependence meant enmeshment, the obliteration of her rights, the squashing of her spirit. The dependent wives and mothers she had known as a child had no rights to speak of. She wanted none of it. Her earliest memories were of arguments with her mother over her independent behavior. She was assertive and opinionated by the age of three, happy to challenge authority whenever she came upon it. Although basically loving, her family was always trying to change her behavior and she was always resisting. I was beginning to see how this opposition of Marie to her family played a powerful role in shaping her later intimate relationships.

Marie found her way out of the pull of her close-knit, large, extended community and into a state university. There she met Tony, who was on campus to give a performance. After a brief, passionate courtship, they were married. As she described it, Marie breathed a sigh of relief that she was finally free of the smothering enmeshments of her family and her culture. No sooner had the sigh left her lips than she realized that she had simply exchanged one type of enmeshment for another. For their honeymoon, Tony arranged for them to visit *his* parents for a *month*.

"Is that when the problem between you began?" I asked.

Marie responded quickly, "Yes, on our honeymoon! In fact, we have had a distance between us since then. There has never been a true connection." She complained that Tony had refused to listen to her when she tried to point out the lies, deceit, and manipulation of his family. She attributed their current marital problems to Tony's refusal to acknowledge the truth about his family life.

Tony quietly agreed that she had been right—there *were* a lot of unhealthy things going on in his family that he hadn't wanted to acknowledge in any way. "I need to understand something more," I said, feeling that I was being left out of some important details. They were presenting little information about Tony's family. "Can you tell me something about what happened on your honeymoon that was so upsetting to the relationship?" They looked at each other and Tony nodded.

"Let me put it this way," Marie began mysteriously. "We ate all our meals with his family. At every single meal the same people were present: his father, his mother, his sister, and a friend named Jack. Jack's relationship to the family was never spoken about openly. When I asked Tony why Jack was always with his father, Tony became annoyed and said it had always been that way—that they were like brothers. I could sense that they did not have a brotherly relationship, though. The affection and connection between them was obvious to any aware person. At meals, Tony's mother acted as if everything was fine, but I could see how depressed she was in between. There seemed to be an unspoken commandment in their household that went something like, 'Thou shall not speak about or question in any way the relationship between Jack and Brandon.' I was astounded that Tony would not acknowledge the obvious, and I was infuriated by everyone's expectation that I would slip silently and unquestioningly into my designated slot."

Tony said nothing and Marie continued, "Tony's mother lived a terrible life, from what I could see. I knew right away what was going on, but nobody would talk about it ever! When Tony's mother was dying two years ago, I sat with her and tried to help bring the secret out—to talk things over. I *know* she wanted to talk. I told her I knew about her husband, and all she could say to me was, 'You don't understand what he gave up to stay with his family.' What *he* gave up! Look what he made her live with! So he stayed with his family, but his boyfriend was always there, too. After she died, Brandon finally lived with Jack openly and the big secret was out in plain sight. But it took *her death* to reveal the truth. I hated being forced to be part of the family secret!"

Tony's face was drained of color. He said that Marie was right, that he hadn't wanted to know the truth. His father's homosexuality wasn't so obvious when he was growing up, Tony said, although there were signs that everyone chose to ignore. "Marie perceived the situation right away, but none of us would talk about it—it was just too hard," Tony mumbled.

"It wasn't too *hard* to see your mother's unhappiness. I think Jack's presence caused her to drink, made her sick, and killed her," Marie exclaimed.

Tony's Childhood

I asked Tony how his family's secret had affected him as a child. As he talked, I formed my own images and impressions of what he was describing.

Tony was the youngest of four children born into a family that was shrouded by this unspoken secret. Under this shroud of secrecy, no bonding occurred. His mother was chronically depressed and torn with conflict. It is not that she did not love her son and want to take care of him. But because her energy was consumed by her defenses, by her need to deny and conceal, she had little left over for Tony. As Tony acquired his Imprint for Emotional Sharing, the emotional climate of the household was silently dominated by the secret of his father's household alliance. To me that signaled that Tony would have to have some confusion over how he really felt about the family environment.

The ambiguities in the family life had to be denied; the implications of his father's having an ever-present male friend had to be denied; the reasons for his mother's depression had to be denied. At the same time, those "reasons" circulated underground in the family's awareness through the transfer of emotions that occurs in any family. Because he was a sensitive child, attuned to the needs of others, Tony attempted to give his mother what she needed—affectionate attention—and to keep her safe from whatever it was that made her depressed. Remember that it is during the boundary-building years that children—like Eric, and also like Tony—who have a parent to protect often have their own needs neglected.

Only when Tony reached the third level of emotional development, the Imprint for Bridging Connections, did his life improve, at least in some ways. His musical abilities provided a new focus that allotted him much-needed attention and approval. The family could rally around his unusual talent without reservation, and his prodigious career was officially launched when he was only twelve. Those years, Tony recalls, were consumed with a rigid schedule of school, music lessons, and practice. He can say little about the way the family lived during this time, except that he has the nagging memory of his mother's dejected emotional state. He once asked her why she was sad so much. She had patted his head and said simply, "Oh, it's just the way I am."

As his musical career solidified during his teens, Tony slid easily into the role of the gifted young musician. On the road, independent, exceptionally mature, he had a platform from which to reach the outer world and escape his childhood—though the pain would linger on. Although always sensitive and attuned to others, he saw himself as needing little from them. He believed his role in life was as a giver, and he took secret pride in his self-sufficiency—sufficient to himself because only then did he feel relieved of the demand to help maintain the family secret.

When he met Marie, he was won over by her warm and vivacious personality. She was bright, intelligent, clearly independent, and from a different cultural background—all very intriguing to Tony. With her he could build a life truly separate from his past. Their life together was harmonious on the surface.

Marie enjoyed her children and was a nurturing mother and wife. By her own admission, however, she always kept what she called "a clear center of myself" within. She recalls an inner strength that she recognized went back to her childhood and was made even firmer by the role given to her in her marriage. She sensed herself to be the emotionally strong one, stronger than Tony and stronger than his parents. She took on and mentored many of the friends in the small social circle they have been part of since the marriage.

But as solid as she seemed to others, there was some nagging insecurity, perhaps as a woman, perhaps from the prejudice she sensed as the child of immigrants who spoke a foreign language. Ever on guard against losing her hard-won independence, Marie was willing to have others depend on her, but deep inside she would depend on no one. Tony never noticed Marie's subtle withholding; he saw only the picture of a wife who ran his home and raised their children with love and care. Accustomed to ignoring the underlying emotional climate, Tony was well versed in accepting things as they were made to appear. Indeed, he'd been required to!

It was not until the death of his mother that Tony began to release the grip of denial that had always been part of his life. He experienced enormous pain as he lifted the lid that concealed a lifetime of lies and recognized the wounds his mother had endured by choosing to stay married to a man whom she knew preferred his boyfriend to her. He also experienced the pain of his father, who was frightened about all he would lose personally and professionally if the truth came out.

Tony went from total silence on the subject to a constant wish to discuss it with Marie, who had known about and understood the situation for almost two decades. She listened at first but soon felt exhausted by his endless angst-ridden self-reflections. She suggested he get help from a therapist. In individual therapy, Tony recognized that the family secret had been a heavy burden indeed. By refusing to listen to Marie's feelings about what was obvious to her the very first time she met his parents, Tony had inserted a wedge of distrust that had separated them ever since. Although Marie was always aware of the wedge, until this time Tony had denied it.

When Tony tried to repair the gap between them, to achieve the close bonding he so desperately sought, he found himself hitting an emotional wall. The more he tried to share everything he was coming to understand about himself and his family's pathology, the more distant Marie became. Her explanation was that the problem had gone on for so many years, she wasn't sure it was resolvable now. She couldn't listen to Tony when he was finally ready to do what she had always asked—to look honestly at himself and his family.

She found his constant need to talk about it oppressive. As she backed away, he would hardly let her out of his sight when he was at home. Their relationship shifted dramatically as she felt him getting too close, encroaching on the space designed to protect her from the turmoil in Tony's family and his denial of it.

The space Marie had originally erected to keep her own family at a distance had served her well after Tony's family became hers—along with their secret. This might have angered Marie, but she was well suited to play the role demanded of her when she married Tony. By this time, seventeen years later, it was perhaps too much for Marie to tear apart her protective "shell" within which she had learned to isolate herself.

Once the secret was brought into the open, the defenses Tony had used all his life were not so necessary. No longer was he a person who needed to deny and isolate himself from the truth. But he was overwhelmed with his mother's death and his father's decision to live an openly homosexual life. Tony knew it was a good decision for his father, but it added to the inner turmoil that he felt.

His clinging attachment to Marie intensified. Simultaneously, all of Marie's defenses seemed to grow stronger. Her attempts to redefine and renew the relationship seemed dangerously distancing to him. She suggested more separate activities, and he felt himself losing her and the life that they had built together. As his world unraveled, he needed constant reassurance and loving acceptance. The greater his needs became, the more angry and detached Marie became.

As in most relationships, the problem was not one-sided. Tony's reaction to his dysfunctional family was not, as Marie maintained, the sole cause of the trouble. As he began to shift in his perceptions, the balance of the relationship changed, and this transformation in him set off her defenses. She had to face her own deeply buried fear of intimacy and connection.

Marie's apparent independence was not supported by the healthy integration of earlier imprints. She was terrified of true intimacy. For her, it meant engulfment and a loss of self so reminiscent of her childhood. She did not know how to maintain her separateness *and* bond with another. She could attune empathically to the needs of others, but this, too, was done from a guarded position where she remained in control. She had learned to equate intimacy with enmeshment with others' needs. Therefore, she was not able to respond with empathy to Tony in his attempts to deny his family's secret, and she had remained unable to empathize with his current emotional turmoil.

So, during the years of their marriage, Marie gave two different messages based on two different imprints. On one hand, she complained that they had never been a couple because of Tony's fears of acknowledging the truth; on the other hand, she resisted every effort Tony made to draw her into intimate relating as he opened himself up in therapy to new truths about himself. Marie began talking more about the need to develop herself and her talents as an artist and designer. She enrolled in school and had plans for a career. She knew what she wanted: she wanted her children, her home, her friends, but not Tony. She saw him as squashing her independence. It was at this point that Marie asked him to move out and he reluctantly did so.

When I spoke to Marie several months later, she said that she felt better apart and would probably go ahead with a divorce. When I spoke to Tony, he was sad, but hoped to find a way to resolve the crisis and reunite. "But," he said, "if we don't, I'll manage. I'll still see my children, I have my work and my friends." With regret he added, "I'll rebuild my life."

Marie and Tony did not reunite, and neither has yet remarried. When I contacted Marie a year later, she remained pleased with her decision, although she was concerned about the effect the divorce would have on the children. They have felt the disruption in their lives, have not done well in school the past year, and seem more isolated from their friends. Defensively Marie added that is was better to come from a divorced home than to do what Tony's mother had done: keep the marriage together and live a lie.

The goal of couples therapy is not always to keep people together. Some relationships may need to end. But all too often we end relationships for the wrong reasons. Partners who choose to break up without understanding that they are caught in old scenarios, without understanding what is hurting them so much, will, in all likelihood, repeat the same destructive patterns in their next relationship. How much better to uncover the old wounds, to peel away the layers, and to see how much is appropriate to the current relationship and how much of it is old business. With this approach, the couple who in the end divorce nevertheless may have learned a great deal about themselves, which will benefit them in future relationships.

Because Tony had learned a great deal about himself, he is not likely to reenact his failed relationship with Marie. On the other hand, I think Marie will need a new relationship in which to begin her growth. She did not see their difficulties as mutually created. Her viewpoint remained fixed throughout their marriage. Any problems between them stemmed from the "problem" with Tony's family. Marie remained unwilling to look at what lay beneath her overwhelming need to function independently. Marie's healing will require that she trust that it is safe to love deeply and to depend on someone else.

Among the tasks of an intimate relationship is to balance the level of independence (relying on the self to meet all needs) with the level of dependence (relying on another to meet some legitimate and crucial needs). The result is a mature dependence that empowers both partners.

Separateness and Togetherness

The more secure you are about yourself, your values and ideas, the more you are able to interact in a mutually dependent relationship. This security within yourself grows out of ties to others—the bonds of love. When you know there is someone who understands you, accepts you, and wants to be with you, then you can give your love openly and freely, without fear of being rejected and humiliated.

But, as noted in Rule #6 for Positive Dependency, you should not expect a partner to meet all of your needs. When you share interests together and also bring into the relationship your separate interests, neither will feel drained by the demands of the relationship; each can be revitalized by the dividends of outside connections and each can give to the other. The more you give, the more you get.

If this does not hold true for your relationship, you must consider two possible causes. You may be with a partner who lacks the interest or capacity to give to you in a mutually enhancing relationship. Or, you may think that you are giving what your partner wants, when, in fact, you are giving your partner what you want and are not paying attention to your partner's desires. You may need to reevaluate your relationship to determine the reality of your situation.

The point of couples therapy, and of this book, is to help people look at what is going on between them, so that whether or not they stay together, *something* changes in their awareness of the issues and strengths of the relationship. With increased awareness and understanding, we can stop continuously reenacting the same old patterns. The way we heal old wounds is to see how we replay early injuries in adult relationships. Recognizing the pattern, we can use our thinking abilities to deduce that we are likely to get the same unwanted results *if* we keep replaying it.

The solution? Try a different pattern. If my inclination is to pull away from conflict with my partner, I can now choose to come closer. If my inclination is to submerge myself in my partner's feelings, I can choose to create some distance. To heal old wounds, we have to go against our habitual tendencies and try different ways of relating. By becoming aware of what is actually happening, instead of operating according to old imprints, we learn to tolerate the discomfort of old emotional wounds, face the fears of venturing into unknown emotional territory, and begin to develop new relationship skills.

Part 3 Healing Attachments: How to Meet Your Partner's Dependency Needs and Grow Together

---

And the Lord said to the rabbi, "Come, I will show you hell."

They entered a room where a group of people sat around a huge pot of stew. Everyone was famished and desperate. Each held a spoon that reached the pot, but each spoon had a handle so long that it could not be used to reach each person's mouth.

The suffering was terrible.

"Come, now I will show you heaven," the Lord said after a while.

They entered another room, identical to the first—the pot of stew, the group of people, the same long spoons.

But there everyone was happy and nourished.

"I don't understand," said the rabbi. "Why are they happy here when they were miserable in the other room and everything was the same?"

The Lord smiled. "Ah, but don't you see?" He said. "Here they have learned to feed each other."

—Merle Shain

7 Intimate Connections: Sex Can Heal or Hurt

*And when, throughout all the wild orgasms of love
slowly a gem forms, in the ancient, once-more-
molten rocks
of two human hearts, two ancient rocks, a man's
heart and
a woman's,
that is the crystal of peace, the slow hard jewel of
trust,
the sapphire of fidelity.
The gem of mutual peace emerging from the wild
chaos of love.*

—D. H. Lawrence, "Fidelity"

Rule #7 for Positive Dependency:
Be generous with your body; not only in sexual intimacy, but also in offering a gentle stroke, a foot massage, a back rub; touch gently or hold firmly depending upon your partner's response. Touch is a basic means of bonding, sharing, and connecting. Remember that a hug goes two ways.

The subject of sex is dear to my heart. After thirty-eight years of marriage, there is always a question of how to sustain an exciting sex life. Will we ever recapture the sexual passion of love anew? Never again will we explore each other as we did when everything was new. But when we have learned each other well, we add a *new* dimension to our lovemaking; knowing the touch that stimulates the most, the words that excite, the fantasies that bring heightened pleasure.

In a sexual encounter we depend on our partner to discover what is satisfying for us; thus, achieving sexual intimacy clearly makes us mutually dependent. But fear of this dependency also makes people avoid sexual intimacy.

Indeed, our sexual encounters are a powerful barometer of our response to dependency issues. How we interact sexually has a lot to do with whether we learned to trust or mistrust the people we have loved and needed. If we learned to fear those on whom we depended, we also learned to build protective defenses to ward off hurt. We do not make conscious decisions about these defenses. They are simply automatic responses that protect us from threat. In adulthood, it can be extremely difficult to give up our habitual defenses and allow the sensations of excitement and merger to flow through the body, when messages imprinted earlier signal that there is danger in such closeness.

To have strong fears of sex is far from unusual. I have listened to a forty-year-old patient talk about the "vagina with teeth" as a way of describing an amorphous but compelling fear of his girlfriend's sexual demands. I have listened to many women talk about the penis as a weapon of violence and describe penetration as an attack. Sexual anxieties are part of many relationships.

When a couple in therapy present a sexual issue, the question becomes, "Is the problem a result of straightforward differences in their sexual needs and desires, a conflict of expectations, or a result of their interlocking imprint needs and wounds?" If the conflicts are caused by differing sexual appetites, problems can often be resolved through simple awareness of their differences and through education in how to meet each other's sexual needs. If the problem is one of differing values and expectations, dialogue and negotiation may be in order. But when problems revolve around imprint issues, a deeper investigation is necessary.

Gender and Sexuality

There are many theories about the differing sexual needs of men and women. When I listen to couples talk about sex, intimacy, and making love, I *know* that they are talking about a wide range of emotions and behaviors, a range that sometimes seems unfathomable. Because men and women have different experiences as they grow up, they typically come to sexual encounters laden with differing, sometimes confused expectations.

When the sexual revolution and the women's movement made both men and women more aware of female sexuality, many men initially applauded. For some men, however, open female sexual expression had an inhibiting effect. Women's sexuality, which included expectations that men would meet their needs, created unintended repercussions and became for some a challenge to male potency. Sex became a kind of competition, as it remains for many couples. Can he "get it up" and keep it firm long enough for her to reach orgasm? Can she lubricate quickly and have multiple orgasms in under twenty minutes? Women often say that sex without other messages demonstrating love makes them feel used. But for many men, sex is the one way they can express love.

No wonder there is so much confusion about sexuality today. While women are trying to break out of centuries-old inhibitions of their sexual expression, many are confronted with men's mixed messages of being desired for their sexiness but *not* for their sexual assertiveness. Men, meanwhile, find they must work hard to prove they are not the "macho male" who dominated in the past, yet must strive to be the superpotent male who can engage in creative foreplay, hold off orgasm, and not fall asleep afterward.

Fortunately, for many men, pleasing a mate is not a problem and, in fact, is an added enhancement to the pleasure of lovemaking. But for men with early wounds who have unresolved feelings of inadequacy and unmet dependency needs, women's emerging sexual messages can feel threatening.

I worked with a couple who had had sexual problems for a long time. I asked both what they saw as ideal lovemaking. The wife had a comprehensive list: "I want you to be gentle and to take time and not rush me. I want you to kiss me in the morning and call me from the office. I want you to let me know you love me during the day." His response was, "What I really want is to fuck and come!" No wonder they had sexual problems—sex was a completely different experience for each of them.

He went on to explain his apparent loss of interest in sex. "It's just too much work. When I get home, I'm tired. I like to relax. When we go to bed, I'd love to make love. But then she begins with the instructions, and I say, 'Forget it.' I just want to go to sleep."

What feels to his wife like an attempt to communicate her sexual needs, to feel loved and accepted, feels to him like unwarranted, controlling demands. Yet he considers himself to be a liberal, open-minded man who has encouraged his wife's independence. He feels confused and angry; she feels betrayed and unloved.

Because sexuality represents a wide range of both emotional and erotic expression, fully understanding how it functions in our lives requires an examination of the way needs arising from our imprints are played out and fought out between partners in the sexual arena. Many of the sexual problems people bring to intimate relationships can be traced back to distortions introduced during early socialization and wounds from injuries during the development of imprints.

It is important to understand how unresolved dependency needs contaminate the sexual arena. Problems are most severe when early imprint patterns are replayed in repeatedly dysfunctional and hurtful ways. Partners have many stages on which they play out these early patterns, but the two most common are making love and communicating needs. Fortunately, dynamic interactions within these same arenas can make an unhappy relationship into a healing one.

This is precisely why I advise people to follow Rule #7 for Positive Dependency, to be generous with touch of all kinds. Touch is a lifelong need, a basic means of bonding; and sensual touch is as important for many people as the sexual act itself. Those who learned early that it is painful or shameful to need touching may avoid it in their adult relationships except when engaged in lovemaking. For most couples a gentle stroke, a massage, or a hug may be an important way to soothe and heal disputes in the relationship that are otherwise nonnegotiable. And while sexual intimacy cannot cure anyone's problems, it can go a long way toward softening the edges that crop up in every relationship.

Sexual Conflicts and Underlying Imprints

Both the most joyful aspects of sexual intimacy and the most agonizing problems of sexual dysfunction have less to do with the sexual act than with the early imprints that each mate brings to the encounter. For example, in problem relationships, sex is unchanging and unsatisfying, often becoming a battleground upon which many nonsexual skirmishes are fought.

Whatever the particulars, the message of sexual dissatisfaction appears in a language we all know. She has a headache, he is exhausted; they go to bed at different hours; they want to engage sexually at different times. Often, these sexual skirmishes actually camouflage efforts to meet differing core needs. It is of prime importance to realize that sexual conflicts in adult life frequently express even more basic longings for unconditional love and acceptance, outstretched arms that comfort as well as excite—positive dependency, at its best.

Hank and Patricia

A couple can easily become locked in a struggled over whose version of making love is the one that will be the standard in the relationship.

"Before we got married, the sex was wonderful," Hank said. "Now, nothing I do pleases her. She even brought home sex manuals. I don't need lessons!"

"He sure knows what *he* likes sexually," Patricia said. "Why won't he let me tell him what *I* like?"

Hank and Patricia are two highly functioning adults who, in most areas of their lives, feel compatible, competent, and capable. They enjoy doing things together, they travel together well, and they have similar values and goals for themselves. They both have their own set of friends and activities, their own careers, and strong, very separate identities. So where was the problem? They stated that their difficulty with sex had been present from the beginning of their marriage. Patricia explained that Hank refused to please her sexually. She knew what gave her pleasure. She knew what she liked and she had told him.

"I didn't like being told how to satisfy her," Hank said gloomily. "It made me feel as though she was accusing me of *not* being a good lover. Suddenly I felt so insecure. Then Patricia brought home books—sex manuals!—and suggested that we take classes! I was horrified and insulted. I'd never had a sexual problem before we were married. I told her it was *her* problem, not mine."

They both stopped talking about it for a while and tried to "make do." The strain, however, was triggering sexual repercussions for Hank—he began having problems with impotence. Thinking that oral stimulation might be the solution, he told Patricia what he wanted. Her response was, "If you won't take care of my needs, why should I take care of yours?"

By the time they came for therapy, the lines of battle had been clearly drawn and the stalemate was several months old. We began to look together at how sex had become a power struggle, a contest, which was creating greater and greater distance between them. When deep emotional attunement and bonding are absent in sex, problems trigger blame and accusation rather than mutual, loving concern. Their problem was not going to yield to the mechanical techniques recommended in the sex manuals. It could only be solved by moving into the more personal realms of unexpressed emotions and needs. To begin this unfamiliar journey, however, Hank and Patricia first had to learn how to communicate with one another. Each was presenting his or her version of reality and not listening to the other. Each was getting angrier and angrier at the other for trying to exert sexual control. We began by looking at each of their versions to uncover clues to buried needs and wounds. What they needed was a foundation of trust, which could only be laid by willing, mutual self-disclosure and the bond of loving acceptance that follows. It would take time.

For adults, intimacy of any kind invariably triggers deep feelings, and sex triggers some of our most primal longings and defenses. To feel comfortable in sex, a couple must be able to experience mutual positive dependency in which partners know one another well and can trust each other when deep feelings arise.

Effect of the Earliest Imprints on Sex

Whether or not we trust our sexual responses as adults is greatly influenced by our earliest relationships. The interactions between infant, mother, and father has an important influence on development of gender and sexual awareness. *Attitudes toward sex develop along with our imprints for bonding and emotional sharing.* The child learns to experience sexuality in the same way that he or she has learned to relate to and rely on others. Either the child has learned, in essence, "It is safe to rely on you; I can trust that my needs will be met"—or the opposite, "I am frightened that I will be hurt if I depend on you."

Parents or other caretakers tend to respond similarly to each level of need the child reveals as he or she matures. Thus, based on prior interactions, children have unconscious expectations of how parents will respond to sexual exploration. Small children learn quickly if it is "bad" to touch themselves. The four year old whose mother flinches anytime he touches himself absorbs her reaction. "Am I a bad boy?" he wonders. The three-year-old who flirts with her daddy as she sits on his lap learns whether it is safe to relate in this way. Does he accept her loving attitudes, or does he respond seductively toward her? A child who is touched inappropriately by a "beloved uncle" may "forget" the specific incident but spend a lifetime reexperiencing confused feelings of excitement mixed with guilt, shame, or fear in sexual situations.

More subtly, children learn a great deal about emotional attitudes toward sexuality through the transfer of emotions that occurs between parents and children, as well as by observing the dynamics between their parents. We are influenced by each of our imprints, and access to all four gives us the widest range of freedom for sexual fulfillment. The first imprint for bonding affects how we relate sexually even though it develops before we have any conscious awareness of gender or sexuality.

• When we feel securely bonded, we are capable of the most passionate form of sexuality—the capacity to be lost in ecstasy. Giving up all control, we experience a pure physical release through union with another.

• When unmet bonding needs lead to lack of trust, a sexual partner may be experienced as "unsafe."

• When there is an unmet yearning for more love in the bonding experience, *being loved* is a more important goal than *giving love*.

• When bonding failures lead to self-soothing, sexuality may be a one-person affair.

• When bonding failures lead to a lifelong need to keep others at a distance, desire and love are only compatible when there is space for emotional escape.

In the Imprint for Emotional Sharing messages flow across boundaries from one person to another. In positive form, this allows us to experience pleasure through attunement to the pleasure of our partner.

• When boundaries were easily and safely crossed in childhood, the sexual boundaries of the adult remain open and responsive.

• Partners with open boundaries "know" what the other wants and give pleasure for the joy of giving.

• When boundaries are in danger of being invaded, there is residing fear that hostile or hateful passions will be released and shared, destroying the pleasures of sexuality.

• When childhood boundaries were invaded, protective defenses are erected to avoid aggressive dumping of emotions.

Even when negative feelings are kept in check or denied, when there are wounds in the imprint for emotional sharing, overwhelming emotions can create turbulence in the sexual arena. On the other hand, when couples trust one another emotionally so that positive feelings permeate relationships, the sex they share reflects a natural ebb and flow of positive dependency.

When sexuality is influenced by the Imprint for Bridging Connections a variety of positive and negative objects may be used to enhance pleasure or, alternatively, to avoid the perceived danger of a sexual relationship.

• Couples may playfully use bridging objects, including films and sexual toys, to enhance their sexual pleasure.
• When bridging is used as a distancer from sexual intimacy, pornographic films, magazines, and the use of people as sex objects can be used as negative bridges that deflect sexual intimacy.
• When bridging is designed to escape closeness, developing other relationships, having affairs, or using prostitutes may serve to cut off an intimate relationship.

Sexuality in the Imprint for Mature Dependence may be the most satisfying when it is enhanced by openness to any of the other imprints. Independence allows us access to dependence on others in a variety of ways.

• When the imprint for mature dependence is activated in a positive form, sexuality and orgasm not tinged with danger can free lovers to descend to the whirlpool of total release, knowing that they can reemerge safely, contented and together.
• With mature dependence couples are interested in pleasing each other, knowing that the giving of pleasure will be reciprocated.
• When mature dependence has not been achieved, sexuality can turn into unilateral demands by each partner.
• When mature dependence is marred by pockets of anxiety, periods of extreme closeness may alternate with times of emotional distance, with sexuality used as the path to reconnection.

The innate sexual drive is influenced by the content of each of the developmental imprints for love. When we make love, we can be in any one of our imprints, though we tend to engage sexually from the particular level that is most comfortable, most protective, and most strongly imprinted. Mutually enhancing positive dependency when meeting sexual needs occurs most effectively when each partner has access to all of the imprints and does not raise a defensive shield during lovemaking. But even in the best of relationships, this ideal situation does not always occur. One or both partners may be under stress, tired, upset about the problems of children, work, or money, or need emo-

tional sustenance more than the excitement of a joyful sexual experience. Even more than sexuality, the mutual exchange of emotional
nurturing in which each may depend on the other is what makes for
intimacy. Observing current sexual interactions can give important
clues to our imprint patterns.

Early imprint messages can lead us to use sex in an attempt to gain

---

Sexual Imprints

Bonding Imprint in Sex

- Feeling bonded and loved through sexual encounters

- Seeking constant affirmation that you are sexually desired

- Becoming obsessed with desire for someone you hardly know

- Fearing a loss of control in orgasm

- Experiencing a sense of merger in the sexual act

Emotional Sharing Imprint in Sex

- Asking for information from your partner to find out how to please him or her

- Expecting unrealistically that your partner know intuitively, without words, what pleases you

- Cutting off emotions and, as a result, feeling bored with sex

- Experiencing a repeated impulse to connect through sex with many partners

- Fear of being attacked or invaded through sexual contact with a partner

Bridging Imprint in Sex

- Wondering if your partner wants you for your body, not yourself

- Using people as sexual partners with no emotional connection

- Fantasizing to enhance sexual excitement

- Sharing fantasy freely with a partner

- Using pornographic movies and books

Mature Dependence Imprint In Sex

- Recognizing differences of sexual desire between partners as normal

- Keeping commitments to a partner even though attracted to others

- Giving as well as receiving pleasure

- Feeling close emotionally as well as sexually

love. Sex serves here as an affirmation and reassurance that one is loved and desired. This can result in a pattern of pretended passion and simulated orgasm to protect a partner from feeling inadequate, while at the same time eliciting the stroking and nurturing that represents the emotional connection so desired. Sexuality is used as a substitute for verbal communication, as a less complicated way of making contact than attempting to share deeply held feelings and needs. But when the sex is over, the participants are still emotional strangers.

Sometimes primitive emotional responses originating in our early imprints create a sensation of something amiss in the sexual arena, even though no words or rational understanding accompany the feelings. People who are otherwise able to function well become extremely troubled with issues surrounding sexuality. In some cases, the trauma of sexual abuse causes amnesia—memories are dissociated, blocked from conscious awareness, so when the child grows up, the sexual need seems clouded by nameless fear.

For others, inappropriately stimulating erotic experiences occurred during a period of life when words, feelings, and thoughts were not sufficiently organized by language. A mother might dress and act in ways that might prematurely expose her child to erotic feelings rather than experiencing sexuality in an adult relationship; a father, frightened of his sexual attraction to his daughter, avoids any touching or, with the emergence of adolescence, initiates verbal battles with her. Unresolved sexual feelings are the result. These feelings, unacknowledged by the parents, can confuse the young child who is trying to make sense of many physical and emotional changes. This confusion leaves a residue of overwhelming feelings, generally kept in check, which sometimes reemerge later during sexual experiences.

If, in your adult relationships, you experience frightening and painful sense memories that interfere with your ability to function sexually, you may have had such an early experience, of which you are not *consciously* aware.

Even though you have no clear memories of specific traumas, there are things you can do to change once you recognize the underlying causes of the problem.

Healing Sexual Trauma

Sexual problems often trigger old imprint feelings of inadequacy, badness, humiliation, and feelings of being judged by the very people you need to love you. This raises defensive patterns. Shame and blame may help protect your self-esteem, but they play havoc with your sexual relationship.

If you want to change the patterns of sexuality between yourself and your partner, there are things you can do to make a difference.

- Be aware of your own needs
- Attune to your partner's needs
- Know when it is important to take care of your partner's needs and when your own needs must come first
- Recognize that sometimes "no" is the appropriate thing to say
- Take responsibility for your part of the sexual encounter and not assign blame or cause shame to your partner

There are many times when meeting a partner's needs is the kind and tender thing to do. There are occasions when providing sexual gratification is a way to reduce tension, to provide a healthy, nonaddictive sleeping potion in the middle of the night. There are other times when watching an erotic movie is an intense stimulus to both, and there are still other times when meeting sexual needs requires a willingness to break out of old habits and explore new areas, emotionally as well as physically.

If you feel that your relationship has multiple sexual problems, consider the possibility that the problems are imprint related. What is missing for you in sex? What is it that you most need sexually? What do you want from your partner sexually that would fill your dependency needs? What sexually could your partner do that would make you feel loved, affirmed, emotionally supported, understood, accepted, responded to? What do you know about your partner's sexual needs? What questions could you ask that might elicit more information about the specific things you can do to respond to your partner's needs? How can you use sexuality in a way that will make both of you feel loved, understood, taken care of, emotionally held?

Mel and Amanda: Mutuality and Sexuality

After a painful divorce, Mel embarked on a long search for a woman to love. When he met Amanda, he thought his search was over. But sexual differences might have broken them up. "I like oral sex," he told her, and despite some hesitation on her part, she wanted to please him. "But just as I climax, she seems to pull away as though what comes out of me is disgusting. It feels as if she doesn't accept all of me, that there is something wrong with me. I want her to accept all of me."

Is there something wrong with her or with me? Mel wondered. Amanda seemed so perfect. But a relationship without the kind of sex that pleased him would be settling for the same kind of unloving, barely sexual relationship that he had had in his twenty-year marriage.

Mel's early bonding failures left him feeling unloved and unlovable. His great fear was that no one would ever want him, just as he believed no one wanted to be around him as a child. Even as he began to change his self-image, the differences in sexual desires made him question the entire relationship with Amanda. "I never felt worthy of love, so I just accepted it. If my own mother thought I was a mess, then I couldn't believe any woman would want me. Now that I am beginning to feel good about myself, I want a woman who doesn't find me distasteful," he said.

"And if she has issues in herself that make her very uncomfortable with what you need sexually, what happens then?" I asked.

"Then I have to decide if I'm willing to settle or if I should just say, 'She's a great lady, but not for me.'"

Amanda had the same decisions to make. Was he worth overcoming her disinclination to engage in oral sex his way? Or was his uncompromising stance a sign of an uncaring, controlling man? Because her early imprints did not include the emotional distortions of controlling or abusive parents, she decided it was worth trying to fulfill Mel's particular sexual and emotional needs. Mel was so grateful that she understood what her concession did for his self-image (as well as for his sexual gratification) that he looked for ways to respond to her vulnerability. Until the age of three, Amanda had lived with her parents in a small farming community in California. On her third birthday Amanda's parents died in an automobile accident.

She had experienced trauma around their death and had many fears that if she loved someone, he would one day disappear. Because Mel seemed so present and so reassuring, Amanda was determined to find ways to meet his needs. Because Mel felt so understood and cared for, he found many ways to remind her that he was available and loving. Both recognized the other's vulnerabilities.

This sexual relationship was the playing field in which each learned to take care of the early needs of the other. As the relationship grew, both of their fears, stemming from early, imprinted wounds, slowly diminished. By the time they married sexuality was no longer an issue.

Sexual Dysfunction and Imprint Distortions

Sex cannot cure a relationship's complex issues, but problems of sexual intimacy can contaminate an otherwise healthy relationship. If we fail to rely on intimacy and touch to bind us to our partner, then we run the risk of undermining the strengths that do exist. When sex is a problem, it can permeate every aspect of a relationship.

Sexual problems can be difficult to understand because a variety of symptoms can arise from similar causes. One person with sexual conflicts suffers from a sexual phobia; a second displays symptoms such as premature ejaculation, impotence, or inorgasmia; another develops a sexual perversion; yet another, displaying no outward sexual symptoms whatsoever, develops allergies or skin rashes. Each of these symptoms is a translation of early imprint messages. In the following cases, both Larry and Kevin suffer from a similar sexual symptom, impotence, but for very different reasons. Larry's wounds are related to his Imprint for Bonding, but Kevin's wounds are related to his Imprint for Mature Dependence.

Larry

Larry and Gina had lived together for years without talking about the issue of sex. When they first came to therapy, they said sex was no problem—they never had it! They haven't almost since they first married twelve years ago. It turned out that Gina had been thinking of leaving Larry for another man. "It's not just the sex," she said. "There's no touching, no intimacy, no words of love." They avoided sex so completely that any physical or emotional reminder of this dangerous subject was put out of mind.

Larry has suffered from impotence for years. Predictably he loses his erection before he and his wife get very far into their lovemaking. She grew suspicious that he might be having an affair. But, in fact, he had the same problem the few times he tried to have sex with prostitutes. In despair, he has wondered if sex will ever be an easy part of his life.

No one would know from Larry's demeanor at work or when he gets together with his male friends for their once-a-week "night out" filled with sexual jokes and innuendos that he feels like an outsider with a secret to hide. He seems like "one of the guys," but in reality, Larry is tortured by his sexual failure.

At first he was ashamed when he talked about his feelings of sexual inadequacy. I asked him to close his eyes and see what images emerged when he focused on those shameful feelings. He described images of dangerous liaisons between aggressive, frightening women and passive, frightened men. Other images emerged of consuming powerlessness. As he felt safer exploring deeper regions of himself, he related fears of "disappearing" inside his partner and losing himself. He would no longer have an identity as a separate person.

Somehow, for Larry, the intimacy of sexual union was tantamount to

emotional engulfment. We realized that Larry was experiencing difficulties from his earliest Bonding Imprint, when fears and terrors have
no words, leaving a nameless dread and a problem that had felt un-
resolvable to him.

Kevin

Kevin loves women and he has been involved with many over the
course of the last twenty years. Although he has never married, he has
had several relationships that lasted a year or longer. Each time he
thinks he has found the right woman and they move in together, he
loses his sexual desire for her and becomes impotent. By finding a new
woman who excites him, he is able to convince himself that it must be
his partner, not he, who has the sexual problem. As a result of this
pattern, he can never be faithful to any woman.

"I *do* want to settle down," he said almost pleadingly. "I *want* a
family. I'm tired of chasing, but it's happening again. Trudy is such a
wonderful woman. I know she loves me because she's been so understanding about my lack of sexual desire. I want us to be together
and I know this is a problem I need her help to resolve."

In his work life, Kevin has a solid sense of himself and excellent
relationships with colleagues and employees. He is an energetic and
avid sportsman and plays as hard as he works.

In therapy, Kevin recalled warm, loving family bonds and a large
extended family. However, his sense of security was shattered when, at
the age of three, he experienced many disruptions. His father's serious
medical condition required the family to move from a city where they
had many ties to a dry climate in the West. In their new surroundings,
the family was emotionally isolated. Kevin's mother, cut off from
friends and family and suddenly having to care for an invalid husband,
clung mightily to her youngest child. Desiring his mother's love but
feeling overwhelmed by her intensity and sensing the jealousy of his
siblings, Kevin handled the conflicting emotional messages in a manner appropriate to his stage of development. He became very independent, distancing himself from any desire for closeness with his
mother. As early as nursery school, he would no longer let his mother
kiss him good-bye when she dropped him off in the morning. In fact,
he stopped letting her hug or touch him in any way very early.

As Kevin described his early relationship with his mother, which was characterized by a strong emotional pull toward her and a compensating flight away from her, he began to recognize parallels in his adult relationships. Somehow, he was confusing these women with his mother. As soon as he became deeply involved with a woman, she became a forbidden, sexually neutral object, and his impotence protected him from vague, unacceptable impulses. At the point of intimacy, when attachment and sex join as erotic love, old danger signals about incestuous wishes and his former desperate need for independence force him to withdraw, literally, from the women he loves.

Sexual Circuitry

Sex is often described as a kind of "electricity." When the sexual "current" flows, excitement "lights up" the emotions—but it can also illuminate the distortions the partners bring to the relationship from the past. As we have seen in earlier chapters, the deeper the emotional connection between the partners, the more likely that wounds from the past will emerge in the relationship. When the emotional "wiring" expressed in the imprints does not work correctly, the attempt to merge can lead to a frightening "short circuit."

Because sex is so powerful, it can often be the key to discovering what is wrong—or what is right—in a relationship.

Consider some aspects of sexuality that correspond with our early imprints:

1. Sensuality through skin contact; total letting go in passion, the oceanic feeling of blissful merger (*Imprint for Primary Bonding*)
2. Attuning to the nonverbal message of each other's sexual needs (*Imprint for Emotional Sharing*)
3. Using pictures, objects, and words as sexual stimulants—romantic dinners, soft music, a sexy video (*Imprint for Bridging Connections*)
4. Taking turns satisfying each other; communicating personal desires without being offensive or defensive; choosing to meet the needs of your partner without always having to be satisfied in kind (*Imprint for Mature Dependence*)

One or more of these ways of connecting may become part of any couple's lovemaking. Some couples seek perfect bonding, while others prefer to maintain an independent spirit. The way a couple achieves sexual pleasure reflects in part the partners' approach to the world based on their developmental experiences. Because we are generally unaware of the underlying imprints that affect our love life, we operate out of unconscious needs, fears, and defenses. We select partners who remind us of important figures with whom we experienced early imprinted interactions and replay in the sexual arena our unique ways of connecting.

We often fall in love blindly, not seeing the other person as more than a shadow. We fill in the unseen pieces with bits and pieces of ourselves. We see a reflection that we like, and it is us. We have an illusion that we will someday fall in love with an ideal person. In fact, we fall in love with an idealized image of who that person is. We create that image out of remnants of our early imprints. It takes time to learn the reality of who our mate is. For some, this is the period when "the honeymoon is over." For others, this is the beginning of true emotional and sexual intimacy.

As a relationship develops over the years, partners either learn to trust each other and find ways to handle the ups and downs in their love life—in which case they experience positive dependency and a safe sexual haven—or they learn to defend themselves against being injured when they are most vulnerable. Those who come for therapy generally fall into the latter group. Some are so cut off from their true needs that they are unaware of the connection between their love lives and their underlying imprint needs. Partners who cope with problems that arise give the sexual electricity a chance to flow between them. Partners whose needs are unaddressed often see their sexual batteries go dead in one way or another.

Bob and Louise: Lack of Sexual Desire

Bob and Louise have not had a sex life for over a year. Louise has never given up feeling that she is not attractive enough or sexually adept enough to keep her husband interested. So she has avoided the subject of sex altogether. They came into marital therapy to resolve arguments over money and household management. It quickly became apparent that Bob's total control over all expenditures, including his extensive income and her much smaller income, was creating serious difficulty between them. With his background in both law and accounting, Bob thought that he could manage their spending and investments in a way that would build a large net worth quickly.

"I'll never let us be poor like my father did all the years when we were growing up," he said.

"You felt powerless to do anything about it when you were a child," I commented. "Now you are going to make up for it, both financially and by being in control of your own destiny. While you are doing that, Bob, you need to understand how it affects Louise." Turning to Louise, I asked, "What happens to you when Bob takes control, and what do you do about it?"

Louise described how his behavior triggers the same insecure helpless state that she felt as a young child, when her parents, fitness freaks, decided she was too chubby and put her on a macrovegetarian diet. She felt constantly hungry.

"How early in your life?" I asked.

"I think they were always nutty about food. I don't remember any time in childhood when I didn't feel deprived. I wanted to please them. I told myself food didn't matter. But when I went away to college, I gained thirty pounds. Even then I wasn't fat. I weighed one hundred and thirty. Bob was really heavy when we met."

"So you were two deprived children when you met, filling up on food." I asked them to consider how this sense of scarcity and plenty played itself out in their financial problems. As we uncovered the layers, I went back to their defensive imprints for handling deprivation—the feelings each of them had that they were not good enough, and the use of food and money as bridging objects to fill up and feel a sense of sufficiency. I then asked about other areas in which the pattern played itself out and the issue of sex arose.

From the beginning of their marriage Bob felt that he wasn't "good enough" sexually. Louise kept telling him how to satisfy her. "Each time she instructed me, it was another stab." He could never get an erection and maintain it long enough to satisfy her. At first the problem was premature ejaculation. Then sex felt like hard work and he had impotence problems. Then he just felt exhausted when the pressures of his successful career kept him up late with work. He simply lost interest.

Louise felt unloved and unlovable, just as she had when she was a child. She felt deprived—as if she had been told to be satisfied with the life she had, much as her parents insisted that she remain on a diet of their design. In a rebellion reminiscent of her college eating binges, she filled up by eating and shopping. Bob took over the finances, fearing that she would bankrupt them.

As we worked to get below the stated problems to their mutual feeling of deprivation, it became increasingly clear that their fights about money were merely a superficial reflection of their struggles to have their needs met. The absence of sex reflected the ongoing failure of their efforts to get emotional nutrition from each other. They were not being generous with each other in any way, including the sharing of their bodies. Generosity, and its antithesis—being stingy and with-holding with each other—pervaded every aspect of their relationship. Issues over money had brought them into therapy, but their sexual problems showed us how they habitually missed opportunities to understand each other's needs. In our two years of work together, we peeled away the layers of their wounded relationship. Resolution of the deeper issues eventually reopened the pathways to sexuality.

Obsessions, Violence, and Emotional Chaos

We have seen how a healthy experience of early bonding endows us with a basic sense of trust in intimate interactions and fosters an ability to surrender completely. Total dependency during infancy, when the baby's body is given over completely to another's care, prepares us to trust physical merger with another in adulthood.

Couples reacting to original bonding wounds may experience a profound unconscious distrust that infiltrates sexual functioning to produce physical and psychological symptoms that appear on the surface to be unrelated to sexuality—skin rashes, asthma, heart palpitations, sleeping disorders. A person with early bonding wounds may have a terror of being "lost" in the sexual act; there is a fear that such intense closeness will somehow engulf, enslave, or cause disintegration. Early bonding wounds may even be the basis of obsessive sexual love. A person who lacks the formative experience of total and *safe* dependency may compulsively seek out intimacy in its most concrete form, yet be unable to sustain a relationship; or, alternatively, may withdraw from even the possibility of sexual intimacy.

Because wounds sustained during the bonding period become our earliest, most "primitive" record, problems during this time can result in extreme responses in adult relationships. There are those, like Kevin and Larry, who have a fear of sexuality; their response is almost phobic. They turn and run, figuratively speaking. An opposite response to sexuality—obsessive attachment—can also originate in our bonding imprint. In obsessive sexual love, one or both partners feels the other person to be a piece of himself or herself and cannot bear the feeling of fragmentation and loss. Clutching tightly, they hold on for dear life. The connection must be maintained because the contact makes them feel whole.

Both of these extreme responses—terror and obsession—are based on what was actually experienced during infancy. Some infants have a greater than normal need to cling to the parent. If the caretaking parent understands the need and is available for a time, development proceeds normally. Some babies find the world outside dangerous. War, riots, earthquakes, fires, or abuse may give a baby an accurate perception of danger. When early years teach that there is danger, any sign of abandonment or loss of love evokes terror.

If you are in a relationship with someone who seems inordinately possessive or jealous, you may be dealing with feelings emanating from your partner's insecure bonding experience. If you, too, feel a fear of separation from the one you love, then the two of you may form a "Siamese twinship." Such relationships can work if each of you recognizes and acknowledges the need openly, then works to find ways to reassure the other, reducing stress and anxiety. I have heard couples describe such a twinship. One patient said he felt "joined at the hip" with a woman he had married after a whirlwind courtship. Although they could barely get along much of the time, being apart from his partner caused him great agitation and he often lost himself in all-consuming thoughts of her. He fears the loss of her even more than the pain of the existing relationship.

When you and your partner are operating out of separate imprints, a different set of problems occurs. Perhaps you lost a parent, or experienced some other trauma as a very young child and carry the fear of premature separation with you as an adult. Meanwhile, your partner carries the seeds of boundary injuries from battling parents who were unaware of the damage they were inflicting on their child. If screaming fights were the order of the day for one of you, with retreat the only answer, and fear of abandonment is the way of being in the world for your partner, these differences will affect your relationship sexually and emotionally. The expectation of frequent sex may become the solution for the one who wants reassurance of love and may be a problem of undue intrusiveness and demandingness for the other. It may also be a sign of voracious unmet needs beneath the sexual quest and intense fears that lie below hasty retreat.

How to Tell If Your Lover Is Obsessed

You my be flattered when you meet someone who can't seem to get enough of you, who calls you three or more times a day from the day you meet. But it may also be a warning sign. You may meet someone who wants to be your friend, who sticks to you like glue, who looks for things you need, and cannot do enough for you. Be aware that such a person is getting something out of it, and it may be that you have come to represent something he or she wants and won't let go of.

Obsessive sexual love can trigger violent behavior because the obsessed person is "thrown back" to primitive infantile experiences of abandonment—experiences that create a mindless, wordless (preverbal) rage. Physical abuse becomes a dangerous possibility. The person's need to *hold on to the other, to fuse, and be joined physically*— thus temporarily creating an illusion of safe *emotional* merger—is so great that he or she has lost the ability to distinguish between mutuality of desire and the exertion of force to gain that end. When the deep inner core of the self has also been damaged by early boundary chaos, it may create a distorted image of who feels the desire and what message is perceived. When there is also anger and rageful reactions to early emotional pain, sexuality and aggression become confused, bringing about serious consequences.

A dangerous scenario, which is to be avoided if you find yourself anywhere in its vicinity, is the one portrayed in the movie *Fatal Attraction* (unlike the situation in the movie, it is men more often than women who are the obsessed partners in these dangerous liaisons). When serious wounds occurred during primary bonding experiences, the need for sexual dominance may remain quite concrete, sometimes culminating in criminal behavior. In *Fatal Attraction*, the obsessed woman's transition from beautiful seductress to rageful murderess, from Jekyll to Hyde, occurred rapidly, triggered by her lover's first refusal to do her bidding. The refusal signaled their separateness and shattered her illusion of being together. For her, the terror of separation was so great that only death could suppress it.

What can you do to avoid such situations? Build relationships slowly. Keep your distance from people who move in closer than is comfortable for you. You may meet someone who seems to be strong and to have the answer to every problem. Such people like to be in control. You may like the feeling of being taken care of. Some may use the assets they have—including money, talent, and access to resources you need—to become a "caretaker of all you desire." But be aware that unless you want someone to take over your life, this could be a dangerous relationship for you. Only willing participants need apply. This kind of relationship, permeated by obsessive love, demands, and sexuality that reflects an excessive need for control, is caused by distortions in the bonding imprint pattern. The unmet bonding needs, perhaps disguised by success and accomplishment, emerge quickly in the relationship and continue to exert destructive and abusive force. Without professional help, the person has no awareness of the cause, and tends to repeatedly blame the partner for problems that emerge.

If you are involved in such a relationship, get away or get help. Don't allow abuse. Join a support group, and *don't* let your lover talk you into going back. Failed attempts to get away reinforce the abusive behavior. Holding on tightly and heaping abuse upon the other reflect the deep need of a wounded child-victim now perpetuating the behavior. You cannot change your partner's behavior no matter how much you try, but you can grow out of the victim state by changing your own behavior.

When an Abuser Recognizes the Danger

Coming out of a twenty-year marriage, dating for the first time, Bill said that he was shocked by the new sexual liberation. Although he had had a number of affairs during his marriage, they were brief and involved little exploration. When he started dating Meg, who suggested "spicing" up their sex life with bondage, he found it quite exciting.

After several experiments, Bill found himself increasingly compelled to tie her up. One day he realized that he actually wanted to hurt her. He could sense the rage welling up, did not know where it came from, and felt very stimulated when he saw how truly frightened Meg became. "She realized I could really hurt her if I chose—and the scary part was that I wanted to more than I wanted to control myself. Suddenly, my mind took over and the spell broke," he said. "It scared the hell out of me." He untied her from the bedposts and "she got up and out of there so fast, I barely saw her go by."

Telling me this story, clearly with much shame, Bill recalled his own terrifying childhood experiences with violence and sexuality. "My father would come home drunk on a Saturday night and beat up my mother," he confided. "I used to see her as the victim and wanted to help her. But then I thought that she must really like the battles, because after he beat her up, they would go into the bedroom and have sex. The walls were thin in our house and I could hear them."

It never occurred to Bill that his father's behavior after the beating was, in fact, another way of abusing his mother. Nor did he realize that his mother's willingness to have sex after the fights was a way for her to survive. Instead, he confused the actions and lived with feelings of trauma, sexuality, and violence all intertwined.

In his own marriage Bill had vowed that he would not become violent like his father. He had denied all angry feelings for fear that any one of them might cause his rage to erupt. The result was an unemotional marriage that lacked vitality and honesty. When, after years of marriage, his anger finally exploded, as he feared, it destroyed the relationship.

In his new relationship Bill looked for safer ways to ventilate his anger. Most of the time he experienced Meg as loving and giving. But at times, her insistence that they do things her way, together with what he experienced as her "sexual demandingness," triggered his violent feelings. He directed much of his violence into eroticized fantasizes of dangerous sexuality. He found ways to enrage her, and once enraged, she would break off the relationship. After she had done so, he then seduced her back. Like his parents, he battled, lost, and then won. Sexually, he vindicated himself. But he was aware that each time the level of violence increased. "Am I turning into my father?" he asked.

Most relationships do not reach this level of behavior and survive. Change can occur if, with help, the damaging imprint pattern can be reexperienced in a healing way. Bill was worried enough about his behavior to seek help and he entered a therapeutic program that led to change. Using imagery, he allowed himself to visualize the experience with his girlfriend and then focus back on his memories of childhood violence. As emotions welled up, he had difficulty breathing, but instead of running from the feelings, he slowly breathed into the terror and rage that he said were encircling him.

Once he was able to "hold" the emotions with his body and his mind, he knew that this was something he had lived with for his whole life. He knew it "belonged" to him, and he was ready to reclaim this piece of himself that had mindlessly driven him. Despite the pain that he had experienced in the process, reowning the emotions that he had warded off for a lifetime made him feel free for the first time. The words he used to describe it were his way of adding a rational component to irrational emotions. "I feel a firebomb in my chest, ready to burst," he would say, describing his experiences while doing his imagery techniques. "I don't know where the destruction will end." Bill acknowledged the need to change. He feared what would happen if he didn't find a way to battle his inner demons.

Once Bill touched these painful and terrifying emotions, he continued using imagery in quiet times at home. He knew it was the chance for a change that would make a relationship with Meg possible. His work requires "holding" the emotions until the mind can moderate between impulse and action. If Meg wants the relationship, it means that she, too, must choose to risk what may happen as Bill undergoes the pain of feeling old wounds and works toward deep changes that endure. Both understand that violent behavior means the end of the relationship. Bill reconnected with old bonding failures, terrors that he felt deeply in the rage-filled battles between his parents. He learned to be conscious about the feelings in his body rather than simply expelling them when he found reasons to be angry at Meg.

Acting out violent impulses is always a choice. It is a quick release of aggression at the expense of another. Violence unchecked always escalates. Therefore, anyone in such a relationship must obtain the support to terminate what can too easily become dangerous. Knowing that he will lose the relationship if there is violent acting out is often the impetus a partner needs to maintain control. There *are* ways to transform the violent impulses, using alternative avenues of communicating the feelings. But, as Bill learned, it takes strong motivation and painful working through. It requires not only the conscious wish to change, but also the development of alternatives to acting out when the inner fires of violence dangerously intensify.

Emotional Attunement and Sexual Connection

The Imprint for Emotional Sharing can transmit sexual arousal from one person to another. It is not unusual for a man to experience in his penis a message that a woman with whom he is conversing is interested in him. Similarly, a woman may feel mild stirrings of arousal in her breasts and genitals when in the presence of an aroused male. The information is transmitted and received through modes of communication that we do not fully understand. The emotional contagion that operates through our Imprint for Emotional Sharing provides an alternative means of communicating at a level much deeper than words— and it is often at work in the sexual arena. One of the most joyful aspects of sexuality is the pleasure one gets from pleasuring another— the erotic stimulation we feel when experiencing a partner's heightening excitement.

A healthy experience of our Imprint for Emotional Sharing during childhood cultivates the ability to empathize with another's emotional responses, to attune to another's needs, pleasures, and fears, and to experience emotional responses as acceptable and safe. Decades later, these qualities contribute to fulfilling adult sexuality by furthering a deep flow of emotion between partners in which physical passion is intensified by emotional attunement, sensitivity, and responsiveness. Positive dependency flourishes in the trust that partners know and accept one another, and sexual expression becomes freer and more spontaneous.

Injury during the early developmental period of emotional sharing creates pervasive emotional distrust, as the child learns to deny or disguise his or her emotions in accordance with the parents' needs. The child learns to discard needs and desires that conflict with achieving the goal of parental approval.

The legacy of wounding in this second, relational imprint predisposes adult partners to use and be used emotionally—to project negative feelings to avoid unwanted sex, or to use sex in an attempt to gain a tenuous sense of emotional connection. If one partner can easily read the other's vulnerabilities, these signals can be used to achieve the upper hand in the sexual arena.

Stephanie was hurt by Charles saying in front of their friends that she is developing a "fat ass." She sat through dinner experiencing shame and feeling too fragmented to think clearly or come back with a retort. But she was enraged at Charles. When they got home, instead of telling him what was really bothering her, she told him that his breath smelled of garlic and he should use mouthwash before coming to bed. When he climbed in bed, she said he still smelled funny, maybe it wasn't the garlic. Charles said nothing, but Stephanie knew that she had hurt him. She created a physical distance because she was hurt and could not express it verbally.

When he approached her sexually, she responded, but with little enthusiasm. Sex between them has never been a problem, and he wondered if he really did have an odor. Somehow he felt turned off and was quite unaware that he was being punished for what he had said earlier. He just knew that he felt a sense of shame and that it was affecting his sexual desire. Each in their own manner had violated the emotional boundary between them in a way that was painful to both.

Sexual Bridges vs. Sexual Perversion

As discussed in chapter 5, the period during which we acquire transitional objects is the time when, as very young children, we learn to use *things* to substitute for people temporarily. The adult's legacy is an ability to connect to others indirectly, through shared activities, interests, political causes, cultural pursuits, and so on.

The Imprint for Bridging Connections also plays a role in sexual intimacy. Positive manifestations include the occasional use of *jointly chosen* "sex toys," movies, and videos to enhance lovemaking. Anything that you and your partner find mutually enhancing to your lovemaking is positive, so long as there is no risk to life and limb. However, whips, chains, and sadomasochistic equipment that can be both dangerous and degrading must be looked upon as perverse, more closely related to the acting out of hate than to the acting out of love.

It is neither uncommon nor necessarily unhealthy to have perverted fantasies during sex or masturbation. A true perversion, however, is a hostile fantasy that is *acted upon*. The acting out of hostility, according to psychoanalyst Robert Stoller, is the defining characteristic of perverted sexual behavior. Perversions, he writes, are the result of a dangerous interplay between hostility and sexual desire. In essence, perversion is the *sexualization of hate*. It includes being aroused by the act of doing something harmful or dangerous to another person. The underlying intent is to transfer intolerable emotions into *someone or something else*. Negative manifestations include the excessive use of alcohol and drugs, and also the *compulsive need* for sex toys on the part of one partner but not the other.[17]

If you are in a relationship with overtly perverse components, you must be aware of the underlying imprint. *You cannot change your partner*. If your partner does not believe a change is necessary, *you can make decisions only about what you do*.

In the following case, pornography was presented as the problem by the wife. As our work unfolded, however, it became clear that the husband was using pornography in retaliation against his wife's attempts to control him sexually and emotionally. In addition, we discovered that serious wounding in the wife's Imprint for Bridging Connections was contributing to their sexual stalemate.

Power Struggles

When Sally and Brice came for therapy, they had many issues. They argued about money, they argued about keeping alcohol in the house for entertaining (an alcoholic who has been sober for six years, she sees the storing of alcohol as an attempt to sabotage her), and they argued about whether her refusal to entertain guests in their home was a retaliation against him. But most of all, they argued about sex.

Sally was outraged at Brice's habit of watching pornographic movies on cable TV. If he wakes up at night and is unable to sleep, or when he is trying to relax after a workday, he likes to tune into one of the X-rated cable television channels. Sally considers this behavior immoral and personally insulting. Saying that it meant he was aroused by other women, she refused to have sex with him. After a month-long campaign to get him to stop, Brice promised "never" to watch the sex channel. Needless to say, he cheated. Sally found out and demanded that he remove the cable, which he refused to do. She again refused to have sex, accusing him of thinking of other women while they were making love. Soon after they had stopped all sexual activity, she began to suspect he was having affairs.

I asked Brice to tell his version of this story. He said that he knew he was addicted to watching pornographic movies, that it was a problem and he should stop, but that he deeply resented being told what he could and could not watch. "After all, I'm a fifty-year-old man!" he said. Clearly, there were all the elements of a power struggle.

Brice said he simply could not understand the depth of Sally's moral outrage. He tried to explain to her that it was "natural" for men to like pornography and that it didn't mean he was having affairs. "I don't understand why you *insist* on taking it so personally—as if my watching those movies were a *personal* rejection of you. It's not! It never has been."

I wondered if Sally would offer a response. "It's true! I do take it very personally," she said. "It makes me feel like I've failed you each time you turn on that damn channel. I know all about performing," she added with increasing vehemence. I wondered at her reference to performing.

"I learned to perform when I was a little girl," Sally continued. "My mother got me tap shoes and then enrolled me in a dance class. She went a little overboard. You would have thought I was a young Ginger Rogers in training. Whenever anyone visited, I was supposed to entertain them. She also got me into child modeling—department-store catalogs and everything. It was all so important to her. By the time I was a teenager, flirting and performing were second nature to me. When it came time to perform for my dates, I learned how to appear sexually aroused. But I reached the point where I hated to do all of those things. That's why I drank—I couldn't stand the phony person I had become. Somehow, those movies remind me of myself. I didn't take it that far obviously, but the emotional prostitution is the same."

Brice nodded his head slowly. "But you never told me why you feel the way you do—you just issued edicts and moral pronouncements. Part of the reason I started to watch the cable channel was to make a statement to you: *I'm an adult and I don't want you to tell me what I can and cannot do.* But when I hear you talk like this, it doesn't seem to have so much to do with control. I can see that it goes much deeper than that."

With Brice's growing ability to listen to her and understand, Sally made an effort to see his need to make decisions as a man. They explored together using the movies for their mutual sexual enhancement. Once she stopped opposing him, Brice no longer felt so compelled to watch pornography. When he did, she carefully withheld her judgment and contained her discomfort. Without the power struggle, their sex life improved. Their ongoing battle for power and control, waged in the bedroom, was finally put to rest once Sally began working on underlying wounds and Brice displayed a willingness to attune to her emotional needs.

Is It Independence or Defensive Distancing?

As we saw in chapter 6, wounds received during development in the Imprint for Mature Dependence leave children feeling prematurely separate and isolated, unable to depend on others in stressful times.

They learn, "I must take care of myself." There are few experiences of positive dependence and many failures in self-sufficiency.

If a child has a healthy period of individuation, he or she will acquire a sense of being a separate, autonomous person and, at the same time, feel part of a family of interconnected relationships. Such children, aware of other people's responses and emotions, are able to interact and cope without losing their own feelings about a situation. They can also allow themselves to be needy or vulnerable, knowing that they won't be punished. In short, they function at a high level of maturity while retaining free access to states of dependency.

In the arena of adult intimacy, this favorable experience of the Imprint for Mature Dependence translates into a willingness to engage in a mutual relationship, both emotionally and physically. There is little fear that a less-than-perfect performance sexually will result in shame, blame, or humiliation. There is a sense that the more one gives, the more one receives. There is also the freedom to let go totally into that oceanic sense of release and union without fear of losing oneself in the closeness.

In adults, distortions in the Imprint for Mature Dependence variously infiltrate all aspects of connections. Commitment and intimacy are viewed as threats to one's individuality; sex with prostitutes and one-night stands are therefore safer alternatives in that they allow avoidance of emotional entanglement. But many such people who are in relationships do not recognize that they are defensively distancing. They believe that they are simply protecting their autonomy and independence from encroachment by an overly dependent or intrusive partner. They do not necessarily want to avoid loving connections. They just fear what it might do to them to be close.

Defensive distancers put much of their emotional energy into regulating the distance between themselves and intimate others. "Don't come close—don't go away," is their underlying message. If you are with a defensive distancer, you may find that periods of warm, loving connection are followed by breaks in the relationship, followed in turn by urgent efforts to reconnect sexually. Many such people also have defects in earlier bonding and boundary imprints, and they never seem able to find comfortable fits. They also seem to gravitate to intimate relationships with others who have similar distance-regulation issues. Closeness and distance, love and hate, wounds and repair, are played out repeatedly in such relationships.

If you are with someone who appears to be a defensive distancer, there is something you can do to check it out. When you feel your partner pulling away, don't try to get closer. Don't ask what is wrong. Don't look for a problem between the two of you that you alone must fix. All these will push a distancer away. What you do instead is pull back. Become less available. Be able to stand alone and a distancer will need to get closer. Such a person seeks an optimum distance—just enough distance draws him or her closer, while being bombarded with efforts for greater closeness raises many of the old anxieties. There are two possible threats: "If I let myself depend on you, I will be smothered, or I will be abandoned and devastated by a separation." Reassurance that you will be there rarely works. It cannot be believed. It takes years of a safe relationship and often many "tests" to believe you will still be there, and determined distancers who select partners who unconsciously play out their "come close—stay away" pattern may never find a right fit.

The defensive distancer may have to look at the history of his or her relationships and ask how close he or she can be. Ask these questions:

Defensive Distancing

- How close were you with your parents?
- Who in your life have you trusted completely?
- What happened?
- Was the trust warranted?
- Have your adult sexual relationships been close or distant?
- Do you pull away or move toward your partner when he/she moves in closer?
- What do you use for an escape hatch?
- How often do you use it?

If you find that you use the idea of independence defensively, you need to slowly allow yourself to get closer to another, a loving friend, a brother or sister, a parent or a child. To make contact, write a letter expressing your feelings; open some conversations with the positive feelings that you have. Take responsibility for your part in keeping the relationship distant and bringing it closer.

If you try to do this with a recently acquired friend or lover, and you notice the other's response is discomfort or emotional distancing, be attuned to the needs and fears of that person and draw back. Remember, you are actually dealing not just with this relationship, but with images from old interactions with other people. Change requires a slow rebuilding, a facing of fears that are out of conscious awareness, an increasing ability to tolerate the discomfort of growing.

Good Sex and Willing Dependency

When sex is good between two people, it provides another way for them to find out about each other's needs, to expand the ability to acknowledge deeper needs, and an opportunity to learn how to fulfill these needs. The woman who is quiet and a little reserved may conceal more vibrant layers that have yet to surface. The partner whom she trusts enough to reveal herself offers the opportunity to help her experience her whole self.

If early experiences were favorable or if old wounds have healed through understanding, it is safe to allow both physical and psychic immersion. Sexuality not tinged with danger frees lovers to descend to the whirlpool of orgasmic release, knowing that they can reemerge safely, contented and together. Couples who achieve this degree of mutual love and trust relate to each other sexually from a perspective of willing dependency. They are interested in pleasing each other, knowing that the giving of pleasure will be reciprocated. They know that the more they give, the more they get. The attention they give each other comes from a place of plenty rather than from a place of deprivation and desperation.

Sexuality can be a battleground for unresolved needs or an arena for mending old wounds. If you find yourself in a relationship where needs are the same or complementary, you will begin to feel fulfilled in a special, mutual way. But when your needs and defenses conflict, you must add a thinking component to your emotions and find new ways of communicating that can increase closeness instead of distance in your relationship. The next two chapters will suggest some further ways to connect to some of your earliest core needs, to look back at wounds that need healing and forward to the ability to depend on one another. This is what leads to the development of an enduring collaborative intimacy.

8 Advise and Dissent: Unconscious Messages in Everyday Life

The feelings I don't have, I don't have.
The feelings I don't have, I won't say I have.
The feelings you say you have, you don't have.
The feelings you would like us both to have,
we neither of us have.
The feelings people ought to have, they never have.
If people say they've got feelings,
you may be pretty sure they haven't got them.
So if you want either of us to feel anything at all,
You'd better abandon all idea of feeling altogether.

—D. H. Lawrence

Rule #8 for Positive Dependency:

Validate your partner's feelings and actions often. Notice his or her positive qualities as if using a magnifying mirror. Comment on what you like. Be free with your compliments. Use selective inattention for the negative qualities. Your partner will think that you are wonderfully perceptive.

Partners can give each other messages that appear to be clear, sensible, and logical, but contain contradictory, convoluted meanings—messages that both conceal and reveal underlying feelings. The context of a message includes not only the literal communication occurring in the present, but sometimes the contents of each partner's imprints.

Matt and I recently had the kind of disconnecting dialogue that so many couples experience. I thought of how I responded and his reaction and realized how easy it is to fall into dysfunctional patterns.

Matt's father, who is ninety-one years old, lives with his wife of fifteen years in Palm Springs, two hours away from us. He has recently taken to calling us a great deal and chiding Matt for not visiting more often. Matt, who retired two years ago, has immersed himself in his new endeavor, the education of our well elders. He is never bored. In fact, he never has enough time to do all he wants.

When he told me last night about his father's complaints, I felt protective of Matt's time. "Why are we the only ones responsible? Where is your sister?" I asked with some annoyance.

"But he is old and his wife is deteriorating. He wants to talk about a convalescent home and he needs to complain to me that I ought to visit him more," Matt said.

"But you can't. You've done a lot more than most children. You support him financially. We take them out to dinner when we are in Palm Springs. What does he want from you—from us?"

"But he's old. And my sister is mad at him and never visits. Like it or not, I'm all he's got."

"Well, I'm mad at him also. No matter how much you give, he wants more. Why don't you tell him we cannot go down to Palm Springs any more than we have been?"

"I thought you liked my dad," Matt said, surprised.

"I think he wants too much from you."

"Actually, I feel guilty for not doing enough."

"Well, you shouldn't," I commented as Matt walked out of the room.

I'm just trying to protect Matt against so many demands, I thought, reassuring myself that what I did was in my husband's best interest.

The next day Matt said, "When I told you about my dad complaining that I wasn't doing enough for him, all I wanted was for you to say, 'I know how hard this is for you.' There's not much we can do about how bad he feels, so I just listen—and I wanted you to just listen and not make it any harder on me."

Of course. As soon as he gave me that message, I knew he was right, and I acknowledged it. Had he not said it, a bit of resentment would have remained. We might forget the conversation and go on. Many people don't notice these injuries or think they are unimportant. But the next time I misread and was unresponsive to his feelings, another bit of resentment would have been added. In time the small pile would turn into a mountain, or perhaps a volcano that could erupt over one small misunderstanding.

When I work with couples, the mountain of miscommunication is piled high and we must dig our way down to understand where the small failures on the part of each were stored away and acted upon to form a destructive force undermining the relationship. At times one remark causes an explosion, but later neither can understand why they were arguing so vehemently.

Although words provide a vehicle to convey our experiences and to communicate with one another, language also brings problems. Words make it possible to decide which aspects of our inner experience to make public and which to keep private. Sometimes our words say one thing, while our body says another. Either our words hide what we feel, or the mismatch between the language of words and the language of the body results in a conflicting double message.

There is a persistent myth that if we simply "think clearly," we will express ourselves clearly. Unfortunately, well-decoded thoughts are a rare commodity. Communication between human beings is never simple, because we do not live at just one level. The subtle communication of relationships embraces both conscious and unconscious messages.

"I didn't mean for us to get into that argument," said Sondra. "It's just that you seemed so distant and I wanted to talk about it so we could resolve whatever was wrong and get closer again." So she said what she thought would get his attention. It did, but not in the way that she wanted. They both ended up screaming at each other.

Couples do not start relationships intending to wound each other. It is the lack of knowing how to help your partner by recognizing and responding to underlying needs that so easily begins a cycle of problems. To begin understanding, we must dig down beneath the mountain of misunderstanding. At times your partner may depend on you only to listen and respond in ways that are healing rather than destructive.

Imprint Literacy

Thoughts, emotions, sensations, and old wounds from our imprints infiltrate the messages we send to each other. Traces of each developmental stage can distort what we perceive as well as what we communicate. We usually attempt to communicate as if we are "rational adults" capable of maintaining an objective distance from our emotions. What we are really feeling may be simmering beneath the surface, often communicated nonverbally, according to the plans encoded in an earlier imprint.

Partners need to develop what I call "imprint literacy," the ability to perceive and understand how each other's history shapes their mutual communication. They learn to decode the deep messages that pass between them, the ones that originate in their imprints and often emerge in disguised form. Keeping a clear channel of communication requires awareness that the other may mean a lot more then he or she actually says in words.

To decode a partner's messages is sometimes a difficult task. For one thing, the four imprints contain different "languages" that, like the developmental experiences themselves, accompany us into adulthood. For another, there is always the possibility of contaminating what we hear with elements of our own deepest wounds. It is a tricky business, listening with empathic emotion and at the same time keeping the response free of one's own hidden pain. All partners can do is to pay attention, knowing that eventually they each will send "cleverly disguised" messages that originate in early imprints. The problem is compounded because messages can be coming from more than one level. Almost any exchange of words on an adult level can contain within it not only messages about deep emotions, but also the context of parental messages that originally triggered the emotional response.

During the early experience when our Imprint for Bonding was generated, primary emotions were our only means of communicating; these responses are inborn, part of our biological heritage. When needs were unmet, it caused intense emotional reactions, incorporated as sense memories that reemerge when later experiences are reminiscent of the preverbal emotional state. When these reactions erupt in adults

The Meaning Behind the Message

Imprint	Adult Words to Partner	Internalized Parental Message About Self	Wounded Self-concept	Healing Words From Partner
Primary Bonding	"You never tell me you love me anymore."	You are too demanding, and I need a rest from you. Don't bother me.	I'm not lovable. I'm too needy.	Words are not necessary—a hug, a hand held out, an emotional communication is desired.
Emotional Sharing	"I get very upset when you are so moody and distant."	You are responsible for my moods. Make me feel better or I won't be available to meet your needs.	Your needs are more important than mine. It hurts me to be so unimportant.	"You read me right. It's because I'm worried about things at work. It's not your problem and you don't have to fix it."
Bridging Connections	"You seem to always be too busy lately. I need to find something to do for myself."	I'm busy now, but I'll be back soon. You can entertain yourself.	I'm alone and frightened. What can I find that will make me feel safe?	"That's a terrific idea. Tell me more about what you'd like to do."
Mature Dependence	"Just listen to me and don't tell me how to solve my problem."	You must do it my way or I will be upset with you.	I feel so inadequate when you tell me what to do.	"I see your point of view, and I'm here to listen if you need me to."

in times of deep stress, they are experienced as unspeakable pain, nameless fear, or rage beyond words.

By the time we develop the Imprint for Emotional Sharing, we are able to experience and express a myriad of *feelings* that arise as part of interacting with important people in our lives.

With our Imprint for Bridging Connections, increasing facility with words and symbols helps us to connect, disconnect, shape, defend, and define ourselves in the temporary absence of others.

Culminating in our Imprint for Mature Dependence is the ability to articulate *our version* of what we experience—*narrations* that contain our interpretations of events in relation to the other. These narrations are our attempts to tell our side of the story, explain our position, justify our responses. More often than not, they are laden with a dizzying array of mixed messages that trigger the battles between parents and children and later, between partners.

In *Parallel Lives: The Story of Five Victorian Marriages,* Phyllis Rose describes marriage as a kind of subjective fiction with two points of view, often deeply in conflict. When the narrations of the partners fit together well, the relationship has strong ties. When differing versions of reality struggle to coexist, we find bewildering, painful patterns of interaction.

When couples fight, they do not usually express their core needs to each other. Most often, they simply hurl complaints, accusations, and mixed messages that camouflage underlying pain and fear. The problems of communication escalate geometrically as each partner's expression of deep wounds rises to drown out the other's.

When couples listen effectively, they learn to sort. out the hidden messages from the way they are presented. In addition, effective communication requires a recognition of how to address the deep needs being communicated. The healing words that truly respond to the deep wound in the other must often address the underlying need not being verbalized.

Exercising the Muscles of Positive Dependency

Now that you have learned about positive dependency and some of the rules that can change the way you think about your relationship, I would like to suggest an exercise that will stretch your ability to change the dynamics of your relationships.

Most people who decide to change their relationship believe that both partners must be motivated and mutually agree to do things differently. And I agree that this is the best way. But it is not the only way. Nothing happens in a vacuum. Any change will have repercussions. If you begin to see things differently and respond with minor changes, then the people around you must deal with a new set of facts.

What follows are affirmations based on the Rules for Positive Dependency. Write one affirmation on each of twenty three-by-five index cards. Take one of the affirmation cards out each day and carry it with you. If your partner and you decide to do this exercise together, each of you can select one of the cards to give to the other to carry for the day. You do not need to do anything but look at the card two or three times during the day. Do not demand of each other any change of behavior. It is a "game" that you cannot lose. You may be surprised by the results.

Affirmations for Positive Dependency

- I will remember that you need love as much as I do. I will give signs of love generously with praise, compliments, hugs, gifts, passion, prayer.
- There are things I will never say to you because I know it would hurt you.
- When the truth includes words of love, I will speak freely.
- I will look for ways to enhance your self-esteem.
- I will recognize your need to be heard and do my best to listen.
- I will try to understand the underlying messages conveyed by your words.
- When we argue about money, family, or sex, I will consider the

underlying dependency issues of each of us rather than look to blame.

- I will strive to recognize the imprints for relationships that you carry from childhood and take care to avoid areas where you have been wounded.
- I will express the needs I consider to be essential to you and not expect you to read my mind.
- I understand that you cannot meet all my needs perfectly.
- When you cannot meet my needs, I will find alternatives that will not damage the relationship.
- I will carefully consider whether the gifts I choose to give are the gifts you truly want.
- If I need to register a criticism or complaint, I will make sure I do it in private and in a way that will not shame you.
- I will choose my battles carefully, evaluating which issues are so important to me that they are not negotiable.
- I will support you in the pursuit of your interests and will encourage your curiosity and zeal for life.
- I will respond your desires sexually as I wish you to respond to mine.
- I will remind myself to magnify your positive qualities and use selective inattention for your negative ones.
- I will work at being the right partner for you.
- I will commit to working on this relationship.
- I will be generous with forgiveness.

The Language of Hurt, Need, and Dependency

Scott and Rhea, the couple we met in chapter 6 who were "perfect" in the early years of their marriage but were now very unhappy, tried hard to resolve their marital problems. Although they had made progress, they were still having difficulties. Scott raised the possibility of a separation to break the impasse. I said that I could understand how separating might facilitate a nonhostile divorce, but I could not think of how a separation could possibly improve their marital relationship.

Rhea felt as though she were living under a constant barrage of

Scott's ideas for improving upon whatever task she was doing, from the right way to put the bacon in the refrigerator to the need to properly manage the house. "You suggested that I tell him to stop criticizing me," she said to me, "but when I do, he gets angry and sulks. Now he starts to talk about a separation, so I'm afraid to assert myself. The message I get is, 'It's best to keep quiet and withdraw.'"

"How do you feel, Scott, when Rhea says this?" I asked.

"I'm used to it," he replied. "Rhea always sees me as too critical and she always withdraws from me. I know what she is talking about, and I do try to say nothing to her that is critical. Things seem fine for a few days. Then we come here to therapy and I get a report card. 'He was good on Thursday, Friday, and Saturday, but Sunday he got upset.' Well, I do get upset sometimes. I grumble a bit, but I feel judged constantly by Rhea, and I hate it."

"So do I," Rhea retorted with more strength than usual. "I can't tolerate the way you hurt me when you're upset. Your stinging criticisms are not something any wife should have to tolerate."

"So you go for several days with everything calm, and then Scott begins to pick on you again," I commented.

"That's right," Rhea said, "and when he's nice, I try to forget how bad things can be. I open up and try to be warm and friendly. Then when I'm open to him, he does it again. It hurts me too much. I can't depend on him to make any lasting change in this area."

I was beginning to get a clue about what might be going on at a deeper level. The next time we had a chance to talk about it, Scott and Rhea had just come back from a vacation. They had picked up their son and one of his friends from camp and had driven them home. "We had a nice time the first week together," Rhea explained. "There were no problems and I was letting myself get close to Scott." Scott agreed that the first week had gone well until the drive home.

"What happened?" I asked.

"I was feeling much closer to Scott," Rhea replied. "I reached over to touch him in the car. He hardly responded and even seemed to get upset."

"She's right," Scott added. "I don't know why, but I didn't feel comfortable with the kids in the back."

"I just reached out for your hand—I wasn't going to seduce you! So it was happening again. I was opening up and Scott pushed me away. So I withdrew."

Scott looked perplexed as we were reviewing this incident. "I wonder about something, Scott," I said. "I'm going to make a guess now, and if I'm wrong, tell me. You complain that Rhea puts up a wall to keep you distant. You say you need more signs of affection and closeness, as you had in the first years of your marriage. But whenever Rhea reaches out to you, when she lets down her guard, you do something to push her away. Is it possible that as much as you want her love, you are afraid of needing it, of becoming dependent on Rhea?"

"I was just thinking that, too," Scott said, smiling slightly.

"Maybe you always wanted to have a relationship where you're not expected to perform and accomplish things—where you're just accepted as you are," I said to Scott. "And if you get a little bit of it . . ."

"Then I want a lot more," he completed the thought.

"What if you want so much from her that you know you'll be disappointed? What if your need feels bottomless?"

"You think I'm pushing away Rhea so I won't be disappointed?"

"Perhaps," I agreed.

Scott shows his well-defined outer face to the world. He is the picture of male power and success, and he remains so even as he willingly peels away the layers to reach his needs and wounds. Allowing the thought that he may be much more dependent than a man has a right to be was somewhat frightening to Scott. But he wasn't forced to confront it prematurely. He was ready to hear the news from deep within. We could now discuss the interactions between them in a new light, using a new vocabulary of words such as *imprints* and *positive dependency.*

In our sessions together, we could now begin to talk about the language of love, neediness, fear, anger, and dependency. By reclaiming his anger and feeling the intensity of the underlying unfulfilled dependency needs, Scott can begin to make choices to stop re-creating his childhood emotions in his current relationship. Meanwhile, Rhea can empathize with Scott's deeper needs and stop blaming herself for triggering his anger. Now, at last, they may have a chance to begin working on recapturing the intimacy they had at the beginning.

Mixed Messages

There are no shortcuts to expressing and understanding our core needs; reaching them takes time and patience. To begin, *listen to the outermost layers of expression*—to the mixed messages in each other's conversations. That is how to gather clues to deeper meanings. Eventually, given patience and a willingness to attune to each other, you can *learn how to accept and not judge your partner's deeper emotions.*

The ultimate goal is to *learn how to identify each other's feelings when they emerge,* even though they are in a disguised form. Be aware that anger is often a camouflage emotion to shield against fear, hurt, and shame. *Feeling understood by another helps us to recognize the reactivation of old wounds,* interrupting the cycle of injury and defense. This is an important function that partners can serve for each other, and *it is one of the hallmarks of positive dependency.*

Sometimes it is as hard to listen to a partner's underlying feelings as it is to express our own deep feelings. We have become so confused about what we are supposed to feel that our true emotions are lost in a haze of cultural edicts.

Today, when asked what is wrong with our intimate relationships, men commonly respond, "Women!" Likewise, many women respond, "Men!" We hear that women are too emotional, too changeable, and love in a smothering way. Men won't grow up, won't commit, and don't know how to love. Meanwhile, contemporary redefinitions of each gender brush up against the old expectations they are supposed to replace. Now, men must be sensitive *and* strong; women must be capable of taking care of themselves and maintaining close connections. And while nobody knows when to display which qualities, everyone seems sure about their right to demand them from their partners. We learn (we think!) how to send clear messages, to be in touch with our needs, to say what we expect from another, and then we cannot understand why there is no one available to give us what we need. That is because our needs and logic are in collision and our cultural expectations are filled with confusion.

Both men and women are the victims of a confusing deluge of mixed messages:

- Be self-sufficient . . . but be near me.

- Know me completely . . . but don't intrude.

- Be sensitive . . . but don't get emotional.

- Be strong . . . but be vulnerable.

- Think for yourself . . . but think as I do.

- Look out for yourself . . . but give to me.

- Open your boundaries to let me in . . . but don't swallow me up.

- Don't come too close . . . but don't go away.

- Be with me . . . but don't ask much of me.

I have counseled countless women in therapy who describe what they want in the man they will marry, and it is a tall order indeed. For a man to be successful with a woman, he must be aggressive, ambitious, and financially successful, just as under the old rules. He must also be a tender parent, a supportive spouse, a good friend, and a gentle but ardent lover.

Our popular magazines provide a detailed description of the perfect mate for that idealized man. The now famous "superwoman" is slender, attractive, well-dressed, and well-groomed. She has the kind of stimulating career that makes good dinner-table conversation. A sexual dynamo at night, a caring mother during the day, she draws from an endless supply of intellectual and physical energy. These impossibly idealized portraits are fraught with conflicting expectations.

Many couples who come for therapy today express the conflicting pressures that come from floating in this "soup" of mixed messages. We can reverse the process to some extent by starting with these mixed messages and seeing where they come from—which core needs are peeking up beneath the surface. In the following case one partner communicates desires that exceed the abilities of the other to meet and is chided for being overly dependent. Neither partner recognizes that dependency needs are normal in times of stress, and the apparently independent partner does not recognize that he, in fact, has many dependency needs.

Don't Come Close; Don't Go Away

Alan and Ginger have been seeing each other for five years, but still live separately. Ginger wants more permanence—if not marriage, at least shared living quarters. Yet she keeps talking about her ability to be independent. Alan is adamant about maintaining separate residences. He says he wants an intimate relationship, but doesn't seem clear about what this entails. During our first session, each became a spokesperson for one aspect of this dilemma. They began by describing their disagreement about whether to marry, live together, or continue as a couple while maintaining separate homes. Their push-pull pattern was a classic one, and one that illustrates well how distortions in the imprint can affect a relationship.

As soon as Ginger pushed for more closeness, Alan pulled away. When she broke off their relationship in reaction, realizing that their expectations were too different and her needs were not being met, Alan fought for a new togetherness. At those times, he sent her flowers and candy and gave her all the words of love that she had been missing.

> ***Mixed Message:*** "Don't come close . . . but don't go away."
> *Alan's wish for secure attachment conflicts with his fear of being so needy.*

"It felt so good to know how much Alan needed me," Ginger said. "I felt loved, so I came right back—and then, it began all over again!"

Once they had reestablished their relationship, Alan reverted to his earlier demand for increased separateness. They could not live together and they could not live apart. Two years later, Ginger was again ready to leave the relationship when Alan suggested that they try therapy.

When I asked about the current situation, Ginger reported that she spent the night at his house two or three times a week and that he came to her house another two nights. But certain nights he refused to see her. "He needs his own time, he tells me. But he throws a fit if I go out of town on business or to visit a friend. He just moved into a new house, but he wouldn't let me help with the move. I can't get close and I can't go away. I just don't know if it will ever feel okay to live this way."

Alan seemed confused by Ginger's discontent. He wondered if there was something wrong with her—then added nonchalantly, "Or perhaps it's me." Alan spent the first session clarifying his need to have separate space and lots of freedom in a relationship he could depend upon.

Mixed Message: "Be self-sufficient . . . but be near me." *Ginger and Alan profess that they are quite able to function independently of each other. And, in fact, they are both capable, accomplished people. Yet at a deeper level, they easily fall into the needy, dependent emotions of unfulfilled bonding. As long as they can maintain the fantasy that the other is there in a loving, nurturing way, the relationship continues. As soon as either feels deprived, however, the balance shifts and the relationship must be renegotiated.*

Many accusations and anecdotes surfaced as each partner defended a position. When they first considered living together, Alan reported, Ginger had gone on a business trip. He had asked her not to go; her trip coincided with an important event for him and he wanted her to be there. Ginger decided not to cancel her business trip. Upon returning, she learned that Alan had been involved sexually with another woman. She insisted on knowing with whom. Alan refused to tell her, adding that Ginger knew that he had had a very active sex life for the fifteen years before they met. He told her that she didn't have the right to know. He was willing to be monogamous if they decided to have a "committed relationship," he explained, but he wanted to be sure that she would not pry or demand more than what was tolerable for him.

As if in defense, to explain his distancing, Alan reported that Ginger had looked at his unopened mail, which enraged him.

"But I didn't open any of the letters," she protested.

"They were addressed to me—even if they are bills, I want my privacy!"

> ***Mixed Message:*** "Know me completely . . . but don't intrude." *One of the most important skills is the ability to attune emotionally to the inner world of another. Some people assume that "if you loved me, you would know what I feel and what I want." This presumption of mind reading as an aspect of love conflicts with a fear of being intruded upon. For people like Alan, a secret life provides safety against emotional invasion and engulfment. Ginger wished to know Alan, to have a closer relationship, to help him decorate his house, ultimately to live together and share a life together. Alan seemed to wish for the same only at times when Ginger pulled away and broke off the relationship. At other times he kept up the barriers.*

Alan described Ginger's tendency to "swallow him up" and "become intrusive," adding that a counselor whom he had seen had supported his decision to live separately and not move toward marriage until he was fully prepared. "I was married once before," Alan remarked, "and it was devastating when it ended. I managed my work and my life so that even my closest friends didn't know how horrible I felt—all alone, living in a hotel. I felt like I was coming apart inside. It's hard to talk about it even now, so there's no way that I would marry again unless I was sure it would be forever. And we have too many problems at this point to think about *forever.*"

Now it was Ginger's turn to be baffled by Alan's reaction: "We get along so well when we are together. Our only fights are about this one issue. I'm not asking to get married right now, just to be allowed to get closer when we *are* together." Turning to me, she said, "When I come over to his house and he is working, he hardly even says hello. I'm busy with my own career, but I need more than this."

As she talked, tears came to her eyes. Alan looked disgusted. "When I try to talk to him about it," she said, "I get upset, and then he won't talk at all. I'm supposed to be sensitive to his needs, but he only gets angry when I express my needs! If I cry, he gets angry at me . . . like now."

Mixed Message: "Be sensitive . . . but don't get emotional."
Many people fear the emotions that are part of our early de-
pendency needs. Reexperiencing primary emotions is in con-
flict with a society obsessed with strength and independence.
Although Ginger is identified as the emotional one, Alan de-
scribes such overwhelming emotions that he would rather stay
holed up in a hotel than let even his close friends see his pain.
Relating through the Emotional Sharing Imprints, *Alan projects*
his painful feelings onto Ginger, then demands that she stop
feeling them—identifying his hurt with hers.

"It's not your tears that upset me so much as the feeling that your
needs are bottomless," Alan responded. Ginger acknowledged that she
needs a lot of reassurance that she is loved. "I don't know if I can love
you as much as you need me to," Alan replied.

"But the times when I broke up with you, it was *you* who began
calling and sending flowers. The moment I'm ready to end this relationship, that's when you give me all the assurance I need and want.
Then I come back and it starts all over again."

"I know. I don't understand it myself."

Alan defensively noted that Ginger's priorities seemed to revolve
around the relationship, but his priorities are developing his career and
maintaining his individuality. "I become preoccupied when I'm working, and since I work at home, even if Ginger is there, I may not want
to talk." He wants her company, but fears her intrusion into his private
space. *(Be with me . . . but don't ask too much of me.)*

Ginger reasserted that she also has a busy career, but she does not
understand the purpose of the relationship if she comes over in the
evening and they do not interact. "It's about being together when it
feels good, and doing our own thing when we want to," Alan responded with confidence.

"But my needs are not getting met," Ginger commented sadly, "and
everyone in my support group says that if you don't love me enough
to commit to at least living together, it is time to end this relationship."

As I listened to each partner's version of reality, I reflected on how
they not only lived in separate houses, but in different worlds. I wondered why they chose to continue their relationship and what they

expected of therapy. Both were clearly convinced of their positions. Ginger attributed Alan's behavior to "commitment phobia." He saw her problem as excessive neediness, leading to unreasonable demands for constant attention. She required that he behave as she expected rather than allowing him just to be himself. He insisted that she be strong and not fall prey to her need for attention. Beneath these common complaints were far deeper issues forged out of the life experiences of both partners.

Ginger acknowledged that her desire for connection was "greater than average," and she related this need to her experience of growing up in a family in which she never felt sure of love from either parent. Her father, a successful writer, had a host of female admirers who arranged to see him whenever he was on his book tours. Her mother became increasingly dysfunctional as she hid through drinking and gambling from the pain of her husband's infidelities. As a response to her parents' absenteeism, Ginger learned to function on her own at an early age. Now, as an adult, she has achieved great success and to all the world appears quite independent. In fact, she could live very well without Alan and is aware of it at times. But beneath her persona as a successful writer, her imprints for bonding and sharing, as played out with Alan, are those of a needy, dependent child feeling unworthy of receiving the love she craves.

Alan chose independence for another reason. It was not to get the love of his parents, but to keep from being "swallowed up" by their unbounded demands. They needed children who were well-behaved—indeed, who acted as perfect clones of their values and ideals, representatives to the community of their perfect standards.

Alan's parents expected and rewarded the close, clinging behavior of their two sons. As Alan was the younger child, there was an unspoken expectation that he would follow in his father's footsteps as a minister. Alan resisted in the only ways he knew. Often, he chose to retreat to the privacy of his room to read, write, draw, or just avoid the demands of his family. He had difficulty in his Imprint for Mature Dependence because dependence was not safe for him; it was engulfing, stifling, and he had to fight to become his own person.

Alan carried his hard-won autonomy into his adult relationships, but it backfired. Accusing him of being emotionally unavailable, his wife, whom he loved, left him. When his current relationship is threatened, he fights to keep it intact. But when Ginger is present, wanting to connect, he becomes defensively distant.

Together and separately, Ginger and Alan are constantly pulled in opposing directions by the mixed messages of closeness *(I need to be close)* and distance *(I need to be separate)* that shield their core needs, rarely finding a workable balance in their relationship. If they are to find a resolution, both will have to be willing to reach and tolerate the deeper needs that are central to each. They can begin by listening to one another's *narrations*.

Narrations

Because most of us were raised by very human, and therefore imperfect, parents, our core human need for love and affirmation is covered by layers and layers of defenses that emerged in response to a variety of childhood assaults and disappointments. We have developed a series of accounts of our experiences that present us in a light we perceive as acceptable and can protect us from our feelings. With the development of language skills, a child gains the ability to express these accounts in words as *narrations*.

When parents punish emotions and feelings, either overtly or through withdrawal of love, it ruptures the direct connection between the child's internal response and the experience that generated that response. A terror of school that is minimized or scorned by a parent must become something else that *is* acceptable. Perhaps the terror is converted into a physical symptom to which the parent *will* respond. The raw terror is now called an illness or an allergy, and in the process, the child has learned to explain emotional responses in a distorted way.

As adults, we all spend a lot of time "explaining" our emotions and the events of our lives in rational terms. We believe in our narrations and often have trouble accepting another person's version of events. Narrations are typically filled with mixed messages and serve as "fronts" for buried wounds. Because narrations were specifically designed to obscure our feelings from ourselves, they are tailor-made to transmit the distortions carried in our imprints. For a couple, genuine communication is largely a process of learning to see beyond narrations to their source and recognize distorted areas of their own and each other's imprints.

Doug's Cat: Choosing Your Battles

Most of the time when we talk to a loved one, we are communicating many different truths, and from any one or a combination of imprints. That is why it is essential to learn to listen for meaning beneath the words to reach deep feelings in your mate. There is the possibility that this deep sharing will transform both partners.

Marcia called for couples therapy. On the phone she quickly described her problem: "I am allergic to cats, but Doug keeps dragging his feet on solving the problem. He is so worried about finding a good home for the cat that the cat is still in our house. When I told him that the doctor said both our son and I are allergic, Doug asked me to get another medical opinion.

"It seems that the cat is more important to him than I am. If that is true, even if he is very good in other ways, I don't see how I can depend on this relationship."

I suggested a meeting with Doug because I wanted to learn his version of this story. When he came in, he spoke of his disappointment with the marriage. "In the time since we married four years ago, Marcia has controlled everything— where we live, who our friends are, where we vacation. When we were first married, we both had furniture. I gave up mine. We used hers. I also had this cat. She never liked it. I told her that the cat was important to me. He is nine years old, and I am very attached to him. She *never* liked the cat, so when she suddenly develops an allergy, I feel suspicious.

"If I have to get rid of the cat, I will. I've been looking for a new home for him, but it has taken some time to get the right home. I think I found someone interested who will take him in, but it's not soon enough for Marcia."

"You sound resentful," I said.

"I feel that I have given a lot to Marcia and I don't feel that she considers what I need. She always has to be right; and whatever it is, we do it her way."

"So the cat was a place where you took a stand. Then, because of her allergy to the cat, her needs take precedence again."

"That's right."

"Are there ways that she takes care of you?"

Doug went on to describe what a good homemaker and terrific mother Marcia is. "She does all of this, has her own career, and manages our social schedule and all of our vacations—and she is doing all of the legwork in getting us a new home."

"So there are a lot of things that are positive ways in which you depend on her."

"Sure, as long as we do it her way."

"How do you resolve it when you want different things?"

"Well, most things aren't that important to me. She plans it and does it, and it's usually okay with me."

"What about the things that are important to you?"

"Well, there's the cat, and the house. I want to move to a larger house, but she says it has to be in exactly the same neighborhood that we live. There are no houses that we want in exactly the same neighborhood. I said to her, 'Let's move a little further east.' She won't do that.

"Then there was the issue of where we would travel for our vacation. I told her clearly where I wanted to go. She explained why the babysitting arrangements wouldn't be good there and we went where she wanted. But where we vacation is least important to me; it was just one more thing building up."

So what at first seemed to be an inconsiderate man, unconcerned with the health of his wife, turned out to be a man (from his point of view) who was increasingly becoming angry with his wife's indifference to his feelings. She seemed to be making decisions based solely upon what was good for her, and not what she knew would meet his needs and wishes.

When Marcia and I met, we talked about how people look to each other to understand and respond to important needs. Marcia believed that she did a lot to take care of Doug. But she also felt that Doug did not understand some things about why she made decisions as she did. "Usually when we disagree, as with the location of the house, it turns out I am right. The children are very close to their school here. If we moved, they would have to change schools or be car-pooled across town." She went on to describe other instances where logic dictated that they do things the way she suggested. Usually Doug ended up agreeing with her. Even with the cat, she felt she was right. If she is allergic, logic says that they must get rid of the cat.

The problem with this couple is beyond logic. At a deep level, they are each feeling the failure of positive dependency. Each feels the other is ignoring important needs, Doug's love for his cat, Marcia's allergic reaction, and hurt and resentment are building up.

We all have issues that should be easy to solve, but somehow become insurmountable problems as Doug and Marcia learned in their on-going fight for control.

What makes people willing to respond to each other?

Positive dependency does not live in the same neighborhood as the fight for control. Being right is not the only issue. How important an issue is to you should be a deciding factor. If everything is of equally high importance, you are not talking about the specific issues. You are in a battle for control.

There are things you can do to move away from the battle. To begin, ask yourself these questions:

- On a scale of one to ten, how important is this issue to you?
- How important do you believe it is to your partner?
- Do you know a way to check this out with your partner?
- How upset will you be if you don't get your way in this?
- What is the upset about?
- Is it worth testing the relationship over this issue?

If the issue is one of your primary objectives, you must take a stand on it. If not, some other relationship problem may be involved, e.g., control, trust, fear, unresponded need. Deal with the underlying concern and the day-to-day issues will be resolved more easily. If you battle over everything, nothing gets resolved. Choose your issues carefully. Pay attention to the imprints.

Primary Emotions

We enter life "prewired" to experience and express terror, fury, joy, disgust, curiosity, and aggression. These are felt simply as strong sensations that occur reflexively in response to events. To the baby, the feeling and the experience are the same, and rationality plays no role in either. The baby does not, for example, differentiate the discomfort of colic from the crying that accompanies it. An infant does not know intellectually what hurts and what feels good, but an infant does know instinctively when he or she is cold, hungry, happy, or getting jabbed by a long fingernail. For a period of time, primary emotional reactions are the baby's only mode of communicating directly with the external world. A mother attuned to her baby understands these emotional messages and responds accordingly.

Sometimes the pain of adulthood is as urgent and compelling as the pain of a baby with colic. When an adult has a primary emotional response, one of the prewired reactions, the response and its stimulus, are nearly the same, just as for a young infant. Terror and the need to cry out are not thought through—the reaction simply occurs. This also applies to "irrational" feelings—such as Mary's fear of abandonment mentioned in chapter 3. Properly speaking, it makes little sense to speak of such experiences as either "rational" or "irrational," but rather as reactions to inner "baby feelings." Intense fear of abandonment results in an instant fight-or-flight response; consequently, anger at being rejected may turn into explosive fury in seconds. When primary, raw emotion is triggered, a little skirmish can suddenly expand into a pitched battle. Primary emotions never lose this immediacy and urgency, no matter how much we analyze them.

Love tends to strip a person down to his or her primary emotions. For this reason, perhaps, the language of love is related to nurturance and is often food-related. "Lips sweeter than wine," "honey," "cupcake," and "I could eat you up," all refer to the level of basic emotion that accompanied our first primary relationship with the person who nurtured us. Because love strips us down even further to the primitive, preverbal level of feelings, our responses within the context of an intimate relationship can be just as thoughtless as those of the infant who cries out for milk.

The difference between primary emotions and thought-through feelings is important. *Primary emotions* and *cognition* (the latter is the ability to think clearly, make rational decisions, and label inner experience with words) are at opposite ends of the developmental continuum. Think about how difficult it can be to identify why you feel terrified by the prospect of having lunch with a particular person or getting up to talk at a meeting or asking your boss for a well-deserved raise. You may have an upset stomach, diarrhea, or a constriction in your throat, but with no logical reason for the intense reaction. These feelings are not only related to the immediate event, but also carry extra baggage from childhood.

It is frightening not to have words to describe an intense internal state. When primary emotions erupt, the adult's reaction to the threatening experience may be as instant, urgent, and mindless as the infant's reaction. Passion, for example, the adult version of the need to be loved and held, may be just as urgent a need as the infant's—and just as primitive. Escalating fury also has its essence in infancy—and people can easily act on it without thought or reason. Physical attack resulting from "baby feelings" of anger occurs more frequently than society admits. We assume that intelligent, sophisticated people do not lose control and strike each other, but they do indeed. Often, the members of a couple who lose control are shocked by the experience and are completely unable to explain the eruption.

Sherry: Feeling Abandoned, Acting Angry

When Sherry encountered her ex-husband, Jim, with his new girlfriend at a social event, they began with a series of pleasantries and exchanged comments about their recent vacations. While they talked about unemotional subjects, Sherry carefully observed the body language of two people "who couldn't seem to keep their hands off of each other." Although she was able to mask her emotions, her heart was pounding, her stomach churning, her face flushed. She felt as if she were "hurtling down an elevator shaft." When her ex-husband mentioned that he could not take the children that weekend because he and his fiancée were going on a trip, Sherry was ready to kill.

At the time, Sherry attributed her rage to the fact that Jim was breaking his commitment to the children. She did not acknowledge the torrents of jealousy sweeping over her, nor the old feeling of terror and the awareness that she had been abandoned for good, this time. She had felt this wrenching feeling when Jim had first informed her that he was leaving their marriage. She thought this dreaded feeling was behind her, that she had gone on with her life and had succeeded in "cutting him out of my insides." But here she was again, feeling as if a piece of herself were being torn apart. Outwardly, she held herself together, as her wish to kill changed into a wish to die. She let him see none of what she was feeling—she wouldn't give him the satisfaction. Instead, she continued the pleasantries for a few minutes, escaped as soon as she was able, and walked over to the lady's lounge where she vomited out everything—food, husband, and the terror she couldn't bear to hold in a moment longer. She vomited repeatedly for the next three days, unable to keep any food in her.

Sherry described the events in therapy a few days later. Jim had been the only man she had allowed into her life. Abandoned by her father when he divorced her mother before her first birthday, Sherry both yearned for and feared a loving relationship with a man. She had had a string of broken relationships before she met and married Jim within a period of six weeks. "I was afraid that I would break it off if we waited," she explained, "and I trusted him completely at first."

But then her fears reemerged. Expecting betrayal, she began to check up on him when he had to work late. She scouted his office and suspected that he was involved with one of the many attractive women who worked there. She began to make "scenes," accusing him when they were out with friends. At first Jim was surprised and hurt, and then angry. He threatened to leave her if she continued to accuse and attack him.

In her more rational moments, Sherry acknowledged that the problem went much deeper than her relationship with Jim. She had no evidence that he had done something to justify her suspicions. Her jealous feelings were only the "tip of the iceberg" and soon descended into primary emotions of terror and abandonment. Her defensive response was to attack and accuse.

Much of the time her fear and aggression had a life of their own, because they welled up from her Imprint for Bonding. The pain of that first ruptured bond and the terror of abandonment surfaced repeatedly whenever Jim was not available or gave her less than total, devoted reassurance. Sherry's "blind rages" did not get her the reassurance that she desperately needed. On the contrary, it got her a divorce. Her Imprint for Bonding, which contained the infant's wordless terror of abandonment, had become a self-fulfilling prophecy.

Larry and Jane

It happens too often to be a coincidence: people who appear successful and independent on the surface actually carry deep, unacknowledged dependency needs and select mates who have *acknowledged* dependency needs to be their caretakers. Each partner has a story to tell about his or her complaints, frustrations, and needs—both met and unmet.

Larry, Jane's husband, complained that Jane talked around in circles. He couldn't get a straight answer out of her.

"Give me an example," I asked Larry.

"Saturday night, we were going to dinner. 'Where do you want to eat?' I said to Jane. It's just a simple question. All I wanted was a suggestion from her. What do I get: 'Well, I don't know,' she says. 'Are you hungry? Do you want to have a quick dinner in and go out somewhere afterward? Or do you want to go to that Italian restaurant where we ate when my folks visited?' She goes on and on and still gives me no answer."

"I just wanted to go somewhere that *you* liked," Jane replied in her defense.

"That leaves me deciding everything. Don't you have a preference or opinion about anything!" Larry's attack was harsh but on target.

Bursting into tears, Jane shouted, "No! No! I *don't* have an opinion about anything! You're right."

She sobbed hard for several minutes, covering her face and collapsing her head into her lap. Her entire body shook with the force of her crying. At first, Larry looked dumbstruck and remained unmoving. Then, as if released from paralysis, he got up swiftly and went to Jane's side, putting his arms around her. He held her for several minutes; gradually her body stopped shaking and her breathing returned to normal. She began to speak, retrieving scenes from her past that, at last, explained her behavior in the present.

Jane's earliest memory was one of being told, "Hold your tongue or I'll slap you!" Her mother was strictly religious and valued discipline and complete obedience above all. Jane learned early to curb all her spontaneous responses and to "test the water" carefully before jumping into a conversation. Now, her painful hesitancies and obsequious behavior were all that remained visible of those painful experiences.

Beneath the surface of her behavior, we realized, Jane wanted desperately to feel the merger of their two wishes. Operating from her Imprint for Bonding, she didn't care one iota where they ate, as long as they were of *one mind.* She feared disagreement above all, because it signaled separation and punishment. Her underlying imprint message was, "If I can find out what you want, and I agree with it, then we will be momentarily joined."

Larry, meanwhile, had his own underlying issues. He feared being controlled and sought the independence and autonomy of his fourth imprint. At first he liked Jane's habit of letting him make the decisions. But the more Jane engaged in indecisive, docile behavior in the hope of securing some merger based on agreement, the more he distanced himself, because the relationship seemed to be drawing him into a caretaking position. "I want to be with a woman who can take care of herself," he said.

Each had narrations of these interchanges, which *never* intersected. Her narration was: "I just want to do whatever you want." His narration was: "Your compliant behavior is actually very controlling." Their communication did not include attunement to one another's core experiences, and there was no atmosphere of positive dependence to contain and safely support the differences. Jane's emotional breakthrough in our session was a turning point for this couple because Larry was now willing and able to attune to her pain and share his own. They both learned to use their initial communications as *signposts* to deeper territory rather than as end points to disagreement.

Feeling-Level Communication

During the time when we develop our Imprint for Boundaries, we begin to be aware of reactions, *feelings,* that occur *interpersonally.* We may experience such feelings as excitement, anticipation, pride, desire, shame, guilt, envy, anger, fear, jealousy, and greed. Unlike *primary emotions,* which are compelling, all-encompassing responses that contain no ambiguities and may or may not include others, feelings are interpersonal and invariably contain shades of gray. Feelings may combine positive and negative qualities, or two different responses simultaneously.

An eighteen-month-old toddler instructed to share a toy with a playmate may want to please her mother by obeying and yet want to keep the toy for herself at the same time. An adult may be proud of her husband, feel desire for a coworker, and experience guilt about her sexual feelings all at the same time. She may defend against her feelings by accusing her husband of thoughts of illicit sex and then become jealous if he looks at another woman. In this process she may silently hold the feelings, openly discuss them, or repeatedly erupt in jealous anger.

We can experience intense feelings and still not lose control (as can occur with primary emotions). We may disagree, get angry, fight, and seek resolution. Like emotions, however, feelings do not initially include the kind of thinking that is associated with the language of our narrations.

Feelings about our experiences *generate* the stories or narrations we tell ourselves and others about old wounds. Thus, as we become adults looking back, we describe our poor self-image and our easily wounded feelings as our *parents' fault,* our frustration and anger as our *partners' fault,* our inability to achieve all we desire as *society's fault.* If we feel jealous a lot of the time, we may attribute the jealousy to the fact that our parents gave more attention to a sibling. In this way we explain our behavior and have a rationale for bringing it into the present and possibly little motivation to change it, even if it is damaging to our current relationship. Because feelings of jealousy, envy, and greed are humiliating to acknowledge, our narrations become even more self-protective. "It's not my fault," "Don't blame me," "You did it first," become habitual protestations we all use to protect our feelings. How much easier it might be to change our narrations if they no longer seemed applicable!

Talk to Me

After he saw the movie *When Harry Met Sally*, a new patient, Ben, said to me, "Everyone laughed at the scene in which Sally faked an orgasm in the restaurant. But women aren't the only ones who fake it. Men fake it, too. We fake *listening,*" he said, smiling slightly, adding that he was determined to be a modern, liberal, sensitive male. Now he was sitting in my office with his wife, Lora, confessing that he had not always been listening after all.

When Lora met Ben, she could not believe her good fortune. Here was a man who knew how to listen! Here was a man who cared about her feelings and wanted to hear her talk about them! After being married to a man who didn't care what she thought or felt and couldn't put two words together when they were alone, she was thrilled that Ben could listen and respond. This was the man with whom she was going to spend the rest of her life.

Ben brought Lora to meet me shortly before they married. As we talked about her views of intimacy, her expectations of a relationship, and memories of her family, she indicated traces of her history of failed connections. She expressed an unfulfilled, driving need to get closer, first to her parents and then to her first husband. She could never find a comfortable way to be in a relationship. There was always a "wall" that kept her locked out. She had tried to penetrate the wall and get closer by communicating her feelings better. But, she said, "I never seem to find the right words. But now, with Ben, all that is different." When she met Ben, she believed that she finally had someone who would love her as she desired. Was it really her dream come true?

She hoped so, but her history of failed relationships seemed to hover close by.

Lora's narration seemed to affect very much her present tense relationship with Ben. In subsequent sessions Lora began to verbalize her fears in a stream of constant recriminations. Is Ben sincere? Did he really want to be with her? Would getting into a relationship with him preoccupy her and keep her running around doing things for him? Would he change? "Why am I feeling so insecure?" she asked. "Why am I doing this to myself?"

Ben responded, "I don't know, but I sure wish you'd stop, because it's driving me crazy."

Lora was jarred. "I'm just trying to tell you how I feel!"

"Why can't we just go out and have a good time for once?" he retorted.

When Ben came to see me for his individual session the following day, he was quite vocal about his discontentment. "I don't know what to do with all the mixed feelings and the stream of doubts she keeps wanting to talk about. It just pours out of her mouth like an overflow of lava." He told me that he thought he had learned how to listen, but now he was wondering if he had "created a monster."

"I would never discuss my misgivings with Lora! If I have doubts, I keep them to myself. Why does she have to express every single feeling that flutters through her?"

Ben's narration collided with Lora's. Ben had learned that it was "bad" to express negative feelings. Harmony, he believed, is essential. In fact, if Lora seemed upset or unhappy, he made a point not even to acknowledge it. The problem was that Lora experienced Ben's constraint as a coldness and indifference, which triggered her doubts and fears. For her, talking about her feelings, disappointments, and fears was helpful and comforting.

By temperament, Ben was calm and steady, not easily excited, and uncertain of what to do with the expression of intense feelings. Lora, on the other hand, was used to the ebb and flow of emotions. Indeed, she experienced *lack* of feeling, positive or negative, as a lack of connection. She began to feel isolated unless she knew someone was present to share thoughts and emotions. "What are you feeling?" she'd ask Ben. "When he says, 'Nothing, I'm fine,' I go ballistic," she said.

The way Lora and Ben each dealt with their own problems became the cause of further problems for both. Their different perspectives on expressing and concealing negative feelings arose from a difference in their imprints. As she told Ben what she was feeling in their relationship, Lora assumed that he would not be personally offended. She did not think of him as capable of being hurt by her words. When Ben, taken aback by her disclosures, decided to refrain from expressing his own growing doubts, he was unaware of the power of his nonverbal communication to cause confusion and anxiety in Lora. In fact, Lora was more hurt by his silence and said things to provoke some dialogue, any dialogue. *No response* was her enemy.

It was no accident that Ben and Lora found each other. Filled with feelings, she was glad to be with a calm person who she thought would not be overwhelmed when she communicated her fears and her need for reassurance. Conversely, because he was not comfortable with his lack of feelings, Ben enjoyed the positive side of Lora's highly charged personality. "She is full of life," he said. "People love her. *I* love her." But after a time together, the very things they each loved became the sources of conflict.

Once Lora and Ben recognized that they were both communicating in a manner that reflected their unique pasts, the tone of their narrations changed from accusatory—"What's wrong with you?"—to understanding—"This is how you are and what you need." They had learned to receive each other's messages in the knowledge that they had different imprint patterns. Lora learned that silence need not be her enemy if Ben could reach out and take her hand. Ben learned to enjoy her intensity once he understood that he was not being blamed for her insecurities and did not have to "fix" them.

Thinking About Feelings

As mentioned earlier, feelings are different from primary emotions because they include a level of awareness that can include thinking. For that reason, feelings are more easily contained and healed than are primary emotions. If you can think about what you feel, you don't

automatically react. You can consider the implications of your response, and although you may feel terrible, you can control your
actions.

Current wounds that bring up core emotional states, reminders of
damage when early bonding needs were not met, are extremely difficult to repair and usually require special accommodation and tolerance
between partners. To repair that kind of early damage, it may also be
necessary to get the help of a therapist.

But before doing this, there are some questions couples can ask
themselves:

- How many of our problems communicating with each other
  have to do with mixed messages and confused expectations?
- How much of our conflict is based on very real differences of
  values, attitudes, temperament, and expectations?
- How many of our arguments make little sense to either of us
  when we try to reconstruct them?
- How important is this relationship to each of us?
- How important is the immediate issue between us?

Your answers to the first two questions have to do with conscious
choices, which, when they differ, can be resolved through negotiation
about what is most important to each of you and by a willingness to
compromise. Your answer to the third question most probably reflects
needs that are out of conscious awareness or with feelings of anxiety,
inadequacy, neediness, and dependency that you experience as too
shameful to acknowledge. The ways that you and your partner defend
against being wounded are the underlying cause of many arguments.

The answer to the fourth question determines your willingness to
tolerate what you learn about yourself and your partner's painful core
needs. When there are few past wounds, this is not a difficult issue.
But, as with many people today who suffer from past physical, emotional, and spiritual abuse, the wounds are deep—the needs are
great—and dependency is a feared if yearned-for desire.

The damage that was done early needs repair. Because the wounds
occurred in relationships, healing can occur only in relationships. Despite the promises of some pop psychology gurus, you cannot love

yourself to health. Immersion into an endless search for self-love leads to narcissism. But you can develop loving bonds with others that become a way toward healing your wounds.

People with damage at the level of their earliest bonding imprint tend to believe that they cannot control themselves when painful or rageful emotions well up. Yet most do, indeed, control themselves . . . at work, in restaurants, in theaters. Only at home does the control vanish. Primary emotions are never an excuse for losing control. By knowing the signals preceding the emotional surge, we can learn to hold, contain, and tolerate the waves of infantile emotions rather than "dumping" them into the world and onto those near and dear to us. When there are core wounds in one or both partners, it is by learning to do this that true communication becomes possible.

There is only one communication that works with people who choose not to contain their primary emotions and lash out when upset. The message is, *if that ever happens again, I'm leaving* —and mean it. Remember, people *can* control their emotions, if they choose to.

Primary emotions cause intense, automatic responses. Our hearts pound, we hyperventilate, we suddenly feel nauseous or faint. Trying to "explain" or override these reactions often seems impossible, but if we learn to recognize primary emotions as they arise and stay with the feelings instead of deadening them or translating them into anger, then we can also learn to control the way we express them.

Mending Our Failures

None of us can respond to each and every need that surfaces in our partners. The feeling of blissful merger experienced by new lovers cannot be maintained permanently in any long-term relationship. The best we can hope for is being understood often enough to maintain the feeling that we are cared for and care for those we are close to despite the imperfections we each carry. There *will* be failures, because none of us is perfect. The good news is that *trust builds from the experience of mended failures.* Indeed, it is the innumerable failures, followed by efforts to repair the damage through deep-level communication, that develop into a language of love that encompasses *all* of who we are.

Failures *mended* provide the experience of containment and well-being; failures *unmended* produce repeated unconscious attempts to re-create and repair earlier damaged relationships on top of the current damage being done. We mend our failures, both with our parents and concurrently those of our present partners, by picking our way through the thicket of mixed messages descending to the deeper region of feelings and below, to the core of primary emotions. This, in essence, is how we and our partners can learn to heal each other.

Creative Dependency

If you have been hurt in the past, you may not have learned that you can depend on others to respond to basic needs for love, affirmation, understanding, acceptance. All of your relationships will include a fail-safe exit provision in case you are hurt or shamed. Without being aware of it you screen all incoming messages and what you hear will be skewed. "What does he mean by that?" "Why did she say such a thing?" "Does he mean he doesn't like me anymore?" "Is she putting me down by that remark?"

The way you process the incoming messages can make it hard to put aside your needs and defenses long enough to pay attention to the needs of another person. Each of you hears only the parts of the communication that can make you feel good or bad, enhanced or devalued. The other exists only as a temporary enhancer of good feelings, a transmitter to fill the emptiness or meet dependency needs. The person you are with may not be recognized by you as a separate individual filled with emotions and needs of his or her own.

You will know whether this is the case by listening to the patterns of communication between you and your partner:

Do simple, nonthreatening conversations end in arguments?

Do you find yourselves frustrated when you try to communicate something important?

Do you end conversations with one or both of you withdrawing but not resolving the issue?

If so, why?

If not, why might either one of you be reacting this way?

Are you afraid of the anger that has come out in past disagreements?

This is a time to stop yourself and consider which of your imprints is at work. What causes your hurt feelings? What needs do you wish were met? What old patterns from your family are being repeated?

What imprint might be at work in your partner?

What are you doing that your partner may be reacting to?

What might he be needing?

Which of her imprint buttons do I push?

Is the reaction that feels so hurtful to me a defense that my partner is using to keep from being hurt by me?

We Choose Our Partners for a Reason

Remember that most of what you feel is probably matched in some way by your partner. Remember that we choose partners who reflect something important in ourselves. Remember that you chose someone whom you hoped would finish some unfinished business from your early imprints.

If you want to change the dynamics of unsatisfying communication you must change the focus from you as injured party to you as part of a two-way interaction. This includes you and your partner as separate people with independent centers of initiative, and individual needs that often overlap. This includes also you and your partner as adult versions of the children you once were. These children contain each of the imprints you developed for relating to important others. The child is still operating within. Even though you have grown-up words, dependency needs remain for a lifetime.

Becoming clear about your partner's needs not only will keep the communication open between you, but will also pull you out of a totally inward preoccupation that was designed to defend against being wounded in the present as you were in the past.

Becoming aware of your own needs will enable you to separate out the emotions and thoughts that are yours from those that belong to your partner. In the next chapter, you will find a model for safe vulnerability that clarifies ways to heal old wounds. You will learn things that you can do to make your relationship a healing partnership. The exercises mid-chapter will enable you to recognize your own unresolved imprints in ways that can begin the healing process. When the wounds of the past no longer drive your behavior in your current relationship, you will have begun the path to collaborative intimacy.

9 Positive Dependency: A Method in the Madness

My true love hath my heart, and I have his,
By just exchange, one for the other giv'n:
I hold his dear, and mine he cannot miss:
There never was a bargain better driv'n.

His heart in me keeps me and him in one,
My heart in him his thoughts and senses guides:
He loves my heart, for once it was his own:
I cherish his, because in me it bides.

His heart his wound received from my sight:
My heart was wounded with his wounded heart.
For as from me on him his hurt did light:
So still me thought in me his heart did smart:
Both equal hurt, in his change sought our bliss:
My true love hath my heart, and I have his.

—Sir Philip Sidney, ''Heart Exchange''

Rule #9 for Positive Dependency:

There will be times when you fail each other, hurt each other, and do things that may feel unforgivable. If you need to register a criticism or complaint, make sure you do it in private. Be generous with forgiveness. To forgive is to begin again, to touch a place of internal transformation, to re-create the relationship.

So you want to hear a happy ending, but happy relationships have little drama. Furthermore, with a nationwide divorce rate over 50 percent, there seem few happy endings to write about.

In *We've Had a Hundred Years of Psychotherapy and the World Is Getting Worse*, therapist James Hillman and journalist Michael Ventura wrote, "If you think [love is] about fulfillment, happiness, satisfaction, union, all that stuff, you're in for even more heartbreak." "Love is madness," Hillman and Ventura continue. "What is the madness looking for?"[18]

What we seek and what we actually get from love are often diametrically opposed. We are seeking answers to the dilemma of intimacy, the search for connection in a world that fosters and even forces fragmentation and disconnection. Too often, we find ourselves on a battleground surrounded by power struggles, conflicting needs, intolerable feelings, collision. Nevertheless, we continue to yearn for the freedom to be vulnerable and to know we are loved.

It is possible, as those who are in happy marriages well know, to make each other feel safe enough to let the tender spots show. Hillman and Ventura, for example, describe the need for positive dependency, but believe it is impossible to experience. "You cannot be vulnerable and be safe," they say, expressing the primary principle of a good partnership as an oxymoron. But there are ways we can move toward the ideal of Rule #9. We can learn to make comments that do not hurt one another. We can learn to register criticism and complaints only in private. Most importantly, we can learn to forgive.

A friend told me with some humor that she discovered her own version of forgiveness after reading Judith Viorst's *Forever Fifty . . . & Other Negotiations*. My friend said, "I got to the point in my marriage where, when my husband made an asshole of himself at a party, I no longer needed to point it out in the car on the way home."

Throughout this book I have described how we internalize our models for relationships early in life when we are most dependent on others for physical and emotional sustenance. From this time we inherit a whole set of interactions and related basic needs that can *only* be met through intimate connection with another. If our early relationships were safe, we internalized imprints for secure intimacy. If we had to

protect ourselves against emotional injury when we were most vulnerable, covering ourselves with a defensive shell was the only realistic
response. But beneath the shell remains an enduring wish to be loved,
affirmed, and understood, even with our deepest pain and anxiety, to
be *safe-in-relation*.

Experiencing needs that are a reminder of childhood can feel shameful or humiliating. We are unwilling to admit that we wish to be taken
care of at times, to feel small and helpless, yet secure in the protective
embrace of a partner. These needs are universal, although men and
women respond to them differently. The need to be touched, held,
nurtured, and affirmed by someone we can depend upon is a lifelong
need as basic as the need for food, water, and oxygen.

It is time to recognize that wholeness and healing come ultimately
only through relationships. Discovering how to function as nurturers
and sounding boards for each other, discovering how to create a relationship that is experienced as a safe haven in a stressful world—
these are the areas we need to study. As difficult as it may seem, we
ultimately have little choice but to risk relationship, to depend upon
others to meet important needs.

As mature adults, we have been taught to deny that we have the very
same needs for positive dependency *now* that we had as children; but
we have different ways to meet them. The sad result is that we neither
allow those feelings in ourselves nor accept the dependency in our
intimate partners. "Grow up," we tell ourselves and each other. But this
injunction addresses only one level of our selves, one face. Like the
nested Russian dolls, this face seen by the world actually contains
many smaller versions of itself—each present and powerful in its own
way.

Looking at my doll collection, I realize again that we all have many
faces, many levels. I think about myself in terms of my Russian dolls.
My outermost level is the face I have learned to show the world; it is
the part of me I want you to know, respect, admire. The next layer is
the part that I share only with my husband and most intimate
friends—my spiritual side, my sexual side, my insecurities, my fight to
heal myself after a bout with cancer. More deeply embedded is that
part of myself that may be obvious to others but of which I am unaware. My husband, listening to me describe myself in terms of the

Russian dolls, told me about a behavior he had seen me carry out for decades.

"When you divide a bowl of cherries," he said, "you always count out *exactly* half. You want to be sure you get an equal share. You do it with everything."

"I want to be sure *you* get an equal share," I protested.

"But you don't see," he continued with a smile, "it doesn't *matter* to me. I would just separate the fruit approximately and assume it would even out. I always thought you needed to be so careful, so *precise*, because you were the younger child, the girl in your family, and your brother was the favorite who got the special privileges. So you are concerned with everything being fair and equal."

He was right, of course. I had never connected my childhood wounds with my lifelong campaign for equal treatment for all (nor with my penchant for counting cherries!). Even my choice of work within my profession reflected this concern (the majority of my work is with couples rather than counseling individuals). This means I am always having to position myself equally between partners, always making certain that each receives a fair share of attention, always wanting to understand each person's unique needs and emotions. Being born the second child, a girl in a family that favored its first-born son, automatically influenced my imprint patterns long before words or conscious thought.

Finally, at the core of the Russian dolls, and of me, is a deeper level still—that part that is unknown to me, to my mate, to the outside world—the part that influences my actions and decisions as surely as my sense of unfairness makes me want to right the wrongs of the world. I would share these parts gladly if I knew what they were. But they are hidden deeply within me, as they are in everyone. I know that these hidden parts lie in my earliest imprints. Even a well-analyzed therapist does not know all that lives in the preverbal realm. To make the situation even more complicated—and more interesting—not only is each of us a "Russian doll," but so are our partners and potential partners. Intimate relationships often play out in the space wherein the deepest worlds within each partner meet.

As I seek ways we can help one another in relationships, I know that to identify dysfunctional behaviors and learn new ways to behave can

Innate, biological, temperamental aspects; a tendency to shyness, an analytic mind, high energy level, etc.

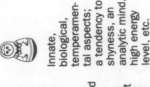

Unconscious, deeply imbedded emotions that may drive my behavior without my being aware of it. The part that comes out in behavior that is hard to understand, or in physical and emotional symptoms.

Aspects that are out of my conscious awareness. Others may see these in me more easily than I do, but I recognize them when made aware. Aspects that would cause me shame for you to know.

The part that I share with the most intimate people in my life. The spiritual, emotional, sexual, private me that can be vulnerable, dependent, excited, or overjoyed, depending on the circumstances.

The part of me seen by the outside world. Wife, mother, therapist, author, a person who tries to show few flaws and looks strong no matter what the inner stresses.

Innate, biological, tempermental aspects; artistic aptitude; intelligence; calm disposition.

Your unconscious. The things that I don't understand and never can change that affect your behavior and our lives together.

The things about you that were different from the image you want to convey to the world. The habits, attitudes, vulnerabilities, imprints for relating to me and to others in your life.

The part of you that I came to know as we began living together. Your values, beliefs, goals in life; what you were willing to do to achieve these goals.

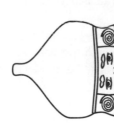

The part of you showed to me when we first met, your success, charm, sense of humor and strength.

be only part of the answer. The other part of the answer is both easier and more difficult. Instead of making sure that we find the right person, we need to focus on *being* the right person. An alternative to asking if we are getting the love we want is to give the love our partner needs. This is difficult, because it implies the risk of vulnerability, of unilateral giving with no guarantee that you will get what you want in return. It is difficult because the world is not necessarily fair. Yet if everyone avoids the risks of love, no one benefits. Sadly, that is where so many people seem to be today.

A Model for Safe Vulnerability

We all have needs, desires, and expectations based on past relationships and past history. We all tend to act in ways that mold relationships to become what we expect. Then, if we don't like it, we go to a therapist and describe what's wrong with the other person.

He drinks, she screams, he ignores, she nags, and so on. The therapist listens and tries to help the complaining partner understand why he or she is staying with someone who is so terrible. Then, together, they work toward the goal of personal growth—independence, self-actualization—and when the therapy is completed, the person emerges stronger, more independent, and unwilling to put up with such a "sick" relationship. This paradigm proves Hillman and Ventura's contention that we all have needs that no one can satisfy and that it is never safe to be vulnerable.

I would like to suggest an alternative—a model in which personal growth and healing are possible *only* in the context of the safe vulnerability found in intimate relationships. This model is based upon the following assumptions:

1. *Understand that we are* all *"adult children."* Maturity is not based upon our degree of independent functioning but on our ability to experience positive, mutual dependence. Children do not survive without a mother's physical and emotional responsiveness. Adults have many of the same needs as children do. We want to be understood. We want to be accepted. We want to be admired. We

want to be listened to. We want our flaws to be overlooked and our strengths to be noticed. We may be ashamed to acknowledge these feelings openly, but that doesn't matter, because they are at the core of each of us.

When these needs are not met, we behave as children do. If scared or frightened, we protect ourselves from being hurt. If emotionally injured, we withdraw. If ignored, we draw attention to ourselves. If we are with people who make us feel inadequate, we try to prove our superiority. If damaged, we get angry and seek revenge. If our needs are not met, we deny those needs or seek another relationship to repair a wounded self.

To have a successful intimate relationship, each partner must openly acknowledge and reclaim the vulnerable inner child. If we can accept the truth that to be human is to have flaws and needs, then we do not have to hide from our dependency needs. When we accept this truth in ourselves, we can respond without blame or shame to our partner's deepest and earliest needs.

2. *An intimate adult relationship contains the possibility of a corrective emotional experience*[7] in which we can satisfy our needs for exclusive and enduring love, connectedness, and positive dependency. For many people, (men even more than women because they have fewer outlets in which to acknowledge emotions and vulnerabilities) an intimate partner is the only one that we can turn to in our desire to be dependent. If we silence our own voice, however, in order to take care of the needs of others, then we lose ourselves. If we listen only to ourselves, then we lose the opportunity to collaborate in the creation of new ways of arranging a life that is part of a vital growing system. A loving mate can meet the needs for both togetherness and separateness.

Many early wounds occurred in childhood when we depended on our parents to understand that growing up often entails meeting dual, sometimes opposing, needs. Needs for connection and autonomy, togetherness and separateness, when frustrated or denied at either end, may cause us to isolate ourselves emotionally from others. It is often these wounds, blocking our dependency needs, that can be healed through corrective emotional experiences in an adult relationship.

3. *Healing takes place at a deep level and it takes place in the here and now.* We tend to think that *deep* means delving into the past. In fact, the past unfinished and unresolved is the present—change the present and you change the past. We do not get well from figuring out the past. *We get well when we stop re-creating the past in present relationships.* Understanding the internal process in the present, as it relates to the past, may free us to tolerate emotions that once were intolerable. Rather than wall off the emergence of painful feelings, we can learn to let emotions arise and to consciously hold them. Psychotherapy is one way to reexperience these intolerable emotions in the safe environment of an empathic therapist. True interaction with an intimate partner with whom we are deeply bonded is another way.

4. *We cannot eradicate our imprint patterns, but we can acquire a new repertoire in our patterns to heal the damage from these early periods of our development.* We needn't be driven by the relationship patterns that worked when we were children, strategies of living and interacting that no longer fit our current situation. In addition to understanding our imprinted needs and emotions, it is also necessary to recognize and "read" our partner's imprint messages. Whatever is unacceptable in ourselves, we tend to reject and denigrate in others. It is the needs and vulnerabilities—the fragile humanness—that we deny and hide from in ourselves that we are most likely to find and complain about in our intimate partner. We are all much more *alike* than we wish to recognize. The more we understand our imprints and accept them as logical outgrowths of our early interactions, the less emotionally charged and shameful they will feel. Not having to hide from ourselves, trusting that our partner will not attack us with our vulnerabilities, makes the relationship a haven for positive dependency.

What You Can Do

Remember that much of what occurs between people operates on both a rational, conscious level and at the level of unconscious Imprints. When you find yourself involved in repetitious patterns of behavior that you can't change, even when you know from the beginning of the interaction that the end result may be disastrous, then you are probably recreating an early Imprint experience of wounding. One way to reach the Imprint needs and wounds is to jog your mind for connections with the past *as you are living it in the present.*

Consider your current relationship (or a recent one). Knowing that Imprints are at the core of any emotional interaction, focus on one incident that created a problem for the two of you. Think about the Imprints of your partner and yourself. Be aware that Imprint needs emerge in times of high emotion, stress, or anxiety. Use the following questions as a guide to which Imprints might be operating beneath the anger, withdrawal, and fighting, beneath any substance abuse, beneath the strong physiological responses (heart pounding, upset stomach, diarrhea and vomiting, etc.).

Imprint #1   You have an unfulfilled wish to feel unconditionally loved in a bonded relationship.

Imprint #2   You have an unmet desire to be heard and empathically understood.

Imprint #3   You are in need of an alternative way to substitute for unmet past needs.

Imprint #4   You are searching for a sense of self-esteem and affirmation as an individual within the context of a solid relationship.

Do you have an unfulfilled wish to feel safe in a bonded relationship?

If problems originate in your *Imprint for Bonding,* you may feel an intense or even obsessive desire to feel safe and secure with someone who totally loves you. If so, you are in need of positive experiences of the *Bonding Imprint.* Review Chapter 3 and join me in thinking of ways in which this most basic need could be fulfilled.

If you are feeling particularly brave, try an "emotional holding" exercise. Begin by flipping a coin to see who is to become the first "caretaker." The winner of the coin-flip gets to be the temporary "child." Select a comfortable space—a couch, a bed, a blanket in front of the fireplace. The "child" is to place his/her head in the lap of the "caretaker."

Silently the child experiences letting go completely to be held and touched gently by the caretaker, allowing any fleeting thoughts or images to flow freely. As the child, reflect on how you would complete the following sentences:

I am most comfortable when you . . .

What I want most from you now is . . .

I would feel safe, warm, and at peace right now if you would . . .

After the exercise is completed, reverse roles. When you are the caretaker, reflect on how you would complete the following sentences:

When I see you like this, I . . .

If you held me like this, I would feel . . .

I resist doing this when . . .

I imagine you feel . . .

Right now I feel . . .

Spend 15 to 20 minutes in each role. If you want more time, redo the exercise. When completed, you may or may not wish to discuss it. Both partners must want to talk or neither should say anything. Deep wounds may arise that should not be forced into the open prematurely. If both wish to share, do so as long as it is comfortable. Because the exercise taps into the earliest preverbal material, the point is not necessarily to talk about it so much as to experience the emotions in *safety*—without having to exchange words.

Do you have an unmet desire to be heard and empathically understood?

If so, you are in need of positive experiences related to the *Sharing Imprint*. Review Chapter 4 and think of ways in which the need to attune empathically to each other can be fulfilled.

You might try an exercise in sharing early wounds. Place two chairs back to back. Close your eyes and sit silently. Sense your partner and yourself breathing in unison. Picture yourself as a child in your parent's home. What age do you see yourself as? What room of your childhood home are you in? Who is there with you? Tell the person in your childhood image what it is you want. Do you want the same thing now you wanted as a child? Do you feel the same way toward this person now as you did as a child?

Now think about what you know about your partner's history and early wounds. See if you can imagine your partner as a child in his/her home and ask the same questions. What age do you see your partner as? What room of his/her childhood home comes to mind? Who is there with him/her? What does your partner want from this person? Does he/she want the same thing now that he/she wanted as a child? Does he/she feel the same way toward this person now as he/she did as a child?

When you have finished, turn the chairs around and face each other. Take a few minutes to discuss any memories that feel important to share. Exchange your images of how each of you experienced his/her childhood. Now share any ways, positive or negative, that your partner reminds you of your parent. Remember, we all select partners after a lifetime of interactions that present our expectations. Share the things that each of you wanted from the people in your childhood home.

Are you in need of an alternative to substitute for unmet past needs?

If so, you may be in need of some new experiences related to your *Imprint for Bridging*. Review Chapter 5 and think of ways that you and your partner can develop together that will help you connect to each other while adding outside interests or people to your lives.

As an exercise in examining the way you make your relationships real for yourselves, sit comfortably on a couch next to each other and consider the following questions.

> *Did you have experiences in childhood when you used sports, music, dance, or studies to help you feel connected to others?*
> *What activities did you do with your friends?*
> *Did you have positive experiences in these activities?*
> *Did you get a feeling of connection, or was there some sense of isolation?*

Share these experiences with each other. Now recall the early days of your relationship together.

> *Were the activities you shared fulfilling for both of you?*
> *Did you take trips early in your relationship?*
> *Who were your friends?*

*What sports events, social, religious, or political activities had mean-
ing for you?*
Have you built on any of your early interests together?
*What things have been lost? Were they replaced with new people, in-
terests, activities?*
Which current interests do you pursue separately? Together?
Select one or two of the activities that you and your partner really
liked—an activity that neither has done in a very long time—and plan
a time when you can do it together. Be sure that neither of you feels
pressured into doing something that isn't really special. Make sure the
child in each of you is pleased.

Are you searching for a sense of self-esteem and affirmation as an individual within the context of a solid relationship?

If so, you are in need of positive experiences in the *Independence
Imprint*. Review Chapter 6 and, with your partner, think of ways in
which this most basic need could be filled.

This exercise should be done outdoors. Go for a walk, go to the
beach, or sit in a park. Sit quietly together, thinking about how you
asserted your independence as a child. Each share a story from your
memory bank about the time you were between three and five years
old. How did your parents respond when your wishes differed from
theirs? What did you do when they disapproved?

Now each share a story from your early adolescence in which your
decision differed markedly from your parents'. Did you feel a withdrawal of love as the cost of doing what felt right to you?

Now consider if separate activities, interests, or friendships create
conflict in your relationship. If so, why? Explore the core issues involved in supporting one another's independence. Is there a difference
between your *parents'* response to your need for independence and
your *partner's* response? Finally, each of you ask for something from
the other that will enhance your feeling of self-esteem.

To Do or Not to Do

Learning the way you and your partner react when basic dependency needs are unmet gives you choices; with these tools you can change the dynamics of how you relate from the foundation up. Do not announce to your partner that you now know his or her infantile needs. It may not even be necessary to discuss the past at all to heal the wounds of early childhood. We do not have to analyze each other's pathologies, perversions, and vulnerable areas.

In fact, that kind of probing is likely to be experienced as a further wound, a blaming for whatever is wrong in your current relationship. Instead, we can learn to recognize what builds self-esteem, what gives affirmation, provides security and trust, and we can choose to meet these needs. Will we get back an exactly even amount? Must the cherries be counted exactly?

Although sharing your knowledge of a partner's imprints is not advisable unless the other brings it up first, choosing to share your knowledge of yourself is always an option if your mate indicates a willingness to listen. Your openness may become the stimulus for a productive dialogue between the two of you. If your partner begins to express core feelings, instead of *discussing* them, simply reflect back what you understand. Consider whether or not you wish to *respond* by meeting the dependent need. If you do not, recognize that your partner may be disappointed, but your response and your partner's response to you will be open for discussion. Make sure you are clear about what your partner says. If you are not meeting your partner's needs because you do not understand what is being communicated, you both lose. The needs go underground, the vulnerability is shamefully hidden away. The issue is avoided but comes out later in subterfuge and distorted ways.

Over time, given interest and practice, you can become increasingly aware of the imprint from which you are responding in different situations. Knowing your needs and painful emotions helps curtail the automatic defensive reactions that cause repetitive problems in your relationship. Even if your partner is not interested in learning how unconscious imprint patterns are affecting your relationship, you can change many things on your own by paying attention to the imprint processes that influence the dynamics between the two of you.

Healing Core Wounds

As we have seen throughout this book, early imprint responses are often communicated through unspoken emotional transmissions rather than through verbal messages. If you do not understand the powerful forces erupting between you and your partner, do not despair. Know that the eruption is a cry for help from deep within; it is by no means a signal that you are in an impossible situation, or a toxic or codependent relationship. Nor does it mean that you are with someone too childlike to be in a committed relationship. Some of the most intense, passionate relationships I have observed were that way precisely because the partners operated from a deep core of their earliest imprints. The very reactions that express unconscious vulnerability can lead to achievement and creativity in adult life.

Many of the people with whom I have worked have willingly removed the cover of their powerful facades to immerse themselves in the anxiety-filled inner places they have described as "the black hole," "the empty core," "the demon," or "the monster" within. They do it with their partners present in the safety of our therapy sessions because they *want* to be *known*. They do it because fleeing from what they felt was intolerable as children has kept them running from relationships for a lifetime. Cutting off deeper parts of one's self also cuts off access to the positive side of the imprints: intimacy, excitement, joy, emotional vitality, sexual passion, and the awareness of others.

Once we arrive at this dangerous destination of our core vulnerabilities, it is often a deep relief. Over the years I have heard clients say some surprising and beautiful things:

Peter to Mary: *I feel so lost and confused at times. I just want you to reach your arms out to me, hold me close, forgive me for hurting you, reassure me that it will be okay.*

Eric to Alice: *I don't want to feel these terrible feelings alone. I want you to share them, feel them, and not think I'm a monster because of what I feel.*

Gary to Betty: *Sometimes I feel like I'm in a pressure cooker that is ready to blow. I try to keep a lid on my feelings, but they want to come out. It feels better just to say it and see that you can hear it.*

What heals the wounds in our imprints? Psychoanalyst Franz Alexander contended that the cure lies not simply in analytic interpretations, not in making the unconscious conscious, but rather in determining what went wrong early in life and providing a "corrective emotional experience." His model proved unworkable because a therapist cannot provide the adult with all that is needed to repair the wounds of missing love. A therapist cannot heal in brief therapy, as Alexander suggested, wounds that took years to develop. We cannot be there for "richer or poorer, in sickness and in health, till death do us part." Therapists have lives of their own, families of their own, values and needs that should not be shared with patients. We can do much to help, but there are things that only a real relationship in the outside world can do.

Healing relationships require knowledge, plus the care and positive intentions of a loving friend, sponsor, teacher, or partner. Therapists can help start the process. We can help couples provide each other with truly corrective emotional experiences—repairing old wounds, understanding deep needs, affirming the positive, respecting the shameful— in essence, completing the work of childhood. Partners move closer to uncovering layers of defenses as they choose to look at how they have used their relationship to deal with vulnerable, underlying needs and intense emotions that had long been buried.

Seeking Help

I hope that this book has opened the lines of communication between deeper parts of the two of you. For many couples, this is enough to create small changes that begin to build a healing relationship. Small changes can make a big difference when they are in the service of understanding each other's ingrained responses and choosing to say and do things that make one another feel affirmed and emotionally connected.

Sometimes it is clear that the relationship needs more than you can

give to each other at this time. This is the point when outside help may
be valuable. There are excellent resources available, possibly through
a marriage-enrichment program connected to your church or syna-
gogue. You can become involved in a formalized couples program
such as Harville Hendrix's *Getting the Love You Want,* which is offered
throughout the country. You can find out more about these resources
by calling (212) 410-7712 or (800) 729-1121, or by writing to the Institute for Relationship Therapy, 1255 Fifth Avenue, Suite C2, New York,
NY 10029.

Additional resources are available through several accrediting orga-
nizations that can make referrals to highly trained family therapists. One
such organization that can be contacted is the American Family Therapy Academy, located at 2020 Pennsylvania Avenue, NW, #273, Washington, DC 20006; (202) 994-2776. Members of this organization are
among the senior professionals in the family-therapy field, who not
only provide services to couples and families but also are experienced
teachers of family therapists. You can get a referral to a therapist in
every state in the United States as well as in many other countries.

Other sources of referrals for specialists in couples therapy are the
American Association for Marriage and Family Therapy (AAMFT),
located at 1100 Seventeenth Street, NW, 10th Floor, Washington, DC
20036-4601; (202) 452-0109; and the American Psychological Association, Division of Family Therapy, 1120 G Street, NW, Suite 330, Washington, DC 20005; (202) 783-7663.

The National Association of Social Workers has a roster of members
throughout the country who specialize in working with problems in
relationships. The training of social workers is particularly useful in
understanding individuals in the context of their relationships. The first
training that I received in the mental-health field was in social work. It
is probably the reason that during all of the training in individual psychology that I have since received, I have continued to think of the
individual in the context of something larger, a family, a group, a
community, or a society as a whole.

A referral to a social worker anywhere in the United States can be
obtained through the National Association of Social Workers, located at
750 First Street, NE, Suite 700, Washington, DC 20002-4241; (800) 227-
3590.

Renewing Our Contract at Different Stages

Think about how you handle your crises. Not the big problems like raising children, handling family finances, and interfering in-laws, but the everyday crises of being together, what to do when you've both had a hard day. Whose responsibility is it to pick up the groceries, start the dinner, tend to the chores? Who gets to relax? Whose stories get listened to? Who initiates lovemaking? What is the usual response? If these kinds of issues become difficult problems, then you are probably dealing with imprint wounds and unmet dependency needs.

If partners are meeting each other's needs in a way that allows for mutual positive dependency, even major crises can be handled without damage to the relationship. Illness, job loss, natural disasters, loss of a home, can lead to the destruction of a relationship or can catalyze a joining together in collaborative partnership to overcome the problem. Such a partnership works if each learns to respect the other's goals, if each knows that it is possible to depend on the other and that it is safe to trust the other's love and goodwill. Then the inevitable crises that come up in the course of living together lead to strengthening the relationship.

Although I had gone to school or worked as a therapist since the day we married, Matt's career provided the primary income for our family. In the early days, mortgage lenders didn't consider women's income, so his income was the one that counted when they approved the mortgage for our home. Our lifestyle was much more related to his world of work than to mine. To take the stand that I wished to have a career and to receive the quiet support of my husband in this decision was enough for me. By the time the women's movement gained energy and women demanded the right to choose home or career, I had already established my career. All I had to do was figure out how to juggle smoothly the demands of organizing our home, raising two children, and running my practice. Matt helped where he could, but the burden was on me. Things hadn't yet reached the point where I expected him to share responsibilities of the home.

When my youngest child left for college and Matt was still working long hours, I had the time to do what I had long wanted to do. I began working on papers and a book describing what I had learned in almost thirty years as a therapist. I moved my office to my home and was very busy.

Then after many years in the business world, my husband said he would like to retire and even wondered how long it would be before I thought of retiring. Retire! I was just *beginning.* My first book was published the same year that Matt took early retirement.

I remembered back to the year before I was married and friends of my parents were in the same situation. Stan had decided to retire. He sold his business on the East Coast and moved to California. Birtha worried constantly, "Will we have enough money to last us? What will I do with him home every day for breakfast, lunch, and dinner? How do I keep him from getting underfoot?" She talked about the woes of retirement incessantly on her visits to our home, and I thought about how unhappy she was. A year after their retirement, they bought a small store and he was back at work, with her helping out during busy times. The following year Stan died. He could have had a happy retirement. Why did she push him so? I wondered.

I remembered my parents' friend. What would I do with a husband at home all day? How would it affect my office at home? Was our nest egg sufficient? Do we have enough for the rest of our lives? I had never viewed my income as money to live on. It was considered extra, for trips, for charity, for savings. Could I retire now even if I wanted to?

But it was Matt's wish to retire and to find something more meaningful than the challenges of business and finance. In order for me to "practice what I preached," I would need to put aside certain old notions that I had about men being stronger, wiser, and earning more money. Where did I ever get such ideas, I now wonder. But such attitudes were ingrained early in life along with my imprints, part of the socializing process. Now, we had to negotiate a new relationship, a new way of thinking about our relationship that incorporated Matt's current needs and values as well as my own. On a scale of priorities from one to ten, I recognized that his ten was retirement. Next, he needed respect, support, and encouragement from me in whatever he chose to do. It did not have to be what I would do if I were in his place, but what he chose, "for better or for worse."

For two years, all he wanted to do was read books. He read everything that he had not had time to read when he was busy as a banker. He read the books that he never got to read in college or graduate school. He was home a lot. He liked company, but I often worked in the office during the day and was on the telephone in the evening. There were no more business events to attend, and I began to travel to give presentations at meetings and conferences.

We continue to change the way we structure our lives together. We continue to seek new balances, and there are some insecurities on both parts. His expectations for himself have changed, and so his expectations of me must be different. Can I still "read" him right? Can he still meet my expectations? My answer—write another book. Is this an answer that will meet his emerging needs? We don't yet know. His answer—go back to school and begin a Ph.D. program in a new field of interest. Is this an answer that will meet my emerging needs? We don't know yet, but we are confident that no matter what is put on our plate, we will make it work.

No one's marriage is static. It changes for everybody, and new stresses bring up old imprint patterns, requiring renewed energy to find new responses in an ongoing, lifelong relationship. Every marriage has within it several marriages, and each stage of the relationship bears a marriage contract that must be renewed to meet the changing needs of both partners.

The search for intimacy continues throughout life. It is the rare individual who can stand alone, without the close support of others, without reducing his or her capacity to function optimally. The "inner child" in each of us continues to seek the security of a closely bonded relationship. Few understand that what they are seeking comes from the intense need for connection in a nurturing relationship that fills these basic lifelong needs.

If the basic need to feel understood and affirmed by someone special is not met, it leaves a residue of loneliness, emptiness, worthlessness, and sadness. When partners are committed to offering such responsiveness to each other, they have the basis of a positive dependency. After a period of time, if each partner is consistently available to the other in

---

In A Healing Relationship Partners Will . . .

- Understand that dependency leaves one vulnerable

- Utilize the relationship to communicate messages in ways that minimize emotional injuries and enhance self-esteem

- Avoid attacking sensitive areas that re-create old wounds

- Translate messages that feel like demands and attacks into understanding of underlying needs and vulnerabilities

- Learn how to move between emotional reactions and cognitive awareness in important transactions

- Use selective inattention on the small negatives that are not significant

- Notice things that are positive and use affirmations often

---

ways that feel mutually beneficial, without defensive attacks, growing trust develops in the security of the relationship and an inner security blossoms in both partners.

I have talked to people who describe their marriage as "the best relationship I ever had in my life." Leslie, a friend and colleague, told me that her husband, Mark, "became my mother when we got married." She relates, "I didn't know how to cook or shop for food. I went to the market and felt overwhelmed. When I went home empty-handed and upset and cried to him, Mark went back with me. He showed me what to do. My mother never taught me anything. Mark was my good mother."

Leslie is now a highly competent professional. But as an eighteen-year-old bride from a dysfunctional family, newly married to a twenty-one-year-old student, she was vulnerable. She turned to Mark and found that she could depend on him. She decided then that she would do anything she could for him and learned that the more she gave, the more she got in return.

Had Mark told her that she was being childish (which she was at the moment), that she was incompetent (which she was at the time), that he would leave her if she didn't stop the crying (which she feared he would say), the relationship would have taken a different track. Caught in old messages of incompetence, she would have reacted to him with all of her defensive barriers up. He, in turn, would have felt her withdrawal and hurt as reflections on his ability to love and be loved. Had the dependency needs of either one gone unmet, the early imprint pattern of defenses that arise would have soon reemerged. Each might have experienced the other's defensive distancing and neither would have felt the relationship to be the safe, healthy environment for the growth of each that it became.

My friend Paula Thomas gave me her view of positive dependency. "My husband is really insecure. His life was not so good. He had a difficult childhood. But as long as I am there for him and take care of his needs, he is a 'happy camper.' And he gives so much back in return. My only concern is that he worries about what would happen to him if he ever lost me. I'm working on convincing him that, now that we've been together and he is getting what he needs, he will be able to function without me if he ever has to. Besides, I have no plans to ever leave! I get so much from him—not money, he is not a great businessman. But money is not security. Knowing that I'm loved, *that's security.*"

Mickey and Gail James, of Vancouver, British Columbia, whom I met on a cruise, responded with tremendous enthusiasm and recognition the moment I mentioned that I was writing a book about positive dependency. Mickey said, "I had a terrible first marriage that lasted sixteen years and a wonderful second marriage to Gail that has lasted almost as long. Gail knew when she married me that she would be taking on a lot. I am older, with four children and lots of problems. But she wanted to be with me and has been there for me, helping me with my business and with the kids. I don't know how I ever got along without her. I would do anything for her." Gail smiled and said, "He takes very good care of me, too. That's why even though he loves golf, for our vacation we're on this cruise!"

Sheila Cluff, owner of The Oaks at Ojai and The Palms at Palm Springs, described to me her understanding of the process. "My husband," she says, "knows of my high energy. He always offered me the encouragement and support I needed to raise our children and develop my business. He is my greatest asset."

"And what do you do for him?" I asked.

"I appreciate him and let him know it every day in every way that I can."

My colleague Rita Lynn had to make new choices when, upon moving from London to Los Angeles, the career of her husband, Jonathan, took off in a major way. Although she filled her therapy practice within two months of relocating to America, she took on nothing new when she saw that his work required increasing amounts of time and support from her. "He always encouraged me when I trained as an analyst, when I worked long hours, and when I needed his help and support.

"It's his time now, and I intend to be there for him. For now it means cutting back on my career. We have lots of years. I'll have lots of opportunities. If I'm there for him now, he'll be there for me later; I can count on that."

When I was young, my mother gave me one of those bits of advice that made a lasting impression. She told me that what a woman looks like the first thirty years of her life depends upon the gifts that God gave her. After that what she looks like depends upon the choices she makes about marriage. I realize now that these choices do not mean simply selecting the right partner. For those who want to share a life with another human being, it is choosing what responses to make, what to say and what to ignore, when to expect changes and when to simply reinforce the best qualities that you find.

The messages of society during the past three decades have not been pro relationships. They have been filled with warnings against being used by unloving partners or against becoming caretakers in unhealthy relationships. Taken to extremes they became messages filled with entitlements, expectations, and "I" messages that often miss the feelings of the other person.

The choices that I made to be pro relationship in my marriage and in my career have worked for me and for many of the people who have consulted me about their lives and loves. Over the years I have carefully considered the things that seem to work for me and for others, and I have consolidated what I learned into the imprints and the rules for healthy dependency in relationships. I offer these to you.

It is not "codependent" to meet the needs of another in the hopes of getting your own needs met. On the contrary it is a healthy, loving exchange. Working together, affirming each other, avoiding messages that hurt, and providing a safe haven within the framework of a relationship not only allows us to depend on each other, but has the power of healing old love wounds. With the right partner, and with the knowledge of how to be the right partner, you can find a path to intimacy. It may be the most important achievement in your life.

And so I end this with the last of my Rules for Healthy Interdependence.

Rule #10 for Positive Dependency:

Accept the fact that your partner will probably not do all of the things you hope for. Most of us have too many obligations and too little time. Agree on what is essential for both of you. Use your energy for the important things—like loving each other. You can depend on that.

Notes

1. M. S. Mahler, F. Pine, and A. Bergman, *The Psychological Birth of the Human Infant: Symbiosis and Individuation* (New York: Basic Books, 1975).
2. M. F. Solomon, *Narcissism and Intimacy: Love and Marriage in an Age of Confusion* (New York: W. W. Norton, 1989).
3. D. W. Winnicott, *Playing and Reality* (England: Penguin, 1971) and *Home Is Where We Start From* (New York: W. W. Norton, 1986).
4. D. Stern, *The Interpersonal World of the Infant* (New York: Basic Books, 1985) and *Diary of a Baby* (New York: Basic Books, 1989).
5. D. W. Winnicott, "Pediatrics and childhood neurosis" in D. Winnicott, ed., *Collected papers: Through pediatrics to psychoanalysis* (London: Tavistock Publications, 1958), 316–21. (Original work published 1956.)
6. H. Kohut, *How Does Analysis Cure?* (Chicago: University of Chicago Press, 1984).
7. F. Alexander, *Fundamentals of Psychoanalysis* (New York: W. W. Norton, 1948).
8. Stern presented these tapes at UCLA, March 28–29, 1992, in a presentation entitled "Narratives: Creating Meaning from Birth Through Adulthood."
9. R. A. Spitz, *The First Year of Life: A Psychoanalytic Study of Normal and Deviant Development of Object Relations* (New York: International Universities Press, 1965).
10. S. Freud, "Dreams and Occulticism" in *New Introductory Lectures on Psychoanalysis*, vol. 22, Standard Edition (1933).
11. These bridges to others used by babies are called transitional objects by British pediatrician and psychoanalyst Donald Winnicott. They are used to alleviate the anxiety of separateness and loss of mother's presence as the child first discoveres that (s)he and mother each have a separate self. Such surrogates temporarily substitute for the needed connections with the caretaking person.
12. D. W. Winnicott, *Collected Papers: Through Pediatrics to Psychoanalysis* (London: Tavistock Publications, 1958).
13. N. Chodorow, *The Reproduction of Mothering: Psychoanalysis and the Sociology of Gender* (Berekely, CA: University of California Press, 1978).
14. This was first noted by psychoanalysist Ralph Greenson and confirmed by Nancy Chodorow and Jean Baker-Miller. R. Greenson, *Technique and Practice of Psychoanalysis* (New Jersey: International University Press, 1967).
15. C. Gilligan, *In a Different Voice: Psychological Theory and Women's Development* (Cambridge, MA: Harvard University Press, 1982).
16. Margaret Mahler, in *The Psychological Birth of the Human Infant,* describes it as healthy refueling, a period when the baby can take strides toward independence if she can look back and be sure mother is there watching. J. Piaget calls this object constancy.
17. J. Piaget, *The Origins of Intelligence in Children,* trans. M. Cook (New York: International Universities Press, 1952).
18. R. Stoller, *Observing the Erotic Imagination* (New York: Yale University Press, 1985).
19. J. Hillman and M. Ventura, *We've Had a Hundred Years of Psychotherapy and the World Is Getting Worse* (New York: Harper, 1992).

Bibliography

Alexander, F. *Fundamentals of Psychoanalysis*. New York: W. W. Norton, 1948.

Beattie, M. *Co-Dependent No More*. San Francisco: Harper, 1987.

Chodorow, N. *The Reproduction of Mothering: Psychoanalysis and the Sociology of Gender*. Berkeley, CA: University of California Press, 1978.

Freud, S. In *New Introductory Lectures on Psycho-analysis,* "Dreams and Occultism." vol. 22, Standard Edition, 1933.

Gilligan, C. *In a Different Voice: Psychological Theory and Women's Development*. Cambridge, MA: Harvard University Press, 1982.

Greenson, R. *Technique and Practice on'Psychoanalysis*. New Jersey: International Universities Press, 1967.

Grotstein, J., M. Solomon, and J. Lang. *The Borderline Patient: Emerging Concepts in Diagnosis, Etiology, Psychodynamics, and Treatment*. Hillsdale, NJ: Analytic Press, 1987.

Hillman, J., and M. Ventura. *We've Had a Hundred Years of Psychotherapy and the World Is Getting Worse*. New York: Harper, 1992.

Jordon, J., A. Kaplan, J. Miller, I. Stiver, and J. Surrey. *Women's Growth In Connection*. New York: The Guilford Press, 1991.

Kohut, H. *How Does Analysis Cure?* Chicago: University of Chicago Press, 1984.

Mahler, M. S., F. Pine, and A. Bergman. *The Psychological Birth of the Human Infant: Symbiosis and Individuation*. New York: Basic Books, 1975.

Miller, J. B. *Toward a New Psychology of Women*. Boston: Beacon Press, 1987.

Piaget, J. *The Origins of Intelligence in Children*. Trans. M. Cook. New York: International Universities Press, 1952.

Rose, P. *Parallel Lives: The Story of Five Victorian Marriages*. New York: Knopf, 1983.

Solomon, M. *Narcissism and Intimacy: Love and Marriage in an Age of Confusion*. New York: W. W. Norton, 1989.

Spitz, R. A. *The First Year of Life: A Psychoanalytic Study of Normal and Deviant Development of Object Relations*. New York: International Universities Press, 1965.

Stern, D. *The Interpersonal World of the Infant*. New York: Basic Books, 1985.

——. *Diary of a Baby*. New York: Basic Books, 1989.

Stoller, R. *Observing the Erotic Imagination*. New York: Yale University Press, 1985.

Wilson-Schaef, A. *Co-Dependence: Misunderstood—Mistreated*. Cambridge, MA.: Harper & Row, 1986.

Winnicott, D. W. "Pediatrics and childhood neurosis." In *Collected papers: Through pediatrics to psychoanalysis,* edited by D. Winnicott, 316–321. London: Tavistock Publications, 1958. (Original work published 1956.)

——. *Playing and Reality*. Middlesex, England: Penguin, 1971.

——. *Home Is Where We Start From*. New York: W. W. Norton, 1986.

Woolf, V. *A Room of One's Own*. New York: Harcourt Brace Javonovich, 1957.